KANT'S PRACTICAL PHILOSOPHY RECONSIDERED

ARCHIVES INTERNATIONALES D'HISTOIRE DES IDÉES

INTERNATIONAL ARCHIVES OF THE HISTORY OF IDEAS

128

YIRMIYAHU YOVEL

(editor)

KANT'S PRACTICAL PHILOSOPHY RECONSIDERED

Papers presented at the
Seventh Jerusalem Philosophical Encounter, December 1986

KANT'S PRACTICAL PHILOSOPHY RECONSIDERED

Papers presented at the Seventh
Jerusalem Philosophical Encounter, December 1986

edited by

YIRMIYAHU YOVEL

The Hebrew University of Jerusalem

KLUWER ACADEMIC PUBLISHERS

DORDRECHT / BOSTON / LONDON

Library of Congress Cataloging in Publication Data

Jerusalem Philosophical Encounter (7th : 1986)
    Kant's practical philosophy reconsidered : papers presented at the
 Seventh Jerusalem Philosophical Encounter, December 1986 / edited by
 Yirmiyahu Yovel.
       p.   cm. -- (Archives internationales d'histoire des idées ;
 128)
    Includes bibliographies and index.
    ISBN 0-7923-0405-5
    1. Kant, Immanuel, 1724-1804--Contributions in ethics--Congresses.
 2. Ethics, Modern--18th century--Congresses.   I. Yovel, Yirmiyahu.
 II. Title.   III. Series.
 B2799.E8J47   1986
 170'.92--dc20   89-15449

ISBN 0–7923–0405–5

Published by Kluwer Academic Publishers,
P.O. Box 17, 3300 AA Dordrecht, The Netherlands.

Kluwer Academic Publishers incorporates
the publishing programmes of
D. Reidel, Martinus Nijhoff, Dr W. Junk and MTP Press.

Sold and distributed in the U.S.A. and Canada
by Kluwer Academic Publishers,
101 Philip Drive, Norwell, MA 02061, U.S.A.

In all other countries, sold and distributed
by Kluwer Academic Publishers Group,
P.O. Box 322, 3300 AH Dordrecht, The Netherlands.

printed on acid free paper

Prepared in cooperation with
Ms Eva Shorr, Managing Editor
The S.H. Bergman Center for Philosophical Studies
The Hebrew University of Jerusalem

Typeset by Studio 'Efrat', Jerusalem, Israel.

Printed in The Netherlands

Contents

IV: *Kant in Contemporary Contexts*

Preface

That Kant's ideas remain vitally present in ethical thinking today is as impossible to deny as it is to overlook their less persisting aspects and sometimes outdated idiom. The essays in this volume attempt to reassess some crucial questions in Kant's practical philosophy both by sketching the lines for new systematic interpretations and by examining how Kantian themes apply to contemporary moral concerns.

In the previous decade, when Kant was primarily read as an answer to utilitarianism, emphasis was mainly laid on the *fundamentals* of his moral theory, stressing such concepts as universalization, duty for its own sake, personal autonomy, unconditional imperatives or humanity as end-in-itself, using the *Groundwork* and its broader (if less popular) systematic parallel, the Analytic of the *Critique of Practical Reason*, as main sources. In recent years, however, emphasis has shifted and become diversified. The present essays reflect this diversification in discussing the extension of Kantian ethics in the domains of law, justice, politics and moral history, and also in considering such meta-philosophical questions as the relation between the various "interests of reason" (as Kant calls them), above all between knowledge and moral practice.

The papers were first presented at the Seventh Jerusalem Philosophical Encounter, held at the Hebrew University of Jerusalem in December 1986. The *Jerusalem Philosophical Encounters* are a series of bi-annual international symposia, in which philosophers of different backgrounds meet in Jerusalem to discuss a common issue. Organized by the S.H. Bergman Center for Philosophical Studies of the Hebrew University of Jerusalem, the series of Encounters have so far produced the following books: *Philosophy of History and Action*, ed. Y. Yovel (Reidel, 1978); *Meaning and Use*, ed. A. Margalit (Reidel, 1979); *Spinoza — His Thought and Work*, ed. N. Rotenstreich (The Israel Academy of Sciences and Humanities, 1983); *The Philosophy of Franz Rosenzweig*, ed. P. Mendes-Flohr (University Press of New England, 1988); *Nietzsche as Affirmative Thinker*, ed. Y. Yovel (Nijhoff, 1985); *Maimonides and Philosophy* (Nijhoff, 1986).

The Encounter owes much of its success to Mr Zev Birger, the Managing Director of the Jerusalem Convention Center and his staff, especially Linda Futterman. I am, as always, grateful to Eva Shorr, Managing Editor of the Hebrew Philosophical Quarterly *Iyyun*, for her meticulous care in preparing the manuscript and her tactful prodding of authors and editor to meet, or approach, the set deadlines. I cordially acknowledge the cooperation of Dr. Alexander Schimmelpenninck, Head of the Humanities and Social Sciences Division at Kluwer, and a philosopher himself, with whom I have already published two former Jerusalem Encounters (on Nietzsche and on Maimonides). Thanks are also due to my colleagues on the Board of the S.H. Bergman Center at the Hebrew University of Jerusalem, Professor Zvi R.J. Werblowski (Chair) and Father Marcel Dubois, for their counsel and support in making this series possible.

Yirmiyahu Yovel

The S.H. Bergman Center for Philosophical Studies
The Hebrew University of Jerusalem

List of Abbreviations

Citations from Kant's writings are identified by an abbreviated form or acronym of their German title. The Arabic numerals refer to the volume and pagination of the Akademie edition of Kant's *Gesammelte Schriften* (GS) (Berlin, 1902-) and to their English translation, separated by a slash; e. g., Rel. 6: 179/167.

Abbreviations used in citing particular works of Kant are as follows:

A/B — *Kritik der reinen Vernunft*, quoted by the pagination of the first (A) and the second (B) original editions.
Critique of Pure Reason, tr. N. Kemp Smith (London: Macmillan, 1963). Also referred to as the first *Critique*.

Anth.— *Anthropologie in pragmatischer Hinsicht*, GS 7.
Anthropology from a Pragmatic Point of View, tr. M. J. Gregor (The Hague: Nijhoff, 1974)

G — *Grundlegung zur Metaphysik der Sitten*, GS 4.
Foundations of the Metaphysics of Morals, tr. L.W. Beck (Indianapolis: Bobbs-Merrill, 1956).
Groundwork of the Metaphysic of Morals, in *The Moral Law*, tr. H. J. Paton (London: Hutchinson, 1953).

I — *Idee zu einer allgemeinen Geschichte in weltbürgerlicher Absicht*, GS 8.
Idea for a Universal History from a Cosmopolitan Point of View, tr. L. W. Beck, in *Kant on History* (Indianapolis: Bobbs-Merrill, 1963).

KpV — *Kritik der praktischen Vernunft*, GS 5.
Critique of Practical Reason, tr. L. W. Beck (Indianapolis: Bobbs-Merrill, 1956). Also referred to as the second *Critique*.

KU — *Kritik der Urteilskraft*, GS 5.
Critique of Judgement, tr. J. C. Meredith (Oxford: Clarendon, 1952). Also referred to as the third *Critique*.

MN — *Metaphysische Anfangsgründe der Naturwissenschaft*, GS 4.
Metaphysical Foundations of Natural Science, tr. J. Ellington (Indianapolis: Bobbs-Merrill, 1970).

MS — *Metaphysik der Sitten*, GS 6.
The General Introduction to the Metaphysics of Morals, tr. J. Elling-

ton, in *Kant: Ethical Philosophy* (Indianapolis: Hackett, 1983).

RL I. *Rechtslehre*
    Metaphysical Elements of Justice, tr. (in parts) J. Ladd (Indianapolis: Bobbs-Merrill, 1965).

TL II. *Tugendlehre*
    The Doctrine of Virtue (DV), tr. M.J. Gregor (Philadelphia: University of Pennsylvania Press, 1964).
    The Metaphysical Principles of Virtue (MP), tr. J. Ellington, in *Kant: Ethical Philosophy*.

Mut. — *Mutmasslicher Anfang der Menschengeschichte*, GS 8.
    Conjectural Beginning of Human History, tr. E.L. Fackenheim, in *Kant on History*.

Prol. — *Prolegomena zu einer jeden künftigen Metaphysik*, GS 4.
    Prolegomena to Any Future Metaphysics, tr. L.W. Beck (Indianapolis: Bobbs-Merrill, 1950).

Rei. — *Die Religion innerhalb der Grenzen der blossen Vernunft*, GS 6.
    Religion within the Limits of Reason Alone, tr. T.M. Greene and H.H. Hudson (New York: Harper Torchbooks, 1960).

Rez. — Recensionen von I.G. Herders *Ideen zur Philosophie der Geschichte der Menschheit*, Theil 1. 2., GS 8.
    Reviews of Herder's *Ideas for a Philosophy of the History of Mankind*, tr. R.E. Anchor, in *Kant on History*.

ZeF — *Zum ewigen Frieden*, GS 8.
    Perpetual Peace, tr. L.W. Beck, in *Kant on History*.

TP — *Über den Gemeinspruch: Das mag in der Theorie richtig sein, taugt aber nicht für die Praxis*, GS 8.
    "On the Common Saying: This May be True in Theory, But it Does not Apply in Practice," in *Kant's Political Writings*, ed. H. Reiss, tr. H.B. Nisbet (Cambridge University Press, 1970).

UG — *Über den Gebrauch teleologischer Principien in der Philosophie*, GS 8.

WiA — *Beantwortung der Frage: Was ist Aufklärung?* GS 8.
    "An Answer to the Question: What is Enlightenment?" in *Kant's Political Writings*.

Henry E. Allison

Empirical and Intelligible Character in the *Critique of Pure Reason*

Kant's conception of free agency has been much criticized and little understood. Since one of the basic criticisms is that it is incoherent, this combination is quite understandable. At the heart of the problem lies the connection between free agency and some of the more problematic and mysterious aspects of transcendental idealism. This connection leads to a familiar dilemma from which there seems to be no escape: either freedom is located in some timeless noumenal realm, in which case it is perhaps conceivable but also irrelevant to the understanding of human agency, or, alternatively, the exercise of free agency is thought to make a difference in the spatio-temporal world in which we live and act, in which case it comes into an irreconcilable conflict with the "causality of nature."[1]

By focusing on the contrast between empirical and intelligible character, as it is developed in the *Critique of Pure Reason*, I hope to show that this standard line of criticism is misguided. More particularly, I shall try to demonstrate that Kant has good reasons for introducing the problematic conception of an intelligible character and that these stem from an analysis of rational agency in general rather than from an appeal to any specifically moral considerations. I shall also argue that this conception complements, rather than conflicts with, the explanation of actions in terms of the empirical character of the agent. The root idea is that, although empirically irrelevant in the sense that it does not enter into the description, explanation or prediction of specific actions, the notion of an intelligible character and the idea of freedom which it

I would like to thank the John Simon Guggenheim Memorial Foundation for their financial support during the period in which this paper was written.

[1] Perhaps the most relentless advocate of this standard line of criticism in the recent literature is Jonathan Bennett, *Kant's Dialectic* (Cambridge University Press, 1974), pp. 187-227, and "Kant's Theory of Freedom," a commentary on an essay by Allen Wood, in *Self and Nature in Kant's Philosophy*, ed. Allen W. Wood (Cornell University Press, 1984), pp. 102-12.

1

Y. Yovel (ed.), Kant's Practical Philosophy Reconsidered, 1-21.
© *1989 Kluwer Academic Publishers.*

involves (transcendental freedom) is nonetheless required for the very conception of oneself as a rational agent with an empirical character. Transcendental idealism enters the picture in that it allows Kant to admit with the determinist and compatibilist the empirical irrelevance of the appeal to an intelligible character without having to admit that it is irrelevant from all "points of view."

The discussion is divided into three parts. The first analyzes Kant's conception of an empirical character in its application to rational agency. It shows that for Kant the "causality of reason" is operative already at the empirical level, so that the empirical explanation of the actions of rational agents is in terms of "reasons" (more generally, psychological factors). The second analyzes the conception of an intelligible character, Kant's grounds (apart from moral considerations) for introducing it, and its role in the conception of rational agency. The third considers some of the problems posed by the simultaneous ascription of both characters to a single action or agent.

I

Kant first presents the contrast between an empirical and an intelligible character in general terms, and only later applies it to the human will and its causality. The initial formulation suggests that it can be regarded as the agency version of the phenomenal–noumenal distinction. "Every efficient cause," Kant tells us, "must have a character, that is, a law of its causality without which it would not be a cause" (A539/B567).[2]

Presumably, this means that every cause or, more properly, causal agent, must have a determinate *modus operandi*, which is described by the "law of its causality." Apart from the ascription of such a character, there would be no grounds for referring to a particular causal agent or type of cause in order to explain a given effect. Insofar as we are dealing with the empirical character of a causal agent, this *modus operandi* must conform to the conditions of possible experience and be describable in empirical terms.

Kant also suggests that, in the case of at least some agents, we may have grounds for assigning an intelligible as well as an empirical character. Since 'intelligible' here is equivalent to 'non-sensible' or 'non-empirical', it follows that the intelligible character of such agents and their activity would neither conform to the conditions of possible experience nor be describable in empirical terms. Moreover, since time is the universal condition of possible expe-

---

[2] Citations from the *Critique of Pure Reason* are, with some modification, from the Kemp Smith translation and references are to the first and second edition pagination.

rience (all appearances are in time), it also follows that, with respect to its intelligible character, such an agent "would not... stand under any conditions of time" (A539/B567). Given Kant's argument in the Analogies, this means that we could not speak meaningfully of something happening in or to this agent or of its being determined by antecedent conditions. In short, with this conception of an intelligible character we have the formula for the thought of the empirically unconditioned activity of a noumenal subject.

Whether this conception of an intelligible character is completely vacuous, as most of Kant's critics contend, or has some relevance for the conception of human agency is the topic of the next section. Our present concern is merely with the empirical character of such agency, which raises problems enough in its own right. These problems stem from the fact that, in applying the general empirical–intelligible distincion to human agency, Kant attributes an empirical character to the "causality of reason." This is implicit in the entire discussion; but Kant makes it fully explicit when, after offering a brief account of how reason can be thought to determine conduct by generating imperatives, he notes, "Reason though it be, it must nonetheless exhibit an empirical character" (A549/B577). Moreover, a few lines later, in a passage which deserves to be cited in full, he writes:

Thus, the will of every man has an empirical character, which is nothing but a certain causality of his reason, so far as that causality exhibits, in its effects in the [field] of appearance, a rule from which we may gather what, in their kind and degrees, are the actions of reason and the grounds thereof, and so may form an estimate concerning the subjective principles of his will. Since this empirical character must itself be discovered from the appearances which are its effect and from the rule to which experience shows them to conform, it follows that all the actions of men in the [field of] appearance are determined in conformity with the order of nature, by their empirical character and by the other causes which cooperate with that character; and if we could exhaustively investigate all the appearances of men's wills, there would not be found a single human action which we could not predict with certainty, and recognize as proceeding necessarily from its antecedent conditions. So far, then, as regards this empirical character there is no freedom; and yet it is only in the light of this character that man can be studied — if, that is to say, we are simply *observing*, and in the manner of anthropology seeking to institute a physiological investigation into the motive causes of his actions. (A549-550/B577-578)

As the passage makes clear, Kant is not only advocating a strict determinism at the empirical level, but a *psychological* determinism. Human actions, regarded empirically, are caused by the empirical character of the agent, defined as a "causality of reason," together with other "co-operating causes." Similarly, the predictability of such actions would require sufficient knowledge of the "appearances of men's wills" (presumably, their mental states), together with the relevant background conditions. Thus, in contrast to most contemporary theorists, who opt for a compatibilist position on the free will issue, Kant's determinism at the empirical level does not rest on the assumption of either the reducibility of action explanations to neuro-physiological ones or of a token–token identity between physical and psychological states. On the contrary, the relevant causal factors seem to be largely psychological in nature, that is, the beliefs, desires and intentions of the agent. Moreover, although the point is not spelled out, it seems reasonable to assume that the "co-operating causes" are supposed to work by influencing the agent's psychological state.

Quite apart from the question of the tenability of such a psychological determinism, Kant's identification of human agency, in its empirical character, with a "causality of reason" raises at least two major exegetical puzzles, which, if unresolved, call into question the coherence of his overall position. First, given Kant's unrelenting insistence on the spontaneous, non-sensible nature of reason and its activity, it is far from clear how he can attribute an empirical character to it at all. Is not reason the paradigmatically noumenal capacity, and how can anything noumenal have an empirical, i.e., phenomenal character? Second, given Kant's rejection of psychological laws, how can he insist on a psychological determinism at the empirical level? If reason does, indeed, exhibit an empirical character, then the study of that character must pertain to the province of empirical psychology (or perhaps anthropology). But Kant denies that empirical psychology is a science, insisting that the most it can provide is a "natural description... but not a science of the soul" (MN 4: 471).[3] Since anthropology, which Kant does regard as the actual "science" of human behavior, seems to differ from empirical psychology mainly in that it prescinds from the question of whether human beings have souls, it is apparent that this stricture must apply to it as well.[4]

---

[3] This denial might seem to contradict Kant's affirmative claims about empirical psychology in the *Critique*. Thus, within the context of his introduction to the Paralogisms, Kant characterizes it as "a kind of *physiology* of inner sense, capable perhaps of explaining the appearances of inner sense" (A347/B405), and, again, in the Architectonic of Pure Reason, after denying that it belongs in metaphysics, he suggests that it will find its home in "a complete anthropology, the pendant to the empirical doctrine of nature" (A849/B877). In reality, however, there is no contradiction because in neither case is it assumed that the "science" is capable of providing anything more than a "natural description."

[4] See *Anthropology* 7: 161, and *Reflexion* 1502, 15: 802. For a brief but helpful discussion of the procedure and scientific status of anthropology *vis-à-vis* both psychology and physiology see Mary J. Gregor's introduction to her translation of *Anthropology*, pp. xii-xv.

With regard to the first question, in order to understand how reason and its causality might be said to have an empirical character, we must first consider Kant's cryptic remarks about the relationship between the empirical and the intelligible character of human agency. The problem here is that Kant offers two versions of this relationship, only one of which seems to be relevant to the question at hand.[5] Sometimes Kant describes this relationship in straightforwardly causal terms. On this view, intelligible character (identified with the causality of reason) is the noumenal cause and empirical character its phenomenal effect.[6] This immediately raises the specter of ontologically distinct noumenal causes and all of the problems that this involves. Moreover, by attributing the causality of reason solely to the intelligible character, it seems to foreclose the possibility of regarding the empirical character as itself an expression or instantiation, rather than merely as a product, of such a causality. In short, on this reading it is not reason, but merely the occurrences in the phenomenal world supposedly produced by it, that can be said to have an empirical character. Sometimes, however, apparently without noticing the difference, Kant also speaks of the empirical character as the appearance or sensible schema of the intelligible character.[7] Unlike the first version of the relationship, this does allow for the possibility that the causality of reason, although intelligible, might nonetheless be said to have an empirical character, namely, its phenomenal expression, appearance or schema. Unfortunately this formulation suffers from the disadvantage of suggesting that there might be an inference route from the empirical to the intelligible, a consequence that the "critical" Kant could hardly accept.

It is clear from the above that what is needed is an account of empirical character that enables us to regard it as in some sense an expression or manifestation (and not simply a result) of an intelligible activity, without requiring us to assume that it yields any insight into the true nature of that activity. Although it is hardly free from ambiguity, some such view does seem to be suggested by the previously cited passage in which Kant describes the empirical character of a human will as

nothing but a certain causality of his reason, so far as that causality exhibits, in its

---

[5] For an account of the distinct ways in which Kant construes the relation between empirical and intelligible character and of some of the problems which this creates, see Bernard Carnois, *La Cohérence de la doctrine kantienne de la liberté* (Paris: Seuil, 1973), and Jürgen Henrichs, *Das Problem der Zeit in der praktischen Philosophie Kants* (Bonn: Bouvier, 1968), esp. pp. 38-42.

[6] See A546/B579, A551/B579, A556/B589.

[7] See A541/B569, A546/B574, A553/B581, and *Reflexion* 5611, 18: 253.

effects in the [field of] appearance, a rule from which we may gather what, in their kind and degree, are the actions of reason and the grounds thereof, and so may form an estimate concerning the subjective principles of his will.

The main ambiguity in this passage concerns the expressions "the actions of reason" and "the subjective principles of his will." If these are taken to refer to an agent's intelligible character, then we are right back at the problem noted above, namely, we are construing Kant to be allowing for the possibility of inferring something about the nature of an intelligible activity or character from its empirical manifestation. This is avoided, however, if we take the expressions to refer to the empirical character of the will. Moreover, this latter reading is strongly supported by Kant's subsequent claim that it is the empirical (not the intelligible) character that "must itself be discovered from the appearances which are its effects and from the rule to which experience shows them to conform." This suggests that the empirical character of the will of a rational agent consists in the subjective principles or "maxims" on the basis of which that agent acts or, more properly, in the disposition to act on the basis of these principles. Construed dispositionally, this character can be inferred from "appearances," that is, from behavior. The basic idea here is that a person's behavior exhibits sufficient regularity so as to enable one to reconstruct the rule or principle on which that person tends to act in given situations. For example, in the case of Kant's honest shopkeeper, one can infer from his behavior that he acts on the basis of the principle of not cheating his customers. This much is empirical, since it is derived from past behavior and can be used (to some extent at least) to predict future behavior. What is non-empirical and, therefore, irrelevant to the description of the shopkeeper's behavior is the ultimate ground of his adoption of this policy.

Finally, even though empirical, this character involves a causality of reason. The key point here is that we are not talking simply about a disposition to behave or to respond in certain predictable ways in given situations (this could be attributed to an *arbitrium brutum*), but rather about a disposition to act on the basis of certain maxims, to pursue certain ends, and to select certain means for the realization of these ends. This, in turn, means that even the empirical study of human behavior, that is, the observation which, for Kant, is carried out in a systematic form in the "science" of anthropology, is, in a very real sense, a study of rational agency.

Unfortunately, this resolution of the initial puzzle also serves to exacerbate the second. Given this account of rational agency, together with his denial of nomological status to the empirical generalizations of psychology or anthropology, it becomes increasingly difficult to understand how Kant could insist upon a causal determinism for human actions at the phenomenal level. Causal determinism, so it would seem, presupposes strict causal laws. Certainly, the kind of predictability to which Kant refers requires covering laws similar (if not identical) to those contained in Newtonian physics. As we have seen, however, Kant denies that there are any such laws in the psychological domain. Moreover, the puzzle only increases if one includes in the picture the distinction drawn in the *Critique of Judgment* between mechanistic and teleological explanation. Clearly, the "causality of reason," even at the empirical level, is inherently purposive. Consequently, explanations of its activity must be teleological rather than mechanistic in nature.

The temptation at this point is to respond that the whole issue of causal law is already settled, or at least it is supposed to have been settled, by the argument of the Second Analogy. Starting with this assumption, it is then reasonable to suggest that Kant's denial of psychological laws can be reconciled with his causal determinism (at the phenomenal level) by attributing to him something like a Davidsonian anomalous monism, which reconciles the anomalousness of the mental with a physicalistic determinism by assuming a token–token identity between mental and physical stages.[8] There are two reasons, however, why this temptation should be rejected. First, although it is impossible to pursue the matter here, Kant clearly rejects physicalism or, as he terms it, "materialism," at the phenomenal level.[9] Second, as I (and others) have argued elsewhere, the Second Analogy attempts to prove only that every event must have some cause, not that similar causes must have similar effects. Accordingly, it does not prove that nature is "lawful" in the sense required to support predictions.[10] The latter conception of lawfulness (empirical lawfulness) is a regulative principle of scientific enquiry, not a constitutive principle of the possibility of experience. Thus, for all that one can infer from the argument of the Second Analogy (or, indeed, the Transcendental Analytic as

[8] Although he does not focus on Kant's denial of psychological laws, an essentially Davidsonian-compatibilist interpretation of Kant's conception of freedom has been developed by Ralf Meerbote. See his "Wille and Willkür in Kant's Theory of Action," *Interpreting Kant*, ed. S. Gram Moltke (University of Iowa Press, 1982), pp. 69-89; "Kant on the Nondeterminate Character of Human Actions," *Kant on Causality, Freedom, and Objectivity*, ed. William A. Harper and Ralf Meerbote (University of Minnesota Press, 1984), pp. 138-63; and "Kant on Freedom and the Rational and Morally Good Will," a commentary on an essay by Terence Irwin, in *Self and Nature in Kant's Philosophy*, pp. 57-72.
[9] On this issue see Karl Ameriks, *Kant's Theory of Mind* (Oxford: Clarendon Press, 1982), pp. 33-47.
[10] See my *Kant's Transcendental Idealism* (Yale University Press, 1983), Chap. 10.

a whole), it remains possible that nature does not exhibit any empirically accessible lawlike regularities.[11]

Nevertheless, none of this undermines Kant's psychological determinism. In fact, it is precisely because Kant, in contrast to contemporary theorists such as Davidson, does not equate having a phenomenal cause with falling under specifiable causal laws, that this species of determinism is reconcilable with his doctrine of the "anomalousness" of the mental. Although Kant denied that the chemistry of his day had achieved full scientific status and contained genuine laws, he would hardly have denied that chemical changes fall within the scope of the Second Analogy.[12] Presumably, the same can be said, *mutatis mutandis*, for organic phenomena and human actions, even though both of them are supposedly amenable to teleological rather than to mechanistic explanation.

Kant makes his position somewhat clearer in the *Critique of Practical Reason*, where, after agreeing with Leibniz that human actions have psychological rather than physical causes, he denies that this exempts them from the "mechanism of nature" broadly construed (5:97). In order to belong to this mechanism, it is sufficient that an occurrence (whether mental or physical) has its determining ground in antecedent time or, as Kant sometimes put it, that it be subject to the "conditions of time." Since psychological phenomena, including the human will in its empirical character, are subject to these conditions, they must fall under the scope of the Second Analogy.

Interestingly enough, this conception of empirical character is capable of providing the basis for a rich and potentially attractive form of compatibilism. It differs from contemporary forms of compatibilism, most notably Davidson's, in ways already noted. Nevertheless, it does leave "elbow room" for freedom in a deterministic (although not Laplacean) universe in the familiar sense that it allows for the description and explanation of human action in terms of the beliefs, desires and intentions of agents and, therefore, for a "naturalized" version of the "causality of reason." Moreover, it is clear from Kant's remarks about a "comparative" or "psychological" concept of freedom in the first two *Critiques*, as well as from his naturalistic account of human freedom as an historically conditioned capacity in the third *Critique*,

---

[11] Admittedly, Kant himself is not very clear on this point and there are many passages that suggest the contrary. See in particular A536/B569. This does not affect the present claim, however, which is concerned with what Kant is entitled to assume about the lawfulness of nature, given his own arguments, not with what he in fact assumes.

[12] For Kant's views on the scientific status of the chemistry of his day see, MN 4:470-71.

the *Anthropology*, and the essays on the philosophy of history, that he was well aware of this fact. Thus, the question inevitably arises: Why did Kant not rest content with such a compatibilist position, particularly since it seems to be in at least rough accord with the main thrust of the Transcendental Analytic?

II

The usual response to this question is that Kant's move beyond compatibilism to an inaccessible noumenal domain is motivated by his concern to ground morality. This is clearly an accurate characterization of Kant's procedure in the *Critique of Practical Reason*, where he dismisses a merely psychological or comparative conception of freedom as nothing more than the "freedom of a turnspit" (5: 97). In the case of the *Critique of Pure Reason*, this reading is suggested by Kant's frequent appeal to the 'ought' or to imperatives. Thus, in his initial discussion of practical freedom, in which he attempts to link it with the transcendental variety, he writes:

For practical freedom presupposes that although something has not happened, it *ought* to have happened, and that its cause [as found] in the [field of] appearance, is not, therefore, so determining that it excludes a causality of our will — a causality which, independently of those natural causes, and even contrary to their force and influence, can produce something that is determined in the time-order in accordance with empirical laws, and which can therefore begin a series of events *entirely of itself*. (A534/B563)

And, later, in an effort to gain entrée for the notion of a causality of reason:

That this reason has causality, or that we at least represent it to ourselves as having causality, is evident from the *imperatives* which in all practical matters [*in allem Praktischen*] we impose as rules upon our executive powers. *Ought* expresses a kind of necessity and of connection with grounds which is found nowhere else in the whole of nature. (A547/B575)

Although these, and similar passages, may suggest the usual interpretation, they hardly require it. Neither of these passages refer specifically to the moral 'ought' or the categorical imperative; and in the second Kant explicitly states that reason imposes imperatives in "all practical matters," which presumably includes prudential as well as moral matters. Moreover, a bit later Kant contends that "the *'ought'* pronounced by reason" is at work "whether what is willed be an object of mere sensibility (the pleasant) or pure reason (the good)." In either case, Kant suggests,

Reason does not... follow the order of things as they present themselves in appearance, but forms for itself with perfect spontaneity an order of its own according to ideas...

according to which it declares actions to be necessary, even though they have never taken place, and perhaps never will take place. (A548/B576)

Finally, in the Canon, after distinguishing between moral laws which dictate our duty and pragmatic laws which dictate the means necessary to the end desired by sensibility, he notes that both count equally as "objective laws of freedom which tell us what *ought to happen*, although perhaps it never does happen" (A802/B830).

These passages make it clear that in the *Critique of Pure Reason*, if not in his later works in moral philosophy, Kant regards the capacity to act on the basis of imperatives in general (not merely categorical imperatives) as the defining characteristic of free agency. They also suggest that the spontaneity presumably required to act on the basis of an 'ought' (whether moral or prudential) is the source of Kant's dissatisfaction with the compatibilist account of agency in terms of empirical character and, therefore, the reason for his introduction of the conception of an intelligible character.

What is not clear at this point is why Kant should think that this is the case. Let us grant, as seems reasonable, that to engage in practical reasoning is to deliberate about what one ought to do (whether in a moral or a prudential sense). Let us further grant that the determination of what one ought to do (even in a prudential sense) requires the "spontaneity" of reason in that it involves the forming of ends or "ought-to-bes" and rules that are not based solely on what one in fact desires at a given moment, but rather reflect what one would choose if one were perfectly rational. Even granting these basic premises, it still does not seem to follow that this requires the abandonment of a compatibilist conception of agency. As we have already seen, even at the empirical level, action explanations refer not only to the agent's desires, but also to chosen ends and maxims or rules of action. Such explanation thus already involves a "causality of reason," albeit in a "naturalized" form. Why, then, did Kant not regard this as sufficient for our conception of ourselves as rational agents, particularly if one abstracts from the peculiar demands of morality?

In order to understand Kant's seemingly gratuitous insistence on a "merely intelligible" moment of spontaneity in the conception of rational agency, one must begin with a consideration of his views on the spontaneity of the understanding and reason in their epistemic functions. Indeed, Kant himself indicates the connection when, in a famous passage, he states that through mere apperception we are conscious of certain faculties, namely, understanding and reason, "the action of which cannot be ascribed to the receptivity of sensibility" (A547/B575). Since Kant's conception of apperception and its spontaneity is obviously too vast a topic to do justice to here, we must be content with a brief sketch of his position. Nevertheless, even the brief sketch should help to cast some light on our problem.

At the very beginning of the Transcendental Analytic, Kant contrasts the receptivity of the senses with the spontaneity of the understanding (A51/B75). Largely against the empiricists, he argues that the senses provide the mind with the data for thinking objects but not with the thought or knowledge thereof. The latter, he maintains, requires the active taking up of the data by the mind, its unification in a concept and its reference to an object. Kant identifies this complex act of unification and reference with judgment, and he regards it as the fundamental activity of the understanding (A73/B94). He also attributes the activity to the spontaneity of the thinking subject.

The essential connection between judgment and spontaneity can be clarified by construing judgment as the activity of "taking as." To judge is to take something as a such and such. In the simplest case, an indeterminate something x is taken as an F; in more complex cases, Fx is qualified by further "determinations" or predicates, e.g., Fx is G; in still more complex cases, distinct takings (categorical judgments) are combined in a single higher order taking (hypothetical and disjunctive judgments). In all cases, however, the activity of "taking as" is constitutive of judgment.

This conception of judgment also accounts for the connection between the spontaneity of the understanding and apperception, which is a central theme of the Transcendental Deduction, particularly in the Second Edition. Eschewing all details, the main point is simply that, although we can perfectly well perceive or intuit x's that are Fs (such a capacity falls within the sphere of sensibility and can be attributed even to animals), we cannot conceive or represent to ourselves an x as F without not only doing it, that is, consciously taking it as such, but also without in some sense "knowing what one is doing," that is, without an awareness (although not an experience) of the activity. Kant terms this non-empirical consciousness of the activity of thinking "apperception," and he distinguishes it sharply from the empirical consciousness of one's mental states, which he assigns to inner sense.[13]

Similar considerations apply to the faculty of reason. Kant characterizes reasoning as "mediate inference" and he usually has syllogistic reasoning in mind. For present purposes, however, the main point is simply that any genuinely inferential process (whatever its logical form) involves drawing

---

[13] See B152-56, *Anth.* 7: 140-42, 161. I discuss this issue in detail in *Kant's Transcendental Idealism*, Chaps. 12 and 13.

conclusions from premises in such a way that the premises are taken as justifying the conclusion. In other words, the premises must not only be good and sufficient reasons for asserting the conclusion, they must be regarded as such. Indeed, the latter is the crucial factor; for even if one's reasons are not good and sufficient, one is still reasoning, albeit badly. Moreover, as before, this "taking as" is a spontaneous, inherently self-conscious activity of the subject. Not only is it something the subject does; it is something that it does for itself and, therefore, self-consciously.

As just described, the activity of reason is essentially of a piece with that of the understanding and involves the same kinds of spontaneity and self-consciousness. Sometimes, however, Kant attributes a distinct, higher level of spontaneity to reason by virtue of its total independence of sensibility and its conditions (something that cannot be said of the understanding because of its need for schemeta).[14] Although it is not perfectly clear what Kant means by this, presumably at least part of what he has in mind is that reason has the capacity to form Ideas and to regulate enquiry in accordance with these Ideas. Such formation and regulation involve spontaneity because rather than simply following the order of nature in borrowing its data from that order, reason projects an order of its own "in accordance with Ideas," that is, it generates a set of norms and goals of explanation, in terms of which scientific enquiry must proceed. In short, it prescribes the direction and standards of such enquiry.[15]

Nevertheless, merely calling attention to Kant's account of the spontaneity of the understanding and reason (henceforth called "epistemic spontaneity") does not of itself suffice to explain, much less to justify, Kant's insistence on the spontaneity of a rational agent (henceforth called "practical spontaneity").[16] The former is an intellectual capacity that Kant regards as the essential feature of a discursive intelligence. The latter is a causal power, specifically, the power to initiate a series of events in the phenomenal world without being determined to do so by antecedent events or states, including the antecedent state of the agent. Given this difference, one can hardly assume

[14] See A547/B575 and *Groundwork*, 4:452.
[15] See Ingeborg Heidemann, *Spontaneität und Zeitlichkeit* (KölnerUniversitäts-Verlag, 1958), pp. 226-27, and my *Kant's Transcendental Idealism*, pp. 274-75.
[16] The theme of a practical spontaneity (and intentionality) in Kant has been treated at length, and with considerable subtlety by Gerold Prauss, *Kant über Freiheit als Autonomie* (Frankfurt am Main: Klostermann, 1983). Although I differ from Prauss on a number of significant points, most of them not directly germane to the specific concerns of this paper, I have certainly been influenced by many aspects of his analysis.

that a being possesses the latter capacity simply by virtue of possessing the former. Moreover, although it does appear that for a period during the 1770s Kant virtually identified these two kinds of spontaneity, grounding transcendental freedom in the mere capacity to say 'I', there is also clear evidence that he rejected such an identification well before the publication of the first *Critique*.[17]

The problem, then, is to understand the connection between epistemic and practical spontaneity, a connection that Kant continued to affirm even after he rejected their identification.[18] Although Kant is somewhat less than fully explicit on the topic, it does seem possible to discern the basic thrust of his position. Put simply, epistemic spontaneity is a necessary but not a sufficient condition of practical spontaneity. That it is not a sufficient condition hardly requires further comment. That it is a necessary condition becomes clear once it is recognized that practical spontaneity or, more simply, practical freedom, involves both a "taking as" and a framing or positing.

The relevance of the second feature should be clear from the earlier discussion. Just as in the theoretical realm the proper, regulative, function of reason is to guide enquiry by framing an ideal order involving the systematic connection of phenomena under laws, so, in the practical realm, its proper function is to guide conduct by framing an order of ends or "ought-to-bes." Like its theoretical analogue, this activity is an expression of the spontaneity of reason (not understanding) because it goes beyond what is dictated by the sensible data, which in this case are the desires and inclinations of the agent. Insofar as one x's because one judges that one ought to x (whether for moral or prudential reasons), one x's for rational considerations. The "necessity" to x is then a rational necessity stemming from "objective laws of reason" (or at least putative laws), not a causal necessity stemming from antecedent conditions. In order to grasp the distinction between the two kinds of necessity, one need only note that it does not follow from the fact that x-ing is rationally or "objectively" necessary that one will x, whereas it does follow from the fact that it is causally necessary. Kant frequently insists that what is objectively

[17] For an account of the development of Kant's thought on this issue see Ameriks, *Kant's Theory of Mind*, pp. 189-203. The virtual identification occurs in the *Metaphysik* L$_1$, 28: 226-69. The key text in evidence of a rejection of this identification is *Reflexion* 5442, 18: 183, where Kant distinguishes between "logical freedom," which pertains to acts of reason, and "transcendental freedom," which supposedly pertains to acts of will.
[18] See A546/B574, *Groundwork*, 4: 447-448 and the review of Johannes Schulz's *Sittenlehre*, 8: 13-14.

necessary is subjectively contingent, and this holds in both moral and prudential contexts.

The practical analogue of "taking as" enters the picture when we consider
the relationship between rational agents and their inclinations or desires.
Although Kant certainly recognizes that rational agents can, and usually do,
act on the basis of their desires, that is, act to realize some object of desire, he
denies that this is to be conceived as a quasi-mechanistic response to the
desire. On the contrary, as we have already seen, even the desire-based actions
of a rational agent involve rules or principles of action. What has not yet been
noted, however, is that it is by being subsumed under these rules or principles
that inclinations or desires are deemed or "taken as" appropriate bases for
actions. As in the epistemic context, this practical "taking as" is a manifestation of the spontaneity of the subject in that it involves a self-determination
that requires a certain independence of the sensible data. Kant hints at this at
the very beginning of his discussion of practical freedom in the Dialectic when
he remarks that in considering a free act we are constrained to consider its
"cause" as "not... so determining that it excludes a causality of our will"
(A534/B562). He provides a somewhat more explicit statement of it in
Religion within the Limits of Reason Alone when he states that "freedom of the
will [*Willkür*] is of a wholly unique nature in that an incentive can determine
the will to an action *only insofar as the individul has incorporated it into his
maxim* (has made it into the general rule in accordance with which he will
conduct himself)" (6: 24/19). The upshot of this is simply that an inclination
or desire does not of itself constitute a reason for acting; it does so only insofar
as we adopt a rule of action which dictates that we ought to pursue the
satisfaction of that inclination or desire.

In fact, the affinity between Kant's conception of rational agency and his
doctrine of transcendental apperception is even greater than the above
account suggests.[19] Thus, one can say that just as "It must be possible for 'I
think' to accompany all my representations" in order for them to be "mine,"
that is, in order for me to be able to represent anything through them, so too,
it must be possible for the 'I take' to accompany all my inclinations if they are
to be "mine" *qua* rational agent, that is, if they are to provide motives or
reasons for acting. Again, just as sensible intuitions are only related to an
object by being subsumed under concepts, so too, sensible inclinations are
only related to an object of the will insofar as they are "incorporated into a

---

[19] Much of what follows in the paragraph, although not the precise formulation, was
suggested to me by my colleague, Robert Pippin.

maxim," that is, subsumed under a rule of action. Finally, and most significantly for the understanding of Kant's position, the 'I take' like the 'I think' can be conceived but not experienced. In other words, I can no more observe myself deciding than I can observe myself judging, although in both cases I must be conscious of what I am doing.[20] That is precisely why both activities are "merely intelligible" in the specifically Kantian sense.

We can see from the above that both aspects of practical spontaneity are essential to our conception of ourselves as rational agents. I cannot conceive of myself as such an agent without regarding myself as capable of pursuing ends which I frame for myself and which I regard as rational to pursue. Correlatively, I cannot conceive of myself as such an agent without assuming that I have a certain control over my inclinations, that I am capable of deciding which of them are to be acted upon (and how) and which resisted. These are, as it were, necessary presuppositions for everyone who regards their reason as practical. Presumably, that is why Kant insists in the *Groundwork* that we cannot act except under the Idea of freedom (4: 448). In the more metaphysical language of the *Critique of Pure Reason*, this means that we cannot conceive of ourselves as rational agents without attributing to our agency an "intelligible character," capable of determining itself on the basis of rational principles, "independently of the conditions of time."

III

So far we have considered Kant's conceptions of the empirical and the intelligible character of rational agency separately. We now have to deal with the question of their connection. This is clearly the most problematic feature of the Kantian account because it involves the claim that one and the same action can, without contradiction, both be explained in terms of antecedent causes and regarded as free in an indeterminist sense. Surely, it is no exaggeration to suggest that the coherence of the Kantian position on freedom stands or falls with this claim.

It will be convenient to begin our consideration of this issue with Kant's own notorious example of a malicious lie, which he presents as an instance of a voluntary action. Faced with such an action, Kant suggests that we first enquire into its "motive causes" *(Bewegursachen)*, and then seek to determine the degree to which the action and its consequences can be imputed to the agent. In other words, we move from the question of explanation to the

---

[20] The key text here is *Reflexion* 5661, 18: 318-19. For my discussion of this topic see *Kant's Transcendental Idealism*, pp. 275-78.

question of imputation.[21] In considering the former question, the operative assumption is that this concerns the empirical character of the action and that it can be answered in terms of factors such as "defective education, bad company... the viciousness of a natural disposition insensitive to shame... levity and thoughtlessness," as well as other "occasional causes that may have intervened" (A554/B582). In short, it is assumed that the action can be explained in terms of a combination of environmental factors and character traits. There are, of course, important questions to be raised regarding the interplay and relative weights of these empirical conditions, but Kant is clearly not concerned with such issues. The main point is merely that "although we believe that the action is thus determined, we none the less blame the agent." Moreover, he continues, we do not do so because of his bad disposition, or even his previous way of life; rather, Kant suggests,

we presuppose that we can leave out of consideration what his way of life may have been, that we can regard the past series of conditions as not having occurred and the act as being completely unconditioned by any preceding state, just as if the agent in and by himself began in this action an entirely new series of consequences. (A555/B583)

Undoubtedly, the most striking feature of the passage is the concluding suggestion that, in order to impute an action to an agent, we must conceive the action as a kind of creation *ex nihilo*, unconditioned by antecedent factors. This sounds paradoxical, to say the least. We seem to be required to admit occurrences in the phenomenal world that are causally unconditioned by antecedent states of affairs, including the antecedent state of the agent. But this contradicts the central teachings of the Transcendental Analytic. At least that is how the situation has appeared to most of Kant's critics.

---

[21] Jonathan Bennett has argued that one of the many problems with Kant's account of freedom is that he fails to distinguish clearly between the problem of agency and the problem of accountability (*Kants Dialectic*, p. 219). Moreover, although he criticizes all aspects of Kant's position, the sharpest criticisms seem to be directed against his views on accountability or imputation, particularly insofar as they are expressed in passages such as the one currently under consideration. In response to this, it must be insisted that, although agency and imputability are certainly distinct, they are also closely related. In fact, as Bennett himself acknowledges, accountability involves agency in that "an action for which a person is responsible is essentially one in respect of which the question arose, for that person, of whether to perform it" (p. 211). This is in accord with the Kantian position. Kant would also insist, however, that in order to conceive of an agent as concerned with the question of whether or not to perform a certain action one must attribute practical spontaneity to that agent. In short, agency, as Kant conceives it, is a necessary condition of imputability.

The paradox can be mitigated somewhat, although not removed, by a consideration of the unusually circumspect language that Kant uses in this passage. Thus, he tells us that, for the purpose of imputation, "we presuppose that we can leave out of consideration" all of the causally relevant factors and that we regard the action as completely unconditioned, "just as if," etc. As I have argued elsewhere, this "as if" should not be taken in a fictionalist sense, but rather as an indication that Kant is merely characterizing the "logic" or "language game" of imputation, not making an ontological claim about the noumenal status of rational agents.[22] In other words, Kant is depicting the conception of agency required for imputation as opposed to the description or explanation of actions.

The root intuition is the familiar one that, insofar as we praise or blame an agent for an action, we assume that, at the time of the action, the agent had a choice in the matter, that is, that the action was not causally necessitated by antecedent conditions, including the state of the agent (even though it must also be somehow connected with this state, as compatibilists frequently remind us). It does not follow from this, however, that we must always deem a rational agent responsible "in spite of everything." On the contrary, Kant insists that we can never be sure in matters of imputation because the intelligible character which we conceive is inaccessible to us. As he puts it in an important footnote dealing with moral responsibility:

The real morality of actions, their merit or guilt, even that of our own conduct, thus remains entirely hidden from us. Our imputations can refer only to the empirical character. How much of this character is ascribable to the pure effect of freedom, how much to mere nature, that is, to faults of temperament for which there is no responsibility, or to its happy constitution (*merito fortunae*), can never be determined; and upon it therefore no perfectly just judgments can be passed. (A551/B579 note)

But this weakening move is unlikely to be enough to satisfy Kant's critics. The essential question, after all, is not whether we are *always* free to act in ways other than we are causally determined to act; it is rather whether, given causal determination, we can *ever* be free in that sense. Kant seems to be committed to the doctrine that we can be. This latter claim may be weaker than the former; but it has certainly struck most of Kant's critics as equally problematic.

Moreover, in order to make sense of the Kantian position, it is not enough simply to point out that Kant is not postulating two distinct causes or causal agents (one phenomenal and the other noumenal), but rather contrasting two

---

[22] *Kant's Transcendental Idealism*, pp. 328-29.

distinct ways in which the causal activity of rational agents can be conceived. Even granting this "two-aspect" reading, one might still agree with Terence Irwin that "if an event is determined, it is true of it under all descriptions that it is determined, even though only some true descriptions, those referring to the relevant laws, show why it is determined."[23] The clear implication of this, which Irwin proceeds to draw, is that Kant cannot coherently claim that an event is determined under a phenomenal description and free under a noumenal one. The most that he can claim is that the noumenal description prescinds from the phenomenal determining grounds, which brings us right back to compatibilism.

Although he does not spell it out, perhaps because he believes that the point is too obvious to require any amplification, Irwin's objection seems to rest on the assumption that being causally determined is a necessary or essential property of any occurrence of which it is predicated. In the contemporary idiom of possible world semantics, this means that if an occurrence is causally determined in any possible world, it must be causally determined in all. Thus, so the argument goes, Kant cannot limit the property of being causally determined to occurrences in the phenomenal world or, equivalently, to occurrences taken under their phenomenal descriptions.

Irwin's point seems to be well taken. Certainly, it expresses in a helpful form the basic difficulty that many philosophers have felt regarding Kant's theory of freedom. At the same time, however, since, implicitly at least, it views the causal principle as an ontological predicate of events considered as *an sich* realities, it also begs a good many questions against transcendental idealism.

As I have argued elsewhere, however, rather than regarding the principles (and their corresponding categories and schemata) as ontological predicates, constitutive of, or even applicable to, things as they are in themselves, Kant regards them as epistemic conditions, necessary for the experience of events in a unified spatio-temporal framework.[24] Moreover, the "critical" limitations of this principle to appearances or, equivalently, to objects of possible experience, does not mean that events only "appear" to be, but "really" are not, subject to this principle; it means rather that a "transcendental location" is left for a different, non-experiential conception of at least some events, namely, those which in their empirical character are regarded as the intentional actions of rational agents.

[23] "Morality and Personality: Kant and Green," *Self and Nature in Kant's Philosophy*, p. 38.
[24] See *Kant's Transcendental Idealism*, pp. 10-13, 65, 86-87, 109.

Finally, it must be kept in mind that, as an epistemic condition, the causal principle functions as a condition of the possibility of the explanation of the actions of rational agents, considered as spatio-temporal occurrences. This entails that, considered with respect to their intelligible character, such actions cannot be explained. Like so much else in Kant's account, this seems quite paradoxical; but it is actually a strength rather than a weakness of his position. Indeed, the point is not that the spontaneity of the agent is supposed to function as a supplemental explanatory factor in some, more metaphysically adequate, super-empirical explanation (this assumption is precisely what makes Kant's whole account seem so objectionable); it is rather that it is necessary to fulfill a distinct, non-explanatory function.

In the example of the malicious lie, this function is imputation, which Kant explicitly contrasts with explanation. This, in turn, suggests the specifically moral reading of Kant's analysis. On this reading, we have conditions of explanation on the one hand and conditions of imputation on the other; correlatively, the force of the appeal to transcendental idealism is to show that these conditions need not conflict with one another. Given the account of intelligible character sketched in the preceding section, however, it seems reasonable to distinguish beween Kant's general point about rational agency and the specifically ethical illustration that he provides of it. As already indicated, the general point is that, in order to attribute an action to a rational agent (whether or not it is for purposes of moral praise or blame), it is necessary to conceive of the agent as endowed with a certain practical spontaneity and this, in turn, involves an appeal to the transcendental Idea of freedom. In support of this reading, it should also be noted that Kant himself presents the malicious lie merely as an example of a voluntary action, and such actions need not have moral significance.

But quite aside from the question of whether or not Kant's account applies only to morally significant actions, the fact remains that the preceding analysis and defense will hardly seem compelling to Kant's critics because it presupposes the truth of transcendental idealism (actually, it also presupposes the truth of a certain interpretation of this idealism). Unfortunately, this is a difficulty that cannot be overcome, at least not without a full-scale defense of transcendental idealism. Kant's whole treatment of freedom, both in the *Critique of Pure Reason* and in his later writings on moral philosophy, is inseparable from his appeal to the transcendental ideality of appearances. Indeed, in a late *Reflexion* (6353, 18: 679) he not only affirms that the ideality of space and time and the reality of the concept of freedom are the two cardinal points around which the system of the *Critique of Pure Reason* turns, which is itself a fairly common claim for Kant, he also contends that one is led analytically from one to the other. Even if this contention is a bit too strong (as I think it is), it still seems clear that about the best one can do is to try to show that Kant's account of freedom is plausible, given the framework of transcendental idealism. This may not seem like much; but it is more than most of Kant's critics will allow.

There is, however, a related criticism that assumes the legitimacy of transcendental idealism and, therefore, that cannot be dismissed simply by appealing to it. This criticism, which has been forcefully developed by Lewis White Beck, turns on the contrast between the standpoints of the actor and of the spectator. Each standpoint, Beck maintains, has its own distinct mode of explanation; the former is in terms of reasons and the later in terms of causes. Moreover, just as one can be either an actor or a spectator but not both with respect to the same action at the same time, so too, one can explain a given action in terms of either reasons or causes, but not in terms of both. Applying this to Kant, it follows that he is not entitled to claim that one and the same action can be both regarded as free and as explicable in causal terms. Finally, in light of this critique, Beck suggests that what Kant should have done is to have treated the freedom–causality conflict in the first *Critique* in the same manner as he treated the conflict between teleological and mechanistic explanation in the third *Critique*, that is, as a conflict between alternative regulative maxims, each of which is required for a certain kind of explanation.[25]

It is not possible to consider here all of the ramifications of Beck's reconstruction of the Kantian position (which is also advocated by other "friendly" critics);[26] but it must be kept in mind that even organic processes, which supposedly require teleological explanations, are subject to the Second Analogy. For present purposes, however, the most important point is that, since empirical and intelligible character both pertain to the causality of reason and, therefore, to rational agency, Kant's distinction between these two kinds of character does not correlate precisely with the familiar contrast between causal and reason-explanation. Thus, as we have already seen, to consider an action with respect to its (or the agent's) empirical character is to consider it in light of its reasons. These reasons, rather than neuro-physiological factors, serve to explain (in Davidson's terms "rationalize") the action. Accordingly,

[25] Lewis White Beck, *A Commentary on Kant's Critique of Practical Reason* (University of Chicago Press, 1960), pp. 191-94 and *The Actor and the Spectator* (Yale University Press, 1975), esp. pp. 123-25.

[26] For similar analyses see Stephen Körner, "Kant's Conception of Freedom," *Proceedings of the British Academy* 53 (1967): 193-217 and John Silber, "The Ethical Significance of Kant's Religion," in the introduction to the English translation of *Religion*, esp. pp. xcvii-ciii.

even at the empirical level, human actions are regarded as expressions of rational agency, not as mere bits of behavior. This is the case even though these reasons are connected with the agent's mental state and are regarded naturalistically both as causal determinants of the action and as themselves causally determined. Correlatively, when an action is considered with respect to its (or the agent's) intelligible character, practical spontaneity is introduced into the picture in order to capture the thought (central to the conception of agency) of the agent deciding to act on the basis of the reasons ("incorporating" them into his maxims).

Moreover, the analogy also breaks down because, as we have likewise seen, the appeal to the intelligible character does not function to provide an alternative explanation that needs somehow to be reconciled with the empirical explanation that rationalizes the action. Instead, it presupposes the legitimacy of the empirical explanation and adds to it a reference to the practical spontaneity of the subject in order to conceive the action in question as an expression of rational agency.

For these reasons, Kant's conception of an intelligible character, at least as it is operative in the *Critique of Pure Reason*, can best be understood as referring to a dimension of rational agency that complements rather than conflicts with the empirical dimension of the same agency. There is no conflict because the complementary factor, the spontaneity of the agent, is empirically vacuous and plays no explanatory role. As Kant succinctly puts it, "This intelligible ground does not have to be considered in empirical enquiries" (A548/B574). But, given Kant's transcendental idealism, which allows transcendental room or conceptual space for what can be conceived but not experienced, it does not follow that it is altogether vacuous and plays no role whatsoever. On the contrary, the main thrust of the preceding discussion has been to argue that it plays a crucial role regulating our conception of ourselves and of others as rational agents.

University of California
San Diego

Christine M. Korsgaard

Morality as Freedom

Elevating though man's privilege is, of being capable of such an idea as freedom of choice — [those who are accustomed only to physiological explanations] are stirred up by the proud claims of speculative reason, which feels its power so strongly in other fields. They are stirred up just as if they were allies, leagued in defense of the omnipotence of theoretical reason and roused by a general call to arms to resist the idea of freedom of choice and thus at present, and perhaps for a long time to come (though ultimately in vain), to attack the moral concept of freedom and, if possible, render it suspect.

Immanuel Kant (TL 6: 378/34-35)

Kantian ethical philosophy has often been criticized for its dependence on an untenable conception of the freedom of the will. Kant is supposed to have asserted that we are morally responsible for all of our actions because we have free will, and that we have free will because we exist in a noumenal world in which we are uninfluenced by the temptations of desire and inclination. If we existed *only* in the noumenal world, we would invariably act as the categorical imperative requires, but because we are also phenomenal beings we sometimes go wrong. The view so understood gives rise to several problems. First, the claim that purely noumenal persons would act as the categorical imperative requires may be questioned. It is not obvious why persons uninfluenced by causality should act morally rather than any other way. Secondly, if it *can* be established that insofar as we are noumena we obey the moral law, then the account of moral imputability becomes unintelligible. If we are only responsible because we are noumena and if insofar as we are noumena we only do what is right, then we cannot be responsible for our evil actions. Or, if we are responsible, it is so radically that no room is left for excuses. For how can we take into account the terrible temptations to which the wrongdoer was subjected, when the choosing noumenon was uninfluenced by those temptations? Finally, the view seems to require an unappealing ontological commit-

I would like to thank Manley Thompson, Andrews Reath, Stephen Engstrom, and Onora O'Neill for valuable comments on earlier drafts of this paper.

Y. Yovel (ed.), Kant's Practical Philosophy Reconsidered, 23-48.

ment to the existence of "two worlds," and to give rise to a variety of puzzles about how what occurs in the one can influence the other.

In this paper my aim is to address these problems. In the first part of the paper, I show why Kant thinks that the moral law is the law of a free will, and why he thinks we must regard ourselves as free. I then argue that the supposed problems about responsibility and ontology arise from a common source: a failure to appreciate the radical nature of Kant's separation of theoretical and practical reason, and of their respective domains of explanation and deliberation. When these domains are separated in the way that Kant's philosophy requires, the problems about responsibility disappear, and we see that Kant's theory of freedom does not commit him to an ontological dualism.[1] In the second part of the paper I show what it does commit him to: a certain conception of the moral virtues.

I. Law as Freedom

1. Freedom enters Kant's moral philosophy as the solution to a problem. The categorical imperative is not analytic, and disregarding its claims is therefore not inconsistent. Yet it is supposed to present us with a rational necessity. In order to show that morality is not a "mere phantom of the mind" (G 4: 445/64), Kant seeks to provide a deduction of (or a credential for)[2] the moral law: he must link being rational to acting on the moral law. The third idea through which rationality and morality are linked is the positive conception of freedom. By showing, first, that a free person as such follows the moral law, and, second, that a rational person has grounds for regarding herself as free, Kant tries to show that insofar as we are rational, we will obey the moral law.

It was making the second of these two connections that troubled Kant — the connection between rationality and freedom. The arguments intended to demonstrate this connection in the *Foundations* and in the *Critique of Practical Reason* are obscure and appear to be different from one another. In *Foundations* III, Kant calls his argument a "deduction" of the moral law

---

[1] For another treatment of some of these same difficulties, but centered more on Kant's views in the *Critique of Pure Reason*, see Henry E. Allison, "Empirical and Intelligible Character in the *Critique of Pure Reason*" in this volume.

[2] The alternative language is used because of the difference in Kant's own two accounts of what he is doing. I discuss this below. (All citations from the *Foundations* are taken from Beck's translation.)

(4: 454/73), and connects freedom and reason through the capacity of reason for pure spontaneous activity which is exhibited in its production of ideas. This spontaneous activity shows we are members of the intelligible world and therefore free (4: 452/70-71). In the *Critique of Practical Reason*, we are instead offered what Kant calls a "credential" for morality (5: 48/49) and told that "the objective reality of the moral law can be proved through no deduction" (5: 47/48). The credential is provided by the fact that freedom can be deduced *from* morality. Kant does not comment on the difference between these two arguments, and his readers do not agree about whether they come to the same thing, or are different arguments serving different purposes, or are incompatible arguments resulting from a change of mind.[3]

But Kant was not in doubt about his success in making the first connection, between morality and freedom. Kant was confident that "if freedom of the will is presupposed, morality together with its principle follows from it by the mere analysis of its concept" (G 4:447/65). In *Foundations* III, the argument for this point takes about a page; in the second *Critique*, it is a mere paragraph, posed as

Problem II
Granted that a will is free, find the law which alone is competent to determine it necessarily.

Since the material of the practical law, i.e., an object of the maxim, cannot be given except empirically, and since a free will must be independent of all empirical conditions (i.e., those belonging to the world of sense) and yet be determinable, a free will must find its ground of determination in the law, but independently of the material of the law. But besides the latter there is nothing in a law except the legislative form. Therefore, the legislative form, in so far as it is contained in the maxim, is the only thing which can constitute a determining ground of the [free] will. (5: 29/28-29)

Not everyone has found this connection so perspicuous. In his well-known appendix to *The Methods of Ethics*,[4] Sidgwick complains that Kant's whole moral philosophy is vitiated by a confusion between two senses of "freedom."

---

[3] For some important discussions of this question see the following works: H.J. Paton, *The Categorical Imperative* (1947), Book IV (University of Pennsylvania Press, 1971); W.D. Ross, *Kant's Ethical Theory* (Oxford: Clarendon Press, 1954); Karl Ameriks, "Kant's Deduction of Freedom and Morality," *Journal of the History of Philosophy* 19 (1981): 53-80; Dieter Henrich, "Die Deduktion des Sittengesetzes," in *Denken im Schatten des Nihilismus*, ed. Alexander Schwan (Darmstadt: Wissenschaftliche Buchgesellschaft, 1975). My own view on the matter is explained in Section 3.

[4] Repr. Indianapolis: Hackett 1981. The appendix, "The Kantian Conception of Free Will [Reprinted with some omissions, from *Mind*, 1888, Vol. 13, no. 51]" was first attached to the sixth edition in 1901.

"Moral or neutral" freedom is the freedom we exercise when we choose between good and evil. "Good or rational" freedom is the freedom we exercise when we act morally, and so are not "enslaved" by our passions and desires. Sidgwick accuses Kant of being unaware of the distinction. This accusation is unfair, for the distinction Sidgwick makes is closely related to Kant's own distinction between the negative and positive freedom. As we shall see, Kant rejects moral or neutral freedom as a conception of freedom; but it is a consequence of negative freedom, or the absence of all determination.

We may put Kant's reply to Sidgwick in these terms. Following John Rawls, we may distinguish the *concept* of X, formally or functionally defined, from a *conception* of X, materially and substantively defined.[5] The Kantian *concept* of free will would be "a will which makes choices independently of all alien influences," that is, a will which is negatively free. A positive *conception* of freedom would be a material account of what such a will would in fact choose. Kant's reply to Sidgwick will then be that there is a single concept of freedom, of which the moral law is the unique positive conception. My aim in the next section is to explain Kant's claim that the moral law is the unique positive conception of freedom.

2. Kant argues that when you make a choice you must act "under the idea of freedom" (G 4:448/66). He explains that "we cannot conceive of a reason which consciously responds to a bidding from the outside with respect to its judgments" (G 4:448/66). You may of course *choose* to act on a desire, but insofar as you take the act to be *yours*, you think you have made it your maxim to act on this desire. If you feel that the desire impelled you into the act, you do not regard the act as a product of your will, but as involuntary. The point is not that you must *believe* that you are free, but that you must choose as if you were free. It is important to see that this is quite consistent with believing yourself to be fully determined. To make it vivid, imagine that you are participating in a scientific experiment, and you know that today your every move is programmed by an electronic device implanted in your brain. The device is not going to bypass your thought processes, however, and make you

---

[5] John Rawls, *A Theory of Justice* (Harvard, 1971), p. 5. Rawls is in turn drawing upon H.L. H. Hart, *The Concept of Law* (Oxford: Clarendon Press, 1961), pp. 155-59. Rawls uses the distinction in separating the concept of justice, "a characteristic set of principles for assigning basic rights and duties and for determining... the proper distribution of the benefits and burdens of social cooperation" from conceptions of justice, that is, various substantive accounts of what those principles are.

move mechanically, but rather to work through them: it will determine what you think. Perhaps you get up and decide to spend the morning working. You no sooner make the decision than it occurs to you that it must have been programmed. We may imagine that in a spirit of rebellion you then decide to skip work and go shopping. And then it occurs to you that *that* must have been programmed. The important point here is that efforts to second guess the device cannot help you decide what to do. They can only prevent you from making any decision. In order to *do* anything, you must simply ignore the fact that you are programmed, and decide what to do — just as if you were free. You will believe that your decision is a sham, but it makes no difference.[6] Kant's point, then, is not about a theoretical assumption necessary to decision, but about a fundamental feature of the standpoint from which decisions are made.[7] It follows from this feature that we must regard our decisions as springing ultimately from principles that we have chosen, and justifiable by those principles. We must regard ourselves as having free will.

Kant defines a free will as a rational causality that is effective without being determined by an alien cause. Anything outside of the will counts as an alien cause, including the desires and inclinations of the person. The free will must be entirely self-determining. Yet, because it is a causality, it must act on some law or other. "Since the concept of a causality entails that of laws... it follows that freedom is by no means lawless" (G 4:446/65). The free will therefore must have its own law. Alternatively, we may say that since the will is practical reason, it cannot be conceived as acting and choosing for no reason. Since reasons are derived from principles, the free will must have its own principle. Kant thinks that the categorical imperative is the free will's law or principle. But it may seem unclear why this more than anything else should be the free will's principle. If it is free to make its own law, why can't it make any law whatever?

To see why, imagine an attempt to discover the freely adopted principle on which some action is based. I ask to know why you are doing some ordinary thing, and you give me your proximate reason, your immediate end. I then ask why you want that, and most likely you mention some larger end or project. I

---

[6] You may take the belief into account in other ways, like other beliefs. For instance, you may decide to warn your friends that you may do something uncharacteristic today, and that if so they should not be upset, since you are, as we say, "not yourself."
[7] This is brought out well by Thomas Hill, Jr., in "Kant's Argument for the Rationality of Moral Conduct," *Pacific Philosophical Quarterly* 66 (1985): 3-23 and in "Kant's Theory of Practical Reason" delivered at the conference *Ethics and Its History*, May 16-17, 1986, at the University of California at San Diego.

can press on, demanding your reason at every step, until we reach the moment when you are out of answers. You have shown that your action is calculated to assist you in achieving what you think is desirable on the whole, what you have determined that you want most.

The reasons that you have given can be cast in the form of maxims derived from imperatives. From a string of hypothetical imperatives, technical and pragmatic (G 4:416-17/34), you have derived a maxim to which we can give the abbreviated formulation:

"I will do this action, in order to get what I desire."

According to Kant, this maxim only determines your will if you have adopted another maxim that makes it your end to get what you desire. This maxim is:

"I will make it my end to have the things that I desire."

Now suppose that I want to know why you have adopted this maxim. Why should you try to satisfy your desires?

There are two answers which we can dismiss immediately. First, suppose you appeal to a psychological law of nature that runs something like "a human being necessarily pursues the things he or she desires."[8] To appeal to this causal law as an answer would be to deny your freedom and to deny that you are acting under the idea of freedom. The answer does not have the structure of reason-giving: it is a way of saying "I can't help it." Second, suppose you claim that you have adopted this maxim randomly. There is nothing further to say. You think you could have adopted some other maxim, since you regard your will as free, but as it happened you picked this one. As we know, Kant rejects this, as being inconsistent with the very idea of a will, which does what it does according to a law, or for a reason. It seems as if the will must choose its principle for a reason and so always on the basis of some more ultimate principle.

We are here confronted with a deep problem of a familiar kind. If you can give a reason, you have derived it from some more fundamental maxim, and I can ask why you have adopted that one. If you cannot, it looks as if your principle was randomly selected. Obviously, to put an end to a regress like this we need a principle about which it is impossible, unnecessary, or incoherent to ask why a free person would have chosen it. Kant's argument must show that

---

[8] To understand this as a law of nature, rather than as a tautology, we must of course understand a "desire" not merely as something we ascribe to a person on the basis of her actions, but as a psychological phenomenon of some sort. This view of desire is also implied by Kant's account of desire as an incentive, which I explain below.

the categorical imperative has this status.

Although Kant does not think that a free will exists in time, we may imagine that there is a "moment" when the free will is called upon to choose its most fundamental principle. In order to be a will, it must have a principle, from which it will derive its reasons. The principle it chooses will determine what it counts as a reason. But precisely because at this "moment" the will has not yet determined what it will count as a reason, it seems as if there could be no reason for it to choose one principle rather than another. Kant calls this feature of the will its "spontaneity."[9]

As the argument stands now, it looks as if the will could adopt any maxim we can construct. If you have a free will you could adopt a maxim of pursuing only those things to which you have an aversion, or perhaps all and only the things your next-door neighbor enjoys. For us human beings, however, these are not serious options, for reasons that come out most clearly in *Religion Within the Limits of Reason Alone*. Kant uses the term "incentive" (*Triebfeder*) to describe the relation of the free person to the candidate reasons among which she chooses. An incentive is something that makes an action interesting to you, that makes it a live option. Desires and inclinations are incentives; so is respect for the moral law. An inclination by itself is *merely* an incentive, and does not become a reason for action until the person has adopted it freely into her maxim (Rel. 6: 23-24/19; 44/40). Although incentives do not yet provide reasons for the spontaneous will, they do determine what the options are — which things, so to speak, are candidates for reasons. And having an aversion to something is not, for us human beings, an incentive for pursuing it, and so will not become a reason. In the *Religion*, Kant claims that it is impossible for a human being not to be moved at all by incentives; our freedom, rather, is exercised in choosing the order of precedence among the different kinds of incentives to which we are subject (6: 30/25; 36/31). So the real choice will be between a maxim of self-love, which subordinates the incentives of morality to those of inclination, and the moral maxim, which subordinates incentives of inclination to moral ones. The maxim of self-love says something like:

> "I will do what I desire, and what is morally required if it doesn't interfere with my self-love."

and the moral maxim says something like:

---

[9] More specifically, Kant associates the will's spontaneity with the fact that it does not exist under temporal conditions and so is uninfluenced by causality, but the important point here is just being uninfluenced — by anything. I discuss the relation between freedom and time in section 6.

"I will do what is morally required, and what I desire if it doesn't interfere with my duty."

More specifically stated, of course, the moral maxim is the maxim derived from the categorical imperative:

"I will act only on a maxim that I can will as a universal law."

It looks at first as if the problem here is to show that there is some reason for the spontaneous will to choose the moral maxim rather than the maxim of self-love. Yet this seems impossible, since the spontaneous will by hypothesis has not yet determined what it counts as a reason. But on reflection we shall see that this problem can be circumvented. We need only consider the *standpoint* of the spontaneous will, and the *content* of the categorical imperative.

At the standpoint of spontaneity, the will must, in order so to speak to commence operations, choose a principle or a law for itself. Nothing provides any content for that law. *All that it has to be is a law.*

Suppose that it chooses the categorical imperative, as represented by the Formula of Universal Law. This formula merely tells us to choose a law. Its only constraint on our choice is that it have the form of a law. Nothing provides any content for that law. *All that it has to be is a law.*

By making the Formula of Universal Law its principle, the free will retains the position of spontaneity. Or, to put it a better way, the argument shows that the free will need do nothing to make the Formula of Universal Law its principle: it is already its principle. The categorical imperative is thus shown to be the law of spontaneity. In a sense, the Formula of Universal Law simply describes the function or task of an autonomous will. The moral law does not impose a constraint on the will; it merely says what it has to do in order to be an autonomous will at all. It has to choose a law.

On the other hand, suppose the will chooses the maxim of self-love. In that case, it departs from its position of spontaneity and puts itself in the service of inclination. A constraint on its choice is acquired. The important thing to see is that there is no incentive for the spontaneous will to do this. Since we are just talking about the will itself right now, and not the whole person, the incentives of inclination cannot provide a temptation to adopt the maxim of self-love. Incentives of inclination cannot move the will to abandon its position of spontaneity, since they cannot move the will at all until it has already abandoned that position by resolving to be moved by them.

This argument, which I will call the Argument from Spontaneity, shows that there are not really two choices, morality and self-love, on an equal footing. The will that makes the categorical imperative its law merely reaffirms its independence of everything except law in general. Its dependence on law in general is not a constraint, for that is just a consequence of the fact that it is a will. Making the categorical imperative its principle does not require the spontaneous will to take an action — it is already its principle. Adopting the maxim of self-love is surrendering the position of spontaneity, and does require an action (Rel. 6: 31-32/26-27). And it is an action for which there could be no reason. Thus, not only are the two options not on a footing, but the choice of the maxim of self-love over that of morality is unintelligible. Morality is the natural condition of a free will. The free will that puts inclination above morality sacrifices its freedom for nothing.

3. A crucial point in the Argument from Spontaneity is that the spontaneous will is not tempted by incentives of inclination. Now, we human beings are not so situated with respect to the incentives of inclination, because we are imperfectly rational beings. Or rather, this is what makes us imperfectly rational beings. Our inclinations may be alien to our purely rational wills, but they are not alien to us, and they do tempt us. Letting our wills serve our happiness therefore does not seem pointless to us. So although the Argument from Spontaneity explains why a purely rational will would have the moral law as its first principle, it does not show us exactly why we should do so. In Kant's language, it does not explain "the interest attaching to the ideas of morality" (G 4:448/66).

Without an account of moral interest, Kant complains, there will be a circle in our explanation of moral obligation (G 4:449-50/67-69). Now, what exactly this circle is is rather difficult to see. Kant has already claimed that, as creatures who must act under the idea of freedom, we are bound by the laws of freedom (G 4:448/66). But he thinks this does not yet explain how "the worth we ascribe" to moral actions (G 4:449/68) can so completely outweigh the worth of our condition — that is, our happiness or unhappiness. We are willing to grant the importance of the autonomy we express in moral conduct only because we already think that morality is supremely important. But it is still unclear why we think so. What is needed is an incentive for us to identify with the free and rational side of our nature. To provide this, Kant introduces the distinction between the intelligible and sensible worlds, or noumena and phenomena.[10] This distinction introduces two new elements into the argument.

---

[10] "World" (*Welt*) is Kant's term, and it is in some respects unfortunate, since it has lent credence to the interpretation of the distinction as an ontological dualism. Actually these two worlds are two standpoints, or ways we have of looking at things; as

The first element is the emphasis on complete causal determination in the phenomenal world. Up until now, I have spoken of the will that adopts the maxim of self-love as adopting an unnecessary constraint. But the addition of the two-worlds picture makes the consequence of adopting the maxim of self-love look even worse. The will that adopts self-love as its maxim is determined by inclinations, and inclinations, in the world of phenomena, are completely determined by natural forces, by the nexus of causal laws. So such a will becomes a mere conduit for natural forces. The person who acts from self-love is in a sense not actively willing at all, but simply allowing herself to be controlled by the passive part of her nature, which in turn is controlled by all of nature. From the perspective of the noumenal world, ends we adopt under the influence of inclination rather than morality do not even seem to be our own.

The other element is introduced with the claim that *"the intelligible world contains the ground of the sensible world and hence of its laws"* (G 4:453/72).[11] Although we can *know* nothing of the noumenal world, it is what we conceive as lying behind the phenomenal world and giving that world its character. To conceive yourself as a member of the noumenal world is therefore to conceive yourself as among the grounds of the world as we know it.[12] And if you hold this position in so far as you have a will, then that means that the actions of your will make a real difference to the way the phenomenal world is.

Combining these two new elements we can generate a very stark contrast between choosing the maxim of morality and choosing that of self-love. We can think of the noumenal world as containing our own wills and whatever else forms part of "the ground of the sensible world and its laws." In particular, the noumenal world contains the ground, whatever it might be, of the laws of nature (for these are not objects of our wills).[13] We can influence

---

I will argue in the next section, they represent a practical and a theoretical viewpoint. I have continued to use the terminology of two worlds, since it is convenient and suits Kant's own usage. I would like to thank Onora O'Neill for urging me to be clearer on this point.

[11] The remark is not italicized in Beck's translation, although it is in the Akademie Textausgabe and the Paton and Abbott translations.

[12] For a different reading than mine of the idea that the intelligible world contains the grounds of the sensible world and its laws, and of why we must conceive ourselves as among those grounds, see Onora O'Neill's "Agency and Anthropology in Kant's *Groundwork*" in this volume.

[13] That our noumenal choices are in some way the ground of the laws of nature is a possibility that remains open; it is enough for the argument that we do not conceive ourselves as choosing these laws.

the phenomenal world, and these other forces do so as well. Of course, nothing can be known about the nature of this influence or its mechanisms, or of how these various agencies together generate the world of appearances. But we can still say this: if by choosing the maxim of self-love you allow the laws of nature to determine your actions, then you are in effect surrendering your place among "the grounds of the sensible world and its laws." The existence of your will in the noumenal world makes no difference to the character of the phenomenal world. For your will is determined by the laws of nature, and those in turn can be accounted for by other forces in the noumenal world. Although you are free, you could just as well not have been. Your freedom makes no difference. But if you will in accordance with the moral law, you do make a difference. You actually contribute — we might say to the rational, as opposed to the merely natural, ordering of the sensible world. The choice of the moral maxim over the maxim of self-love may then be seen as a choice of genuine activity over passivity; a choice to use your active powers to make a difference in the world.

Recall that all of this is supposed to solve the problem of moral interest. Kant thinks of the idea of our intelligible existence as being, roughly speaking, the motivating thought of morality, and so what makes morality possible. In the *Religion*, Kant tells us that one who honors the moral law cannot avoid thinking about what sort of world he would create under the guidance of practical reason, and that the answer is determined by the moral idea of the Highest Good (6: 5/5). In the second *Critique*, Kant says in one place that our intelligible existence gives us a "higher vocation" (5: 98/91). This vocation is help to make the world a rational place, by contributing to the production of the Highest Good.[14]

This argument also explains why Kant thinks that unless the Highest Good is possible the moral law is "fantastic, directed to empty imaginary ends, and consequently inherently false" (KpV 5:114/118). The difficulty arises in this way. We have explained moral interest in terms of a stark contrast between being a mere conduit for natural forces on the one hand and making a real difference in the world through one's intentions on the other. But in between these two possibilities we discover a third — that our intentions and actions will make a real difference in the world, but that we will have no control over what sort of difference they make — because the consequences of our actions

---

[14] In a footnote in "On the Common Saying: 'This may be True in Theory, but it does not Apply in Practice'" Kant speaks directly of the moral incentive as provided by the idea of the highest possible earthly good, as "attainable through his [man's] collaboration [*Mitwirkung*]" (TP 8: 280n/65n).

will not be what we intend. This can happen because we are not the only elements of the noumenal world and the various forces it contains combine, in ways we cannot comprehend, to generate the world of appearances. The forces of nature and the actions of other persons mediate between our intentions and the actual results of our actions, often distorting or perverting those results. This possibility then makes the appeal of freedom seem like a fraud. If the motivating thought of morality is that freedom means that we can make a difference in the world, but we then find that we have no control over the form this difference ultimately takes, then the motivating thought is genuinely threatened. Postulating God as the author of the laws of nature is a way of guaranteeing that other noumenal forces will cooperate with our good intentions, and leaves our moral interest in place. In the *Foundations*, Kant says:

the idea of a pure intelligible world as a whole of all intelligences to which we ourselves belong as rational beings... is always a useful and permissible idea for the purpose of a rational faith. This is so even though all knowledge terminates at its boundary, for through the glorious idea of a universal realm of end-in-themselves (rational beings) a lively interest in the moral law can be awakened in us. (4:462/82)

The Two-Worlds Argument is worked out better in the *Critique of Practical Reason* than in *Foundations* III. In *Foundations* III, Kant wants to argue that the idea of our existence in the intelligible world suggests our freedom to us: our capacity for pure spontaneous activity, which reveals itself in reason's production of ideas, makes us members of the intelligible world. As such we may regard ourselves as free. In the second *Critique*, Kant develops the reverse argument that freedom leads us to the conception of our existence in the intelligible world. It is morality, in turn, that teaches us that we are free. So morality itself "points" us to the intelligible world (KpV 5:44/43). The argument of the *Critique of Practical Reason* is superior because freedom requires not just that we exist in the intelligible world, but that we exist there insofar as we have wills — that we can be motivated from there, so to speak. The *Foundations* argument places our theoretical capacity to formulate pure ideas in the intelligible world, but that by itself does not imply that we can be moved by them.[15] And the latter is what the argument must show. The second *Critique* argument starts firmly from the fact that we can be motivated by pure ideas. That we can be so motivated is what Kant calls the Fact of Reason.

---

[15] For a different and perhaps more sympathetic account of the argument of *Foundations* III, see Onora O'Neill, "Agency and Anthropology in Kant's *Groundwork*" in this volume, especially section 6.

But the function of the idea of our intelligible existence as an incentive is essentially the same in both books. The famous address to Duty in the *Critique of Practical Reason*, like *Foundations* III, demands to know the source of the special worth we assign to morality (5:86-87/98). And the answer is again that respect for the moral law is produced by the thought of our intelligible nature. Kant says that the incentive of pure practical reason is

nothing else than the pure moral law itself, so far as it lets us perceive the sublimity of our own supersensuous existence. (KpV 5:89/91)[16]

The Argument from Spontaneity shows why a free and spontaneous will, uninfluenced by anything, makes the moral law its principle. The Argument from the Two Worlds shows us why we imperfectly rational beings, influenced by sensibility as well as morality, should do so as well. If we are free we are members of the intelligible world, the ground of the sensible world and its laws. This gives us a "higher vocation" than the satisfaction of our own desires. We can help to bring about the Highest Good in the world. The thought of that higher vocation is the motive of morality.

4. But the result of the Argument from Spontaneity may seem too strong. If the will *is* free, moral evil is unintelligible, for if this argument is correct, moral evil is the pure will's wholly unmotivated abandonment of its freedom. However, this is exactly Kant's view: evil is unintelligible. Neither a good will nor an evil will admits of explanation, for both must be regarded as grounded in the person's own free and spontaneous choice. If these choices could be explained, they would be derived from something else, and then they would not be the spontaneous choices that they purport to be (Rel. 6:21/17). Yet it is evil that is unintelligible, for it is in the evil choice that the will falls away from its freedom. Kant says:

Evil could have sprung only from the morally-evil (not from mere limitations in our nature); and yet the original predisposition is a predisposition to good; there is then for us no conceivable ground from which the moral evil in us could originally have come. (Rel. 6:43/38)

Moral evil is a Fall, in the Biblical sense, and it is exactly as hard to understand as the Fall in the Bible (Rel. 6:19/15; 41ff/36ff).

---

[16] The view that the idea of the intelligible world plays a motivational role can also be supported by appeal to Kant's writings on moral education, especially in the Methodologies of the second *Critique* and *The Metaphysical Principles of Virtue* (my references here are to the Ellington translation). In both, there is an emphasis on awakening the child to the sublimity of the intelligible existence which freedom reveals.

In fact, Kant goes so far as to deny that what Sidgwick calls moral or neutral freedom, the freedom to choose between good and evil, is really a conception of freedom at all:

> freedom can never be located in the fact that the rational subject is able to make a choice in opposition to his (legislative) reason, even though experience proves often enough that this does happen (though we cannot comprehend how this is possible)... Only freedom in relation to the internal legislation of reason is properly a capacity; the possibility of deviating from it is an incapacity. (MS 6:226-27/26-27)

Many readers, among them Sidgwick,[17] have complained that so strong an identification of freedom and morality should force Kant to give up his account of moral imputability. If the moral law is the unique positive conception of freedom, then it seems as if only morally good actions are really free. Kant does say that if we were solely members of the intelligible world we would always act in accordance with the moral law. How then are we to account for the imputability of bad actions and characters? Your noumenal self would not have chosen them. Your phenomenal self, being wholly determined, cannot be held responsible.

But these complaints ignore the status of the positive conception of freedom, and its corollary, intelligible existence, in the Kantian system. The positive conception of freedom, understood as noumenal causality, is a postulate of practical reason, in the sense developed in the *Dialectic* of the *Critique of Practical Reason*. Kant explains the basis of such postulates this way:

> The postulates of pure practical reason all proceed from the principle of morality, which is not a postulate but a law by which reason directly determines the will. This will... requires these necessary conditions for obedience to its precept. These postulates are not theoretical dogmas but presuppositions of necessarily practical import; thus, while they do not extend speculative knowledge, they give objective reality to the ideas of speculative reason in general (by means of their relation to the practical sphere), and they justify it in holding to concepts even the possibility of which it could not otherwise venture to affirm.
>
> These postulates are those of immortality, of freedom affirmatively regarded (as the causality of a being so far as he belongs to the intelligible world), and of the existence of God. (5:132/137)

A postulate of practical reason is an object of rational belief, but the reasons for the belief are practical and moral. The person needs the belief as a condition for obedience to the moral law, and it is this, combined with the categorical nature of that law, that justifies the belief. Although the beliefs are

---

[17] *The Methods of Ethics*, p. 516.

theoretical in form — the will is free, there is a God — their basis and their function are practical. As Kant says in the passage quoted above, and as he constantly emphasizes in the second *Critique*, the postulates play no theoretical or explanatory role whatsoever. They provide us with concepts that define the intelligible world, but we have no intuitions to which we may apply those concepts, and consequently no theoretical knowledge of their objects (e.g. 5:54-56/55-57; 133/138; 136/141).

The fact that the postulates of practical reason play no theoretical role has two important implications. One is that we cannot conclude from the Argument from Spontaneity that evil is impossible, or that a person who does something evil has not done it freely. A free but evil will is shown to be unintelligible *from the standpoint of pure practical reason*, but not to be theoretically impossible. It cannot be explained, but no act of freedom can be explained. And we are whole persons, not just pure spontaneous wills. Unlike the pure will in the Argument from Spontaneity, we are imperfectly rational, because we *are* subject to temptation from inclinations. There is no problem about explaining how *we* go wrong.

A central feature of Kant's philosophy as a whole is brought out here. The deliberating agent, employing reason practically, views the world as it were from a noumenal standpoint, as an expression of the wills of God and other rational agents. This is the philosophical consequence of the fact that we act under the idea of freedom, and of the way in which freedom leads to the other practical postulates: the ethical world replaces the world of speculative metaphysics. Kant tells us that "a moral principle is nothing but a dimly conceived metaphysics, which is inherent in every man's rational constitution" (TL 6:376/32). The theorizing spectator, on the other hand, views the world as phenomena, mechanistic and fully determined. The interests of morality demand a different conceptual organization of the world than those of theoretical explanation (MS 6:217/17; 221/20; 225/25). Both interests are rational and legitimate. And it is important that neither standpoint is privileged over the other — each has its own territory. Or, if either is privileged, it is the practical, because, according to Kant, "every interest is ultimately practical" (KpV 5:121/126).[18] From the explanatory standpoint of theoretical reason, nothing is easier to understand than that a human being might evade duty when it is in conflict with her heart's desire. From the normative standpoint of practical reason her sacrifice of her freedom for some mere object of inclination is completely unintelligible. These two standpoints give

---

[18] The metaphysical conception of the world also provides the regulative principles used in the theoretical sphere — but what those do is regulate the *practice* of science.

us two very different views of the world. To suppose that the Argument from Spontaneity shows anything at all about what can *happen* is to mix the theoretical and explanatory standpoint with the practical and normative one in an illegitimate way.

The second implication follows from the first. The standpoint from which you adopt the belief in freedom is that of the deliberating agent. You are licensed to believe in the practical postulates because they are necessary conditions of obeying the moral law. Thus it is primarily your own freedom that you are licensed to believe in, and, as a consequence, it is primarily yourself that you hold imputable. The result is that the business of praising and blaming others occupies a somewhat unstable position in Kantian ethics. It is true that you are supposed to regard others as free, and to treat them accordingly. But the necessity of doing so comes from the moral law, which commands the attribution of freedom to persons, and not from theoretical reasoning about how their wills actually function.[19] The moral sentiments of approval and disapproval, praise and blame, are, when directed to others, governed by the duties associated with the virtues of love and respect. And these duties, as Kant understands them, may actually demand attitudes of us that exclude or curtail theoretical reasoning about the motives of others. To the extent that we respect others and regard them as free, we must admit that we do not know the ultimate ground of their motives. And not knowing it, we are obligated wherever possible to take a generous attitude. Even when dealing with an actual wrongdoer, Kant says we must

not deny the wrongdoer all moral worth, because on that hypothesis he could never be improved either — and this latter is incompatible with the idea of man, who as such (as a moral being) can never lose all predisposition to good. (TL 6:463-64/128-29)[20]

And Kant urges us to "cast the veil of philanthropy over the faults of others, not merely by softening but also by silencing our judgments" (TL 6:466/132).[21]

---

[19] In Kantian ethics moral concepts are ideals of practical reason that are imposed on the world, by the command of the moral law, and for practical and moral purposes only. When we praise and blame we are, so to speak, applying the concept of "freedom" to another. The moral law both commands and regulates the application of this concept. I discuss this way of regarding moral concepts in "Two Arguments against Lying," *Argumentation* 2 (1988): 27-49.

[20] I give a fuller explanation of the attitude Kant thinks is required and the moral basis for it in my "The Right to Lie: Kant on Dealing with Evil," *Philosophy and Public Affairs* 15 (1986): 325-349.

[21] In these respects Kant's views stand in sharp contrast to the British Sentimentalists whom he admired: Hutcheson, Hume, and Adam Smith. All developed their ethical

The positive conception of freedom, then, is not to be given a theoretical employment. The idea of positive freedom is not supposed to show that moral evil is so irrational that it is impossible. Indeed, Kant does not propose that we should explain actions theoretically by referring them to the free choice of maxims in an intelligible world. The role of the idea of freedom and the intelligible world is, rather, a practical one. It provides a conception of ourselves which motivates us to obey the moral law.

In Kant's philosophy, freedom of the will *cannot* be theoretically established. To establish it would be to achieve knowledge of the noumenal world, and this is something that we cannot have. The freedom of the will is asserted, but as a practical postulate, and so only from a practical point of view. But surely, one is tempted to say, it cannot simply *fail to matter* to the moral agent who is to be motivated by this conception whether she is in point of actual fact free or mechanistically determined.

In one sense Kant's response to this worry is contained in the idea of the Fact of Reason. The Fact of Reason is our consciousness of the moral law as a determining ground of the will (KpV 5:31/31). Kant says: "We can come to know pure practical principles in the same way we know pure theoretical principles, by attending to the necessity with which reason prescribes them to us and to the elimination from them of all empirical conditions, which reason directs" (KpV 5:30/29). The moral law is thus presented to us by reason "as soon as we construct maxims for the will" (KpV 5:29/29) and it reveals our freedom to us. It does this by showing us that we are able to act against even our strongest inclinations, because there are cases in which we ought to. Kant says that a person considering such a case:

judges... that he can do something because he knows that he ought, and he recognizes that he is free — a fact that, without the moral law, would have remained unknown to him. (KpV 5:30/30)

Putting this together with the argument from the *Foundations* about acting under the idea of freedom, we arrive at an account of the possibility of morality with a rather complicated structure. (i) We must act under the idea of (at least negative) freedom; (ii) we must therefore act on maxims we regard

---

theories from the point of view of the spectator of the moral conduct of others, and took approbation and disapprobation as the central concepts of ethics, from which the other concepts of moral thought are developed. Hutcheson and Hume believe that the best moral agent is not thinking about morality at all, but acting from admirable natural affections. Smith comes closer to an agent-centered theory, for he takes the agent to act from specifically moral thoughts, but they are generated from an *internal spectator*.

ourselves as having chosen; (iii) by the Argument from Spontaneity (or, as Kant puts it here, by eliminating all empirical conditions, as reason directs) we are led to the moral law (the positive conception of freedom); (iv) our ability to act on the moral law teaches us that we *are* (negatively) free; (v) if so, we are members of the intelligible world, and have a higher vocation than the satisfaction of our desires, and (vi) this provides us with the incentive to be positively free — that is, moral.

But all of this still remains at the level of the practical postulate. For the sense in which our ability to act on the moral law teaches us that we are free (step iv) and so are members of an intelligible world (step v) is that we must believe these things in order to obey the categorical imperative. And articles of belief we hold because they are necessary conditions of obedience to the moral law are practical postulates, with no theoretical employment.

And, in a sense, Kant's answer to the question whether it matters if we are in fact (theoretically) free *is* that it does not matter. Kant's deduction of freedom from the moral law in the *Critique of Practical Reason* concludes:

Thus reason, which with its ideas always became transcendent when proceeding in a speculative manner, can be given for the first time an objective, *although still only practical*, reality; its transcendent use is changed into an immanent use, whereby reason becomes, in the field of experience, an efficient cause through ideas. (5: 48/49; my emphasis)

Reason becomes an efficient cause by telling us how a free person would act and by providing the conception of our higher vocation that motivates us to act that way. For if the moral law does indeed provide the positive conception of freedom, then we know how a person with a completely free will would act. Motivated by the idea of the higher vocation freedom gives us, we can act that way ourselves. But if we are able to act exactly as we would if we were free, under the influence of the idea of freedom, then we are free. Nothing is missing: the will in the Argument from Spontaneity, when making its original choice of a principle, could not do more. It chooses to act on the moral law for the sake of maintaining its freedom; and we can do the same. *By acting morally, we can make ourselves free.*

II. Virtue as Freedom

5. At this point a natural objection arises. The proposed solution to the free will problem depends on our being able to act according to the moral law for the sake of our freedom. I have claimed that what interests us in our freedom is the higher vocation of contributing to the Highest Good. But if this interest

determines our moral actions, how can we be free? To answer this question, we must turn to Kant's theory of virtue, or "internal freedom."

It is Kant's view that all human action is purposive. A human being always acts for the sake of an end. Kant speaks of this as being the result of our finite and sensible nature. In a footnote in *Religion* I Kant says:

All men could have sufficient incentive if (as they should) they adhered solely to the dictation of pure reason in the law. What need have they to know the outcome of their moral actions and abstentions...? Yet it is one of the inescapable limitations of man and of his faculty of practical reason (a limitation, perhaps, of all other worldly beings as well) to have regard, in every action, to the consequence thereof — which consequence, though last in practice... is yet first in representation and intention.... In this end, if directly presented to him by reason alone, man seeks something that he can *love*; therefore the law, which merely arouses his respect, even though it does not acknowledge this object of love as a necessity, does yet extend itself on its behalf by including the moral goal of reason among its determining grounds. (6: 6-7n/6-7n)

The objective necessity in the law ought to motivate us directly, but a human being always acts for the sake of an end. This is why, in the *Foundations*, it is *after* explaining the Formula of Universal Law that Kant embarks on the project of showing the possibility of reason determining conduct a priori, and launches into a discussion of ends (4: 427/45). The Formula of Universal Law explains the objective necessity of moral conduct, but it does not explain the subjective necessity: that is, it does not explain how pure reason secures "access to the human mind" (KpV 5: 151/155). Pure practical reason itself must gain access to us through ends. Thus it is necessary to introduce the Formula of Humanity, which directs that we make humanity, and other aims which may be derived from it, our ends. The *Religion* footnote continues:

This extension is possible because of the moral law's being taken in relation to the natural characteristic of man, that for all his actions he must conceive of an end over and above the law (a characteristic which makes man an object of experience). (6: 7n/7n)[22]

Kant also says that it is because of our susceptibility to temptation that ethics extends to ends.

For since sensible inclinations may misdirect us to ends (the matter of choice) which may be contrary to duty, legislative reason cannot guard against their influence other than, in turn, by means of an opposing moral end, which therefore must be given a priori independently of inclination. (TL 6: 381/38)

---

[22] The mysterious-sounding parenthetical phrase is "*welche Eigenschaft desselben ihn zum Gegenstande der Erfahrung macht.*" I take the point to be to equate sensibility and the need for an end.

This sounds like a different account of the need for ends, but I believe it is not. The same element in our nature — the passive, sensible, representational element that makes us require an end, is also what makes us susceptible to temptation.[23]

What this implies is that for human beings, freedom must take the form of virtue: the adoption and pursuit of moral ends. Kant explains why, in *The Metaphysical Principles of Virtue*, by setting up a problem (6: 388-89/47). Every action has an end, and choice is always determined by an end (G 4: 427/45; TL 6: 381/38, 384-85/43; Rel. 6: 4/4). So a maxim of action, or of the means to an end, is adopted freely only when you have adopted the maxim of holding that end. But the moral law only says that the maxim we adopt must have a certain form, not that we must have certain maxims. How can it be necessary to have certain maxims? The answer is that if there are ends that are duties, there will be maxims that it is a duty to have: maxims of actions that promote those ends. Since we must believe that we are morally obligated (that is, that there are maxims we ought to have), we must believe that there are such obligatory ends. For example, Kant says that the (external) duties of justice can be done from a moral motive and so done freely by one who makes the rights of humanity one's end (TL 6: 390/49). The possibility of internal freedom is secured by the "Supreme Principle of the Doctrine of Virtue" which runs "Act according to a maxim whose ends are such that there can be a universal law that everyone have these ends" (TL 6: 395/54). This principle is deduced from pure practical reason by the following argument:

> For practical reason to be indifferent to ends, i.e., to take no interest in them, would be a contradiction; for then it would not determine the maxims of actions (and the actions always contain an end) and, consequently, would not be practical reason. Pure reason, however, cannot a priori command any ends unless it declares these ends to be at the same time duties; such duties are then called duties of virtue. (TL 6: 395/54-55)

In the introduction to *The Metaphysical Principles of Virtue*, Kant says that the obligatory ends are one's own perfection and the happiness of others. But in fact, a number of different ends appear in this text and elsewhere in the ethical writings. One's own perfection includes moral perfection and so subsumes the whole of morality, as well as natural perfection, which involves the development of our physical and intellectual capacities. The duties of respect make the rational autonomy of others an end. Securing the rights of

---

[23] In the Introduction to the *Metaphysics of Morals*, the faculty of desire is "the capacity to be by means of one's representations the cause of the objects of these representations" and the capacity to act in accordance with representations is identified as "life." (6: 211/9)

humanity is an end (TL 6: 390/49). In the political writings, the development of republican forms of government is made a necessary end for sovereigns (RL 6: 340/112), and peace is an end for everyone (RL 6: 354-55/127-29). The Highest Good, the whole object of practical reason, is a necessary end, as we have already seen (KpV 5: 108-14/112-18; Rel. 6: 3-6/3-6). It is because there are various ends, Kant says, that there are various virtues, even though virtue is essentially one thing (TL 6: 395/54; 406/65). All of these ends are determined by the moral law and so are necessary ends (ends of reason); and all of them can be derived from the unconditional value of humanity. When we act for the sake of these ends, we act from the moral law, for it determines them. It is because the law determines ends that creatures like ourselves, who always act for ends, can be free.[24]

6. But this may not seem to resolve the problem. Clearly it is not enough that we act for moral ends; we must also do so *because* they are moral ends. We must adopt the ends themselves freely, as ends determined by the moral law. But if we must be free in order to adopt moral ends, then adopting moral ends cannot be what makes us free.

The answer to this objection lies in the special nature of internal freedom. To explain the answer, we must take a detour through another problem about the adoption of moral ends. Kant argues that the duties of virtue are all of broad obligation; they do not require definite acts which may simply be discharged (TL 6: 390/48).[25] The duty to *advance* a moral end is one of broad

---

[24] It might seem to be a problem that the Highest Good is supposed to be conceived as a divine end. How can God have an end if that is a need of sensibility? Kant explains: "For while the divinity has no subjective need of any external object, it cannot be conceived as closed up within itself, but only as compelled by the very awareness of its own all-sufficiency to produce the highest good outside itself. In the case of the supreme being, this necessity (which corresponds to duty in man) can be envisaged by us only as a moral need" (TP 8: 280n/65n).

[25] The question of the relation between the two distinctions, perfect/imperfect, and broad/strict, is a very difficult one. These have sometimes been thought to be simply alternative terms for the same distinction, but Kant explicitly asserts that all duties of virtue are of broad obligation, while mentioning many that are perfect. He does not explain himself, and his own use of the terms does not provide clear guidance. Two important discussions of this problem are in Mary Gregor, *The Laws of Freedom: A Study of Kant's Method of Applying the Categorical Imperative in the Metaphysik der Sitten* (Oxford: Basil Blackwell, 1963), pp. 95-127, and in Onora (O'Neill) Nell, *Acting on Principle: An Essay on Kantian Ethics* (New York: Columbia University Press, 1975), pp. 43-58. The main justification I have to offer for the way I use these terms in the text is that they enable me to make the explanation that follows.

obligation because it is an imperfect duty; the law does not say exactly what or how much we should do to advance the end. But what about the duty to *adopt* a moral end? Kant thinks that the adoption of an end is necessarily a free act, for he says:

> Another may indeed force me to do something which is not my end (but is only the means to some other's end); but he cannot force me to make it my own end, for I can have no end except of my own making. (TL 6: 38-39/381-82)

Making something your end is a kind of internal action, and it is these internal actions that are commanded by the Supreme Principle of the Doctrine of Virtue. The duty to adopt these ends (and so also the duty not to act against them) is a perfect duty. The law does say exactly what we must do. So why does Kant count such duties as creating only broad obligations which may not be discharged?

   One of the things we expect of a person who has an end is that she will notice facts that are associated with that end in a certain way, and things that bear on the promotion of the end will occur to her. This is a general point about ends, and does not apply only to moral ends. To see this, imagine that I claim that I am Charlotte's friend, and that I have her happiness as my end. But imagine also that it seldom or never occurs to me to do anything in particular to make Charlotte happy. When I see something in a shop window that suits her taste exactly, I do not think, "now that is something Charlotte would really like," and go in to purchase it. When I look at the calendar on what happens to be her birthday, it does not occur to me that it is her birthday, and I should telephone. When I hear of some catastrophe happening in her neighborhood, I do not wonder about the possible bearing of this event on her safety and comfort. These things just do not come to me. Under these circumstances, surely Charlotte would be entitled to complain that there is no real sense in which I have her happiness as my end.[26] It would not be pertinent for me to reply that I have no direct control over what occurs to me. To find certain features of the world salient is part of our notion of what it is to have an end. To have an end is to see the world in a certain way. But what determines

---

[26] In one sense I may still claim to have her happiness as my end. I may hold an end merely negatively, as something I will endeavor not to act against. The Formula of Humanity says that we must never use another merely as a means, and Kant says in the *Foundations* that humanity is conceived negatively, as "that which must never be acted against" (4: 437/56). But Kant makes it clear that *virtue* is going to require a more positive pursuit of the end. He says: "It is not enough that he is not authorized to use either himself or others merely as means (this latter including also the case of his being indifferent to others)" (TL 6: 395/54).

salience most directly lies in our sensory and representational capacities — and so in the passive part of our nature. To adopt an end is to perform an internal action. But it is also to undergo certain changes, changes in your representational capacities. It is to come to perceive the world in the way that having the end requires.

When the end is one that is suggested by natural inclination, we are already inclined to perceive the world in the relevant way. Indeed, that you are inclined to perceive the world that way is the form that the incentive takes. Our sensible nature here helps us out. But when the end is one prompted by reason this may not be the case. Here, you are imposing a change on your sensible nature, and your sensible nature may, and probably will, be recalcitrant. Although adopting an end is a volitional act, it is one that you can only do gradually and perhaps incompletely.

This is why the duty to adopt an end is of broad obligation. You cannot, just by making a resolution, acquire a virtue or recover from a vice. Or better still, we will say that you can, because you are free, but then we must say that only what happens in the future establishes whether you have really made the resolution or not. I do not mean that only the future will produce the evidence: I mean that only what you do in the future will enable us to correctly attribute a resolution to you. There is a kind of backwards determination in the construction of one's character. Whether you have made it your maxim to be more just, helpful, respectful, or honest depends on what you do in the future — on whether you make progress towards being the sort of person you have (presumably) resolved to be. Because the materials we have to work with in these cases are recalcitrant, it is in the progress, not in the success, that Kant places virtue (TL 6: 409/69). But the work must show up in progress. Suppose, for instance, that I am selfish, but resolve to be more attentive to the needs of others. As a selfish person I will also be self-absorbed, and fail to notice when others are in trouble and to be perceptive about what they need. At first, others may have to draw my attention to the cases where I can help. But if I continue indefinitely to *fail to notice* when others are in need and I can help, then I just did not resolve. On the other hand, if I do progress, I will count as having resolved, even if I am not consistently unselfish all of the time.

This is Kant's explicit view in *Religion Within the Limits of Reason Alone*. According to Kant, we must think of our free actions and choices as being unconditioned by time. If they were conditioned by time they would be subject to causality and so not free (6: 40/35). Still, time is a condition of our thinking, and this means that for us, temporally unconditioned choice must be represented as choice that either is before or in a certain way follows from the events of our lives. For purposes of holding ourselves responsible, we think of the free adoption of our most fundamental maxim as if it were before our phenomenal choices: the evil in us is present from birth, Kant says, as if it were innate (Rel. 6: 21-22/17; 41/38; see also KpV 5: 100/103). But if our maxims were innate, we could not change for the better, for our most fundamental reasons would be self-interested ones. So, for purposes of regarding ourselves as free to change, we see the free choice of our character as something to which the whole conduct of our life adds up. Kant explains:

> duty demands nothing of us which we cannot do. There is no reconciliation possible here except by saying that man is under the necessity of, and is therefore capable of, a revolution in his cast of mind, but only of a gradual reform in his sensuous nature (which places obstacles in the way of the former). That is, if a man reverses, by a single unchangeable decision, that highest ground of his maxims whereby he was an evil man (and thus puts on the new man), he is, so far as his principle and cast of mind are concerned, a subject susceptible of goodness, but only in continuous labor and growth is he a good man. That is, he can hope... to find himself upon the good (though strait) path of continual *progress* from bad to better. For Him who penetrates to the intelligible ground of the heart (the ground of all maxims of the will [*Willkür*]) and for whom this unending progress is a unity, *i.e.*, for God, that amounts to his being actually a good man (pleasing to Him); and, thus viewed, this change can be regarded as a revolution. (Rel. 6: 47-48/43)[27]

The appearance of freedom in the phenomenal world, then, is virtue — a constant struggle to love and respect the humanity in oneself and others, and to defeat the claims inclination tries to make against that humanity. So far from committing him to a mysterious dualism, Kant's theory of the atemporal nature of freedom permits him to harmonize freedom with a temporal account of the acquisition of virtue. One achieves virtue through a gradual habituation, and, as in Aristotle's ethics, the sign of success is gladness in its practice. In the *Religion*, Kant says:

[27] See also this passage from the *Religion*: "we may also think of this endless progress of our goodness towards conformity to the law, even if this progress is conceived in terms of actual deeds, or life-conduct, as being judged by Him who knows the heart, through a purely intellectual intuition, as a completed whole, because of the *disposition*, supersensible in its nature, from which this progress itself is derived" (6: 67-68/60-61); and from the *Critique of Practical Reason*: "Only endless progress from lower to higher stages of moral perfection is possible to a rational but finite being. The Infinite Being, to whom the temporal condition is nothing, sees in this series, which is for us without end, a whole conformable to the moral law" (5: 123/127). This is why Kant thinks that ethics leads to a view of the "immortality" of the soul, which gives us a prospect of an *endless* progress toward the better. Only an endless progress is adequate to the achievement of freedom, and to wiping out the original evil in our nature (Rel. 6: 72/66; KpV 5: 122-24/126-28).

This resolve, then, encouraged by good progress, must needs beget a joyous frame of mind, without which man is never certain of having really *attained a love* for the good, *i.e.*, of having incorporated it into his maxim. (Rel. 6: 21n/19n)

To the extent to which moral ends have really become our ends, we will take pleasure in the pursuit of them. Indeed we have all of the emotions appropriate to having an end. In the *Metaphysical Principles of Virtue*, Kant speaks of gratitude (TL 6: 454-56/119-21) and even sympathetic feeling (TL 6: 456-58/121-23) as being required. He is quick to qualify these remarks, for we have no direct control over our feelings. Yet it is his view that one who does adopt an end will normally come to have the feelings that are natural to a person who has this end. If the end were suggested by sensibility, we would already have had the feelings, but though the end is adopted on moral grounds we should still come to have them eventually.[28] When explaining the relation between inclination and morality in the duty of beneficence, for example, Kant says:

Beneficence is a duty. Whoever often exercises this and sees his beneficent purpose succeed comes at last really to love him whom he has benefited. When therefore it is said, "Thou shalt love thy neighbor as thyself," this does not mean you should directly (at first) love and through this love (subsequently) benefit him; but rather, "Do good to your neighbor," and this beneficence will produce in you the love of mankind (as readiness of inclination toward beneficence in general). (TL 6: 402/61)

Kant does not mean that we will come to act solely from the inclination, but rather that the inclination will be in harmony with reason and so will no longer be an impediment. As long as we do not act from inclination, but because the ends are dictated by the law, this is no detriment to our moral character. On the contrary, it shows that we have advanced toward the complete control over our sensuous nature that is implied by freedom.

So we do not exactly need to adopt moral ends freely in order to be free. If we come, over time, to act purely for the sake of moral ends, it will come to be true that we are, timelessly, free.

---

[28] This is not guaranteed. The *Foundations* contains a well-known discussion of the worth of a man who is helpful although "by temperament cold and indifferent to the sufferings of others, perhaps because he is provided with special gifts of patience and fortitude" (4: 398/14-15), which shows that Kant thinks moral worth may be combined with a recalcitrant temperament. The discussion has unfortunately often been taken to suggest that Kant thinks moral worth *must* be combined with a recalcitrant temperament.

7. Kant's theory of the freedom of the will involves neither extravagant ontological claims nor the unyielding theory of responsibility which seems to follow from those claims.[29] These problems arise only from a misunderstanding of a fundamental feature of the Kantian philosophy — the radical split between the theoretical and practical points of view. The idea of intelligible causality is a practical conception, and our belief in it is an article of practical faith. It is not supposed to be theoretically employed, and it cannot be used to explain anything that happens. It is true that the positive conception of freedom makes practical freedom possible — but not because it explains how it is possible. It makes practical freedom possible because we can act on it.

Kant sees positive freedom as pointing to a higher vocation, the thought of which moves us to moral conduct, and explains how we can take an interest in such conduct. This interest leads us to adopt moral ends, and so to struggle against the temptations that beset us. If we reach the point where we are indeed moved wholly by ends determined by the law, we are in fact free — practically free. Nothing in this development requires any ontological claims, or requires that we be radically different sorts of creatures than the mundane rational animals we suppose ourselves to be. All that Kant needs is the conclusion that the moral law does indeed represent the positive conception of freedom. The idea of freedom motivates us to cultivate the virtues, and, in turn, virtue makes us free.

The University of Chicago

---

[29] Kant's theory of free will is sometimes described as "compatibilist" because both freedom and determinism are affirmed. This description seems to me to be potentially misleading. Most compatibilists, I believe, want to assert both freedom and determinism (or, both responsibility and determinism) from the same point of view — a theoretical and explanatory point of view. Kant does not do this, and could not do it without something his view forbids — describing the relation between the noumenal and phenomenal worlds.

Nathan Rotenstreich

On the Formalism of Kant's Ethics

(1)

Kant himself described his system as formal idealism. He distinguished this
type of idealism from material idealism — a philosophical position which
"doubts or denies the existence of outer things in themselves"
(A491n/B519n). This description does not afford us a clear insight into the
meaning of formalism as it occurs in the ethical context, because of the
difficulty inherent in the terms 'form' and 'formalism'. This difficulty is due to
an interesting transformation (i.e., the special use of the root 'form' in this
context), whereby *forma* as the Latin equivalent of the Greek *morphē* does not
connote essence but, rather, something which is external and thus a mere
framework. Thus, according to Kant, when we speak of the forms of knowledge, we refer only to logical forms which are "the formal ground of the
objects" (A93/B125). Form is a condition in the sense that only through it can
appearances be present and thus empirically intuited or given. Even when we
add the feature of condition to the framework, there remains a gap between
that which belongs to the realm of form as condition, and that which is
brought within the scope of awareness and is conditioned by the form. That is,
the fact of its being a condition does not deprive form of its externality
vis-à-vis that which appears within its framework. This aspect of form
becomes prominent in the conjunction of form and law (KpV 5: 35/35), since
law as such does not entail the presence of material or its direction. Form
understood as law is the form of universality. Even as there is a gap between
framework and material, so is there a gap between universality and the
particular cases which can be subsumed under it but cannot be derived from
it. Hence, when we try to decipher the meaning of form or formalism in the
context of ethics, we must be more specific, so as to appreciate the impact of
universality on the very direction of ethics. This will be the first step in our
exploration.

49

Y. Yovel (ed.), Kant's Practical Philosophy Reconsidered, 49-62.
© *1989 Kluwer Academic Publishers.*

(2)

In order to account for the context in which Kant's notion of form or formalism emerges, it is important to note another expression he uses. Kant mentions a reviewer of his book who argued that it contained no new principle of morality but only a new formula (*Formel*). Against this critical comment, Kant asks: who would want to introduce a new principle of morality and be, as it were, an inventor? He adds that those who know what a formula means to a mathematician will not regard a formula which performs a similar function for all duties (i.e., moral concepts and attitudes) as insignificant or unnecessary (KpV 5: 8n/8n). The analogy with mathematics is obviously significant with respect to Kant's introduction of variations on the root 'form' in the context of the ethical system. But here it may be appropriate to go back to Kant's own distinction between forms of intuition and forms of understanding, because the synthesis of the two is essential to the exploration of the structure of mathematics. To begin with, Kant identifies the notion of form with that of function. Function is understood as the unity of the activity of ordering different "representations under one common representation" (A68/B93). We must note here the status of unity: it is the function that brings about unity. Indeed, this aspect of bringing about is emphasized, since Kant speaks about activity, and the combination of unity and activity in turn points towards the bringing about of an order. This, it seems, refers to functions as such, though Kant distinguishes between intuitions which are grounded in what he calls affections, and concepts which rest on functions. Functions appear within the context of concepts and not of intuitions. And indeed, all our propositions or judgements are functions of unity (A69/B94). Perhaps we could illuminate this notion by saying that as functions, they exhibit a tendency towards unity. Given this point of departure, we may propose a distinction between forms of intuition, i.e., space and time, on the one hand, and forms of concepts on the other. To be sure, space as a form is the subjective condition of sensuality (A26/B42). The meaning of 'condition' is that all things are set side by side in space, and only under this limitation are these things viewed as objects of our sensuous intuition (A27/B43).

Hence, the form of intuition, being the form of sensuality, can be interpreted as a framework in which data or objects are placed. The forms embrace objects, let us add, and do not shape them. Possibly, since the sensuous intuition as a faculty "is strictly only a receptivity" (A494/B522), receptivity mediates between the objects and our perception. Applying pure intuition of space and time does not shape the data. It receives them, and the very act of reception places them, as noted above, within the framework of space and time. From this point of view, forms of understanding as categories differ from forms of intuition. Kant's use of the expression "making" when he says "the making of knowledge" (B288) indicates the active or forming character of the forms of thinking. There is a connection between this use and categorial statements. The fact that through these forms alone no object can be thought or determined, does not diminish their active or formative character and may even emphasize it. Since the forms are active, they require data in order to effect the synthesis between themselves and the data. The activity inherent in the forms has to be restrained by the data. But this, of course, belongs to Kant's theory of knowledge. What is relevant to his description of forms as such is their presentation not only as embracing frameworks, but as activities shaping that which is given. The summing up of this active character of the forms of thought is articulated in the statement that they are "the mode of determining an object for the manifold of a possible intuition" (A254/B309) — the word 'determining' here makes the activity quite conspicuous. The basic duality between that which is given, and thus related to reality, and that which is determining or ordering, and hence related to understanding or reason, is central in the context of this inquiry.

(3)

The active character or essence of morality is inherent in the statement that morality necessarily presupposes freedom as a property of our will (Bxxviii). The concept of duty, the central concept of morality, is related to empirical concepts such as pleasure or pain, desires or inclinations. The active character of duty is associated with these empirical notions whereas duty itself is supposed to lead us to overcome them, or to look at them as a temptation which must not become a motive. Practical philosophy is not included in transcendental philosophy because of these motives and feelings, which are not merely data in need of ordering, but must be overcome. But the concept of duty, which contains the element of activity as an essential component, is related to reason, and as such can be seen, from the point of view of form, as a conceptual order. Form consists in universality — and this is a central issue in Kant's explication of the relation between morality and form. Universality is expressed in universal laws; hence, "maxims must be chosen as if they had to hold as universal laws of nature (G IV: 436/107). Here the notion of universal laws in general is a paradigm or model for the universality of law applicable to the realm of morality. Kant tries to bring the concept of 'the universal formula' as close as possible to our common understanding. Yet universality is not a feature borrowed from the sphere of the universal laws of nature, but, rather, is inherent in the notion of law as such, and applies to the sphere of morality as it does to that of reason.

In the *Groundwork* Kant brings together the formal principle of volition and the notion of duty (G 4: 400/68). Duty is "the objective necessity to act from obligation" (G 4: 439/107). Duty comprises the interrelation between *making* a universal law and being *subjected* to it (G 4: 439-40/107). Duty implies a negation or an overcoming of self-interest (G 4: 397/65). It therefore implies universality, because the direction towards self-interest by definition pertains to a singular human being, but also implies the forming of action by guiding the agents in the direction of universality. If this is so, then the form or formula referred to within the context of moral philosophy as being identical with law is not form in the sense of encompassing data but in that of shaping our attitudes and behaviour. The activity of the form, or the activity inherent in the adherence to the form, is the first major point which has to be made in our attempt to undersand Kant's notion of form and the formalism of his ethics. "The moral disposition is necessarily connected with a consciousness of the determination of the will directly by a law" (KpV 5: 117/121). It should be emphasized that the context in which this statement is made is that of the moral disposition. That disposition is not a datum, but reflects the determination of the will directly (in the original text, *unmittelbar* 'immediately') by the moral law. Hence, the position of the moral law, which in turn exhibits the position of the form, is one of determination, and immediately so, thus bringing about a primary synthesis, if the term can be used, or integration, of the will and the law — will being the faculty of deciding and law being the formative component of the decision. In this sense, it will be noted, Kant's formalism does not refer to an abstract formula, but to a factor of shaping, which, as such (as a priori) is independent. It finds its realization in ordering the will, but also in directing it towards universality. The integration of these aspects is meant to remain within the scope of form. But it gives the notion of form the meaning of a manifold of components — and we must obviously distinguish between a manifold and a clash of its components.

The conjunction of form with that of law endows form with the essence of a principle which introduces order, or more precisely, order alone, because the data are there, by definition 'given', already organized either in a temporal sequence or as spatially coexisting. The laws of understanding bring into that primary ordering of the data either a structure of correlation, like the relation between substance and accident, or that of a series, as in the case of the principle of causality. Within practical reason or ethics, laws introduce a component additional to that of ordering, which could be described as that of shaping. Through a play on words we might arrive at the 'formative essence of the form'. The difference between the realms of knowledge and of ethics stems from the difference in their *raison d'être*: knowledge takes cognisance of that which exists, while ethics guides conduct. Hence the formal principle of ethics is meant to be the anchor of guidance. That is, form occupies not only the position of law, but also that of duty. What is characteristic of the formalism of Kant's ethics is the conjunction of law and duty that transcends the position of law as a principle of order, as in the realm of knowledge. An examination of some characteristic features of the concept of duty will lead us to the analysis that follows.

(4)

The concept of duty, like the realm of ethics in general, presupposes the presence of will, here understood as a faculty determining the causality of human beings through the conception of a rule. Will leads to decisions, rule directs them. Hence, the law has the form of an imperative. This can be understood in the following way: since will as a faculty of decision may push in different directions, law *qua* imperative guides the faculty of will in the determinate direction which is prescribed by the moral law. Kant calls this the moral constraint imposed by practical reason. It is in this context that the notion of duty is analysed or described as that aspect of the guiding of decisions which is not caused by the so-called subjective causes but, rather, by the purely objective grounds of determination. Duty implies the aspect of constraint as well as that of reason and its objective law (TL 6: 379f/DV 36f). The realm of knowledge, being that of order and its identification, is the realm of subsumption of data under order and its law. The realm of ethics is that of the *free* submission of the will to law. The inevitable constraint imposed on our inclinations does not, however, affect the freedom of that submission. In this sense, the concept of duty refers to a fundamental integration of freedom of the will and law. Duty curbs inclination and points to determination by law (G 4: 399/67). This aspect of imposition turns the moral law or duty into a formative principle. Kant himself emphasized the importance of that principle by pointing to the respect it inspires. However, this respect is not a manifestation of feelings or inclinations already present at the empirical level, but is, rather, a response, not only guided by the moral law, but emerging out of its acknowledgement. To be sure, the account of the concept of duty as encompassing that of good will (G 4: 397/65), is perhaps imprecise: although duty pertains to will, it does not include it as a part even when it is good will that is at issue. This formulation, on the other hand, is Kant's attempt to provide an integrated profile of the concept of duty, and in the context of the elaboration of the concept of form we could say that it is his attempt to overcome the association between form and that which is external. Since duty is the universal aspect of the law, it is opposed to purposes determined by self-interest. Hence, obligation, as a different expression of that which is termed duty, makes room for emphasis on the aspect of "necessitation" (TL 223/DV 21). Duty is, therefore, acting in conformity with the law of reason. It is conformity with a universal formative or shaping factor as the real incentive of action (KpV 5: 151/155).

(5)

The formative character of duty, or the shaping essence of form, is expressed in the place accorded to character within the realm of ethics. One of Kant's descriptions of character is "a consistent practical habit of mind [*Denkungsart*] according to unchangeable maxims" (KpV 5: 152/156). According to this description, character is a consistent habit, that is, a permanent attitude, as suggested by the notion of order, which in turn is related to the notion of law, and in this context maxims occupy the position of laws. The notion of character exhibits the shaping essence of law in its permanence. We could also generalize by saying that the very position of character is something which has been determined and is not simply given. It is not enough to maintain objective laws of morality which we merely admire and esteem in relation to man in general; the idea of the law has to be seen in relation to man as an individual. The law appears in a form deserving high respect. The notion of character is presented in this context as related to the consciousness of man's moral disposition, and the conjunction between that disposition and his character proper is what Kant describes as the highest good in man (KpV 5: 161/165). This description is meant to lead us to the conclusion that law, as a form taking the shape of duty and manifested in character, which connotes the person as morally shaped, is not an external factor, but one which, as formative, permeates the person and, in Kant's sense, elevates him from the sphere of inclinations and urges to that of being determined by moral principles, i.e., by law and duty. The intelligible character of duty is, again, reflected in one of the descriptions of its position and direction. Possibly the emphasis on intelligibility enables Kant to bring about a correlation between it and freedom, which is a non-sensuous fact, and can be viewed as akin to intelligibility (KpV 5: 19ff/17ff).

We can sum up this part of our inquiry by emphasizing that formalism in ethics has to be seen as bringing together different components, all of which emphasize the active or shaping character of the moral law. This shaping character finds its expression not only negatively with respect to the overcoming of inclinations, but also positively as guiding the ethical attitude through acknowledgement of or respect for the universal character of law. One could say that the activity is already expressed in the overcoming of the self-interest imbuing inclinations through adherence to the universality of law. Yet, as we shall see, this universality is not solely an aspect of the systematic position of law, but, rather, it points to the universality of humanity. As such, law, in its essence, turns out to include in its content moral guidance. Hence, the formalism of Kant's ethics has to be construed in its qualified formulation insofar as the status of form is concerned, and all the more so due to the conjunction of law, the guidance of humanity, and an additional aspect of Kant's system. This third factor is the relation between man as a being who posits ends, on the one hand, and the distinctive role of ends with respect to moral law and the ethical approach in general, on the other.

(6)

Form as a shaping factor is also rendered by Kant as matter or content. How can this conjunction of form and matter be explained? Kant says that matter is an end. This would imply that form as a shaping factor is the elevation of the moral agent's choice to universality or rationality. In this sense, universality becomes, as a shaping focus of the moral decision, the content of that decision. The law, as universal, thus directs the decision towards the overcoming of merely relative and arbitrary ends, as, apparently, a relative end is an arbitrary one. If one of the formulations of the moral law as universal is the conversion of the maxim into a universal law, this conversion is understood as a complete determination of the agent's will. Kant himself brings together the various aspects of the position of an end by presenting the law in the following way: "A rational being, as by his very nature an end and consequently an end in himself, must serve for every maxim as a condition limiting all merely relative and arbitrary ends" (G 4:436/104). From the point of view of empirical human beings, the universal law is an end because it is not stated in terms of sensuous traits. Being an end is an end in itself, but at the same time it turns the position of the human being into an end. This can be interpreted in the following way: the rational human being determined by the universal law — and this is part of the definition of the rational human being — elevates himself into an end in himself by assuming the obligation to obey the law as an end. To adhere to the law is to adhere to the rationality of human beings. This shift from sensuality to rationality through the positing of human beings as ends, is probably interpreted by Kant as the matter of the universal moral law, which, as such, is identical with its position as form. Since form becomes a motivating factor, as such it is also the goal of the moral attitude.

To be determined in accordance with the idea of certain laws is a power or faculty found in rational beings only. The aspect of end is relevant in that context because of the element of self-determination of the will which, from this viewpoint, is a subjective ground of self-determination. Yet, since that ground is not an impulsion, but a law, it is described by Kant as an objective ground. "Practical principles are *formal* if they abstract from all subjective ends; they are *material*, on the other hand, if they are based on such ends and consequently on certain impulsions" (G 4: 427/95). Kant introduces into the context of that exposition the notion of an absolute value, which is identical with that of an end in itself, and as such is a motivation of the categorical imperative (ibid.). Hence we may conclude that the position of a universal law, as inherently of absolute value, is an end in itself. The meaning of the end in itself may be twofold. It is a goal for human beings to aspire to, and since it does not serve any end beyond itself, it is an end in itself. Here we may find the explanation for this attempt to integrate the various descriptions. What is most consequential for Kant's system is ultimately the identification of form with content. That identification precludes the possibility of interpreting Kant's ethical system as formalistic in the external sense of that term, since the form becomes the motivation, and the motivation is raised to the level of adherence to universality. Thus the circle is closed in that the relationship between motivation and universality generates a structure of ethical motivation and adherence.

(7)

From another point of view, we can examine this integrated structure by emphasizing the position of the end, which is an object of free choice. Every action has its end. The moral action brings about the conversion of oneself as the object of choice into an end. Since that shift to the position of end is not confined egotistically to one's self alone, it creates a situation whereby every human being becomes an end. The universalization of the human sphere is, within the horizon of the agent, an end to which he adheres and to which he directs himself. The aspect of duty is also an elaboration of the position of the end in terms of universality: "the moral doctrine of ends, which treats of duties, is based on principles given *a priori* in pure practical reason" (TL 6: 385/DV 44).

An additional perspective is introduced from the point of view of the conjunction of ends and duties. This conjunction is expressed in the concept of one's own perfection and the happiness of others. These two obligatory ends are duties of each person. When we look into these two duties, we find that it is the component of the happiness of other human beings which is emphasized rather than that of one's own happiness. This is so because according to the universalistic trend of Kant's ethics the happiness of others is, so to speak, trans-egotistic or trans-egoistic, and thus can be seen as congruous with universality. The ends of other human beings are adopted as my own ends not by turning myself towards my own happiness, but by making the happiness of others the end or the goal of morality. The commitment to the happiness of others is from this point of view congruous with what is described as moral integrity (TL 6: 388/DV 47).

One's own perfection amounts to the duty to cultivate one's powers — the highest of which is understanding — which are described as the powers of concepts. One's own perfection is the activation of the end, so to speak, that is, one has a duty to strive to raise oneself up from the crude state of one's nature. This is the humanity by which the agent alone is capable of setting ends. Self-perfection is connoted by the traditional term as a virtue, and one has a duty to cultivate one's will so as to attain the purest attitude of virtue. Essentially, the locus of overlap of self-perfection, will, virtue and universality turns out to be a position in which the law is the motive as well as the norm of one's actions; one obeys the law as a norm out of duty. The aspect of duty therefore has two directions: one towards fellow men — the pursuit of whose happiness is viewed as a duty — and a second towards the agent himself and his practical perfection, which is not a kind of enjoyment but rather a duty.

The position of the notion of virtue is described by Kant as a "moral strength of will" (TL 6: 405/DV 66). Because of the obligation inherent in virtue, Kant says, "full perfection is represented, not as if man possesses virtue, but rather as if virtue possesses man" (TL 6: 406/DV 67). This position of virtue ultimately reflects the position of the form, which, as we saw before, turns out to be what Kant calls matter or content. In this sense, the broad ethical consideration is that of ends, and ends are realized in the two directions — vis-à-vis one's fellow men and vis-à-vis oneself. The conjunction of being obligated and obligating oneself is related to the position of the moral law. What is significant from the systematic point of view in this context is not only a kind of basic synthesis between form and matter or content, but also the synthesis between universality and end. Thus morality is intrinsically related to the conception of man as an end, and that conception contains both the agent and his fellow men. Both poles, as it were, are pertinent to the ethical obligation. They are related to the interpretation of the position of human beings as representatives of mankind or humanity at large. The anti-egotistic status of man, which is indeed the core of the ethical attitude, is thus related to the interpretation of human beings as representatives, on the one hand, and as striving towards ends, on the other. As noted above, Kant considered the obligation towards humanity and towards individual human beings, including oneself, essentially both as a formal determination and a material one. From this point of view, to put it like that, formalism is not formalistic. We shall look into this topic from yet another point of view, when we realize that the inherent capacity of human beings for setting themselves goals is a kind of link between the empirical human situation and the situation aimed at within the realm of morality.

(8)

Being a goal adds to the moral law the component of being the ultimate end of human aspirations. In Kant's texts we do not find a fuller analysis of what being an end is. Moreover, Kant does not analyse the relation between what he calls the power to set oneself an end, which is characteristic of human existence as distinguished from animality, and the end in the strict moral sense of the term, that is, humanity as mankind and not as human essence, as well as humanity as requiring acknowledgement or respect beyond any instrumental or pragmatic considerations. Hence when Kant refers to the "anthropological"[1] aspect of the end, he refers to "any end whatsoever," not to the end in the moral sense of that concept as inherent in the position of the moral law. The brevity, or perhaps imprecision of this presentation is perhaps attributable to the systematic issue before us, namely, the relation between the empirical human being, who as such is capable of transcending himself, and setting an end to his aspirations or even existence, including the moral end in the delineated sense of that term. It goes without saying that that issue is of systematic significance for Kant's theory in general, and his ethical theory in particular. But from the point of view of the alleged formalism of Kant's

---

[1] Kant eventually goes beyond his own statements. It is not enough to refer to anthropology for the sake of the applicaton of ethics to man. The aspect of positing an end indicates that man, anthropologically regarded, is the ontological precondition of ethics (G 4: 412/79).

ethical system, it can be said that since the form is a law, and as such is an end, it certainly goes beyond the external aspect of that which is described as a form. It has bearing on human behaviour, both in terms of implying the setting of an end for it and in terms of eliciting responses. Thus the moral law is to be viewed from two angles. From the point of view of human existence it is a goal, and from the point of view of the role of reason in the human context it is a law (G 4: 428/95). In this sense Kant attempts to bring together not only will and reason as such, but also will and reason aiming at an essential end, which is in itself of an absolute value.

The question of the empirical level of existence comes to the fore in this connection, because in dealing with everyday conflicts and affairs rather than with the law and the ultimate end, it is inevitable that we interpret and apply these general notions to the particular circumstances at hand. One could say that since the law and the end are of universal — hence absolute — significance, the transition from absoluteness to contingent conditions constitutes a fundamental issue of principle.

Plato's system is a paradigm of a situation where the realm of ideas is fundamentally separated from the world of particular facts, appearances, conditions, or however one wishes to refer to empirical reality.

(9)

When we have gone beyond the terminological issues involved in Kant's analysis we can conclude that what we shall describe now as the trans-formal meaning of the ethical laws in Kant's system can be explicated by employing the concepts of freedom and equality. In terms of the self-determination of the will, and concurrently in terms of the overcoming of the inclinations and impulses, Kant stresses the aspect of freedom inherent in the moral law. Only a free being or a being determined by free will can set universality and humanity as his ends, or regard every human being as an end in himself. Only rising above and beyond the narrow concerns of selfishness or the particularity of one's involvement with one's fellow men can lead to the perspective of universality and to all that is entailed by it. Freedom implies going beyond that which is empirically given, and in this sense, freedom is both a precondition for the ethical attitude and a goal for such an attitude. To this extent, it is a goal activating the response of subduing the limiting effects of urges and impulses.

At the same time, however, Kant's system implies the concept or idea of equality, for every human being has to be regarded as an end or as a representative of mankind at large. Every human being is entitled to be acknowledged and respected — the attitudes comprising the response of consciousness to the law as such. In this sense, in acknowledging their position as ends as a principle guiding human behaviour, they are thereby guided by the principle of equality. We could say, in addition, that in order that the principle of equality become a principle within the horizon of the ethical attitude, it presupposes one's being guided by the principle of freedom. At the same time, one could say that since freedom is not confined to the empirical human being here and now, but is the predisposition of the ethical attitude and its principle, the acknowledgement of human beings as free is inherently the acknowledgement of equality. One could argue that this relation between freedom and equality is to some extent circular: to acknowledge equality presupposes freedom, and the principle of equality guides us in looking at freedom both as an end and as a condition. Yet, this circularity is perhaps an additional feature of the trans-formalism of Kant's system. For, more generally, merely formal connections lend themselves less readily to circularity than connections imbued with contents. In any case, we may sum up by saying that the presentation of Kant's system by Kant himself should guide us in regarding that system as actively adhering to a form which is more than a mere form. That addition to mere formalism becomes apparent in the various aspects discussed above.

The formative character of the moral law in Kant's interpretation gains prominence in his attempt to incorporate the concept of virtue into the system. Virtue is understood as related to moral disposition in conflict. Negatively described, it is not holiness in the sense of the perfect purity of the intentions of the will (KpV 5: 84/87). The conflict is due to the duality of the inclinations perceptible to human sensuality as opposed to moral law. Virtue is related to the impact of moral law on the human response and thus essentially, or even by definition, involves conflict. As a matter of fact, Kant suggests several subdivisions of the moral virtues, grounded in the two principles dealt with above, namely, one's duties to oneself and the concern for the happiness of others. Related to the first principle is one's duty to preserve oneself, and what is entailed by that, such as the repudiation of suicide, and even more everyday matters such as the rejection of the immoderate consumption of food and drink. Moving from what is described as the carnal level of human existence to the moral domain proper, lying is mentioned and the moral consideration against it is grounded in one's being regarded as a person. Even the notion of wisdom is brought here, "for wisdom consists in the harmony of the will of a being with his final end" (TL 6: 441/DV 107).

Within the context of one's duties to others, love and respect are mentioned, as well as benevolence, gratitude, etc. The formative character of the moral law is systematically expressed in a statement which criticizes "the uselessness of the Aristotelian principle that virtue consists in the middle-way between two vices" (TL 6: 432/DV 96). This brief critical comment is significant both for the understanding of Kant's architectonical approach and for the understanding of the substance of the system. The shaping evoked by moral law is not just an intervention in the workings of given inclinations of human beings, as Kant apparently understood Aristotle's concept of the mean. It is an attempt to present moral law as giving rise to human response out of the sources of the moral law itself. The shaping character involved is thus the expression of the sequence starting with the moral law as such, and percolating, as it were, into the profile of human beings, as shaped by moral law, and expressing its shape in the various virtues. Hence, Kant's exposition can be summed up by saying that it presents the ultimate origin of moral behaviour, grounding it in the law.

Hence, the well-known critical analysis by Max Scheler cannot be accepted. Kant's system is not what Scheler describes as *logonomie*.[2] This characterization is inappropriate for several reasons. Logos is not the sole element within the context of Kant's system; the system is based on a primary synthesis or integration of reason and will. In addition, that synthesis or integrated interrelation between reason and will shapes the character of the person, and as was just observed, it leads to virtues as moral attitudes involved in the struggle. When Scheler presents the opposition imputed to Kant between the autonomy of reason and the autonomy of the person — if we accept this presentation at all — his comment disregards the impact of the autonomy of reason on the autonomy of the person. According to Kant there can be no autonomy of the person without the impact of the autonomy of the basic integration of reason and will. It is not that the person, according to Kant, is the logical subject as Scheler points out (p. 38). The person is, rather, an integrated entity, though his formative factors do not derive from the given data of his existence, but from the primary synthesis. When Scheler speaks about evidence of preference accessible to intuition (p. 110), he is certainly describing a view which is different from Kant's. For according to Kant the relation between the person and the synthesis inherent in the moral law cannot be based on intuition. Still, the preference is expressed there through acceptance of the law, reverence for it, and making it the shaping factor of

---

[2] Max Scheler, *Der Formalismus in der Ethik und die materiale Wertethik*, 4th rev. ed. (Bern: Francke, 1954). Further references are to this work.

one's attitude. Since Scheler's theory attempts to present material values as opposed to formal ones, and Kant is thereby understood as representing the formalistic approach, we may wonder whether the polemic in Scheler's theory does justice to Kant's system, and can thus serve as a point of departure for a different approach to the problem of ethics.

Thus we conclude that Kant formulated a system which cannot be viewed as merely formalistic, because it is a view related to the attitude of human beings. The attitude of a moral character in the strict sense of the term is not continuous with the empirically given inclinations or dispositions of human beings, but is rather a fusion of the different impacts of the moral law.

The Hebrew University of Jerusalem

Onora S. O'Neill

Agency and Anthropology in Kant's *Groundwork*

1. The Frameworks of the Groundwork

Recently Bernard Williams described Kant's *Groundwork of the Metaphysic of Morals* as "the most significant work of moral philosophy after Aristotle, and one of the most puzzling."[1] This seems to me right on both counts. The puzzles would be fewer if we had a *strategy* for reading the entire *Groundwork* and making sense of its multiple transitions between distinct frameworks of argument. One central strategic task is to make sense of Kant's account of action and agency. He discusses agency under various headings — including willing, rational willing, and freedom — throughout the work. The discussion is complex not only because of this variety of headings, but still more because it is conducted in three distinct frameworks, and because the transitions between these coincide only approximately with the transitions between chapters. The first chapter analyses our common account of morality and claims that it centres on the idea of good willing; the second chapter undertakes a metaphysics of morals by analysing good willing in terms of an abstract account of rational willing as such; the last chapter (in the sections from 450 onwards) argues from the perspective of a critique of reason that rational willing is free and yet compatible with the causality of nature.

Throughout the text the discussion of agency is closely linked to the account of morality: willing is dissected in order to discover what good willing is. However, agency is clearly the more fundamental concern, since moral considerations will be vacuous if there are no free and rational agents. Until the later parts of chapter III (from 450 onwards) the moral theory is presented without argument that we are or can know ourselves to be beings for whom such a theory is binding.

Acknowledgement. I would like to thank Jay Bernstein, Christine Korsgaard, Otfried Höffe, Alan Montefiore, David Smith and Yirmiyahu Yovel for helpful comments.
[1] *Ethics and the Limits of Philosophy* (Fontana, 1985), p. 55.

Y. Yovel (ed.), *Kant's Practical Philosophy Reconsidered, 63-82.*

A strategic reading of the *Groundwork* can postpone treatment of many problems to do with Kant's account of morality. The interpretation, justification and application of the Categorical Imperative, as well as the deep connections drawn between autonomy and morality, need not be discussed initially, puzzling though they are. These topics can be bracketed while we explicate the overall structure of Kant's account of agency.

2. The Status of Anthropology

Kant denies repeatedly that anthropology — the theoretical study of human nature — has any place in a metaphysic of morals. The *Groundwork* as a whole is an argument about the possibility and necessity of practical reasoning; it is not specifically about the embodiment of practical reason in human beings. So discussion of specifically human characteristics would presumably be out of place. There is plenty of textual evidence for this view. In the first *Critique* Kant wrote

the metaphysic of morals is really pure moral philosophy, with no underlying basis of anthropology or of other empirical conditions. (A842/B870)

In the Preface of the *Groundwork* he insists that it is

a matter of the utmost necessity to work out for once a pure moral philosophy completely cleansed of everything that can only be empirical and appropriate to anthropology. (4: 389; cf. 410, 425, 427).

The principles of morality to be discussed are to hold for all rational beings and not just for human beings. Even when pure moral philosophy is applied to man

it does not borrow in the slightest from acquaintance with him (in anthropology), but gives him laws *a priori* as a rational being. (G 4: 389)

This is to be "universal practical philosophy" (G 4: 390) and so must

investigate the Idea and principles of a possible *pure* will, and not the activities of human willing as such. (G 4: 390)

Yet anybody familiar with the text of the *Groundwork* knows that it contains many empirical claims and observations about human nature, that the central notion of duty is defined in terms of

a good will, exposed, however, to certain subjective limitations and obstacles (G 4: 397)

and that the notorious examples are examples of human duties, and some of them of human duties under quite specific social circumstances which include shopkeepers, money and debts. These apparent discrepancies between the prefatory claims of the *Groundwork* and its actual content have produced recurrent controversy about the scope of the work and scepticism about its success. Hence one reasonable test for a strategy for reading the entire work might be whether it could reduce or dispel these controversies by shedding light on the relation between prefatory comments and actual content. Such an interpretive strategy would have to locate the anthropological passages of the *Groundwork* within a wider framework, or sequence of frameworks, and show why Kant both denies that anthropology is basic to his task yet says so much about human nature and the human condition in the text.

We might begin such a reading of the text by distinguishing the treatment of agency in each of the three frameworks. While Chapter I articulates the view of specifically *human* agency that is implicit in our common understanding of morality, Chapter II and the early pages of Chapter III (up to 450) develop a *general* and abstract account of the agency of possible rational beings who are subject to the Categorical Imperative. Chapter III (after 450) explores what grounds we may have for holding that human beings are agents of this general sort, although also clearly parts of a natural and causally ordered world.

The status of anthropological comments will depend on the framework within which they are placed. Remarks about human nature and specific human social relations and duties that are unproblematic in the context of our common understanding may be problematic in the context of a metaphysic of morals. Here they can perhaps serve only as *familiar illustrations* of a more general and abstract theory of agency, and must not be taken either as presuppositions or as proofs of human agency or of the duties of rational beings as such. Anthropological remarks may have yet another status in the argument in Chapter III, which is undertaken from the quite different standpoint of critical inquiry into the limits of human reason, and seeks to adjudicate the allocation of the burden of proving human agency. If we adopt an interpretive strategy that distinguishes the several frameworks of the *Groundwork*, we will neither seek clues to the basic argument of the text in the examples of Chapters I and II, nor attribute the failure of the text to limitations in those examples. Nor will we be likely to interpret Chapter III (beyond 450) from the perspective of rational agency as such, rather than from that of critical inquiry.

3. Anthropology and the Opacity of Human Self-Knowledge

A helpful starting point for exploring Kant's attempted vindication of agency is to ask a sceptical question about agency. We may wonder whether agency is not perhaps a complete illusion, since all action, including all human action, can be explained in terms of natural causality. What we grandly take to be our own spontaneous choosing is perhaps no more than the natural play of desire. Possibly there is no profound difference between the activities of animals — even of simple life-forms — and human activities. If so the enterprise of morality is an illusion based upon an illusion. This familiar line of thought makes it plain enough why some view of agency is vital for any discussion of the basis of moral principles. Even an abstract metaphysic of morals, let alone a detailed determination of human duties, must take some stand on agency.

Scepticism about agency is peculiarly pointed for Kant because he maintained a view of self and other knowledge which makes it particularly hard to establish or rebut claims about agency. In particular he argued that neither inspection nor introspection can tell us whether an action reflects natural causes (such as desires or inclinations, understood in the sense that naturalists conceive them) or free agency. Although we commonly distinguish behaviour caused by natural events from action that is freely chosen, we cannot so readily vindicate this popular distinction. Kant denies that we can either have transparent self knowledge or know others as they are in themselves. All that we have is incomplete empirical knowledge of ourselves and of others. We cannot simply point to action that is (for example) caused by desire or to action that is not so caused, but results (for example) from reasoned choosing. No theme recurs more often in the *Groundwork* than that of the opacity of human self and other knowledge. It is this opacity that prevents us from knowing whether there has ever been a single instance of good willing (G 4: 387–88, 406–8), and from forming a determinate conception of human happiness, which would allow us to work out principles rather than counsels of prudence (G 4: 418). More generally, the opacity of self and other knowledge means that we cannot be sure what desires we or others may have, or whether claims that particular acts are not caused by desires are true. In denying that we have transparent self knowledge, or equivalent insight into others, Kant rejects claims that we have scientific, empirical, intuitive or introspective knowledge of the determinants of human action.

This insistence on the opacity of self and other knowledge vindicates Kant's prefatory claim that anthropology cannot settle questions about human agency, but leaves it unclear how they might be settled. It also leaves an apparent tension in the first chapter of the *Groundwork*. Ostensibly the chapter argues from "common rational knowledge of morality" to a certain view of agency and morality. But we *know* that Kant thinks common rational knowledge of morality inadequate to demonstrate that human beings are agents in the required sense, or subject to morality. What then can the chapter be meant to establish?

Perhaps the matter can be seen in this way: within the total structure of the *Groundwork* it makes sense that the method of the first chapter should not be adequate to establish whether or not all agency is based on desire, so naturally caused. The chapter shows, and is intended to show, that a vindication of rational agency can *begin* but not *end* with "common rational knowledge of morality," which is theoretically unsatisfactory because it is inconclusive and practically unsatisfactory because it is liable to corruption (G 4: 404–5). This is why an inquiry into agency and morality has to go on to a metaphysic of morals, and (if that too proves inconclusive) to a critique of practical reason. The numerous anthropological remarks of Chapter I are neither problematical nor incompatible with the warnings of the preface: for we know that Kant's method in that chapter is "analytical" of common human understanding, and that he holds that the philosophical inadequacy of that perspective, within which these anthropological remarks are located, can be shown.

However, the first chapter is not redundant. It allows Kant to make considerable headway with his task, by showing that the conception of free agency is deeply embedded within "common rational knowledge of morality." It is revealed in the most basic of ordinary moral distinctions, such as those between an (unconditionally) good will and other (conditional) goods and between action done out of duty and action which merely accords with duty. These reminders about the deep structure of our common moral views are important if Kant is to sustain his claim that

the concept of a will estimable in itself and apart from any further end... is already present in a sound natural understanding (G 4: 397),

if his philosophical discussion of the basis of morality is to have practical relevance to "the great mass of men" (B xxxiii) and if that discussion is to be an appropriate object of a critique of practical reason.

4. Anthropology and Exemplary Duties

The anthropological content of Chapter II is another matter. Here we are supposedly considering a metaphysic of morals, so no longer focussed on ordinary views of human duty, but on a more abstract account of principles of action for rational beings as such. The method of the chapter is still "analytic" (G 4: 445), but we are no longer analysing common conceptions of human morality but the more abstract notion of rational willing as such. If this is the method of Chapter II it seems odd that Kant should make any specifically anthropological comments. Yet he does. Why does he discuss what are clearly not the duties of rational beings as such, and in some cases apparently not even the duties of human beings as such, but (at most) the duties of human beings with special social relations, rather like those of late eighteenth century Königsberg?

We can make sense of the anthropological content of Chapter II if we note that it is *illustrative*. Human actions, duties and institutions are mentioned in *examples* that are intended as hypothetical applications of more abstract principles. These principles ought never "depend on the special nature of human reason" (G 4: 412), yet ethics "requires anthropology for its application to man" (G 4: 412).[2] To illustrate the duties of (finite) rational beings as such Kant has to offer examples chosen from the case of the only species of rational being with which we are acquainted. His problem is like that of a biologist who illustrates a claim about a phylum of which a single species survives. That lone species (which may be far from typical) serves to illustrate the phylum, and may mislead the biologist into unwarranted generalizations. Kant was well aware of this problem, and the barrier it presents to accounts of specifically human species nature. At the end of *Anthropology from a Pragmatic Viewpoint* he remarks

It seems, therefore, that the problem of giving an account of the character of the human species is quite insoluble, because the problem could only be solved by comparing two species of rational beings, but experience has not offered us a comparison between two species of rational being. (7: 321; cf. KpV 5: 12/13)

Immediately after this passage he speculates about the place of "this race of terrestrial rational beings" "among other rational beings of the universe (unknown to us)" and suggests that if there were rational beings who unlike us "could not think in any other way but aloud" this would greatly alter moral relations. (Presumably deception, or at least face-to-face deception, would be impossible.) In the essay *Idea of a Universal History from a Cosmopolitan Point of View* he refers to "our neighbours in the cosmos" (Prop. 6, note). If human agency is but one illustration of rational agency as such, and our self and other knowledge is limited, we cannot prove anything about the *differentia* of specifically human agency or nature.[3]

---

[2] This suggests that we must take the remark that moral philosophy "must not borrow from acquaintance with man" (G 4: 412) to mean that it must not draw on anthropology to determine its own principles, but that reference to specific circumstances and forms of agency is needed in actual deliberation. Cf. Maximilian Forschner, "Reine Morallehre und Anthropologie," *Neue Hefte für Philosophie* 22 (1983): 25-44.

[3] See, for example, his discussion of our lack of insight into the fundamental maxims, *Religion within the Limits of Reason Alone*, Book I.

It is not hard to understand Kant's repeated reference to human duties in Chapter II when we take account of our lack of alternative illustrations of the duties of rational beings as such. Still, local illustrations of rational agency cannot show much about the general character of rational agency. Biologists can use the case of the lone surviving species not only to *illustrate* but to determine the characteristics of the phylum of which it is a member. They can draw on evidence from the fossil record, from palaeobotany, from the theory of evolution and from geology to check and discipline inferences drawn from the case of the lone surviving species. But what can those who make claims about rational beings and their agency rely on for like discipline? An answer to this question might show a lot about the strategy and success of the *Groundwork*.

5. Between the Holy Wills and the Beasts: Agency and Desire

Much of Kant's strategy in the first two chapters is a matter of providing a *typology* of possible sorts of agency, distinguishing how differing types of agent depend on natural causality. Although these chapters implicitly classify human agency as free agency, but not untrammelled by desire (arbitrium liberum sed sensitivum), Kant does not seek to *prove* where on this spectrum of agency human agency falls.

On a certain (perhaps common) construal of the notion of agency, action which is the outcome solely of natural causality does not reflect *any* sort of agency. However, Kant's idiom allows even that sort of action to count as displaying a certain sort of will, an *abritrium brutum*. This point seems to be of merely terminological interest: if we do not want to allow action which is wholly determined by natural causes to count as *any* sort of agency, then we (unlike Kant) will exlude *arbitria bruta* from the spectrum of agency and treat a narrower range of action as reflecting agency. But since it is the *upper* end of the spectrum that is significant for a discussion of morality, disputes about placing the lower bound of agency are a subsidiary matter.[4]

However, it is significant, and perplexing, that Kant should conceive of naturally caused action as action caused by desires, inclinations and instinct. We are more familiar with the thought that naturally caused action is action caused by drive states or physiological processes. For us the theories that appear to threaten human agency go behind surface(?) phenomena of desire and suggest that there are far more specific natural causes of action. Kant's

---

[4] See the Introduction to the *Metaphysic of Morals* for a systematic account of the spectrum of agency.

contrast between action which reflects desires and that which reflects reason is often criticized for assuming a supposedly unconvincing dualism between morality and nature. More concretely, passages in the *Groundwork* that can be read as saying that what we ought to do must be other than what we want to do, or that human duty is a matter of denying and thwarting our own desires, are criticized for being psychologically and ethically implausible.[5]

When Kant distinguishes actions that are determined by reason from those determined by desire he is concerned only with distinguishing free from naturally caused action. He is bothered by the implications of a purely naturalistic interpretation of agency. He does not deny that desires are essential to human agency (they supply the material which we discipline in the light of moral reasons); and he neither denies nor discusses whether a different, moralized conception of desire might have a more central role in the moral life. He denies only that a purely naturalistic conception of desire (e.g. that of Hobbes) is sufficient to ground free agency.[6] The lowest level of the spectrum of agency is defined as that at which all action is naturally caused (we might say *physiologically* caused and Kant might say *pathologically* caused), and there is no free agency. Kant's picture of the role of desire in human action is likely to be radically distorted if we attribute any but a naturalistic conception of desire to him.

Kant defines the lower bound of the spectrum of agency, where all action is naturalistically determined, in Chapter I, and illustrates this with the case of animal action. He then immediately argues that what we might take for the next region of the spectrum — the case of action determined by nature plus limited, merely instrumental, reasoning capacities — is empty. Any organic being where "the real purpose of nature" is "his preservation, his welfare, or in a word his happiness" (G 4: 395) has *no* practical use for reason, since

the whole rule of his behaviour would have been mapped out for him far more accurately by instinct. (G 4: 395)

The opacity of self knowledge, which also precludes any introspective demonstration of agency, means that for beings whose sole aim is their happiness

nature would have prevented reason from striking out into a *practical use* and from presuming, with its feeble vision, to think out for itself a plan for happiness and for the means to its attainment. Nature would herself have taken over the choice not only of

[5] Susan Mendus, "The Practical and the Pathological," *Journal of Value Inquiry* 19 (1985): 235-43, shows why this is an unconvincing reading.
[6] It is less clear to me that he would deny a Humean view of desires (motives) as causes of action; he might regard this as innocuous (if beside the point) because a Humean causal claim asserts no necessary connection between desire and the resulting action.

ends but also of means, and would with wise precaution have entrusted both to instinct alone. (G 4: 395)

Where ends are fixed, reasoning is apparently redundant, indeed counterproductive. The *conclusion* of this argument is important: beings whose reasoning is *solely* instrumental are not to be found. Either an agent does not reason at all, or its reasoning capacities are not merely subservient to given ends. Even within the confines of common rational knowledge we are driven to the view that

since... reason has been imparted to us as a practical power — that is, as one which is to have influence on the *will*; its true function must be to produce a *will* that is *good*, not as a *means* to some further end, but *in itself*. (G 4: 396)

However, the *argument* itself is of restricted significance. Since it occurs within a chapter which assumes the framework of common rational knowledge of morality whose philosophical inadequacy is foreseen, and also depends on an adaptive (teleological or evolutionary) view of nature — indeed, specifically on the view that nature works for the best — the conclusion cannot simply be carried beyond this framework. At most we learn from Chapter I that our daily views of human agency do not accomodate the possibility of beings whose rationality is solely instrumental. However, this alone cannot tell us whether to think of ourselves as wholly lacking in rational capacities — beasts with illusions of grandeur — or as able to guide our choice of ends as well as of means by reason. Even so, this argument in the restricted context of Chapter I is an important *polemical* move, for it casts doubt on the supposedly "common sense" and recently influential view that human reason is merely instrumental.

It is in Chapter II, within the broader and more abstract framework of a metaphysic of morals, that Kant tries to define the upper end of the spectrum of agency. He offers us the thought experiment of beings for whom reason never appears as an "imperative,"

for the *divine* will, and in general for a *holy* will, there are no imperatives... Imperatives... are only formulae for expressing the relation of objective laws of willing to the subjective imperfection of the will of this or that rational being — for example, of the human will. (G 4: 414)

We do not have to imagine that holy wills are devoid of desire: it is rather that they never act on desires in ways that would conflict with the Categorical Imperative.[7]

---

[7] From this alone we can tell that the Categorical Imperative underdetermines action, for if it provided a principle for generating a required action in each situation the

Kant's spectrum of possible types of agent runs from beings who are wholly guided by desire or instinct, to the holy wills, for whom the notions of obligation and duty are superfluous (G 4: 439). It therefore stretches not merely from the beasts to the angels, but beyond. For angels, as tradition conceives them, are subject to temptation and capable of evil. Notions of obligation and duty are superfluous (G 4: 439). It therefore stretches not finite rational beings, who are capable of reason and also capable of flouting it, Kant identifies several hypothetical possibilities: there might be non-terrestrial rational beings, devils or angels. But it appears that human beings will not be acquainted with practical reasoners unless they themselves reason practically.

However, nothing in Chapter II demonstrates that human beings are actually practical reasoners. A metaphysic of morals delineates a range of possibilities, but its conclusion is only hypothetical. *If* we are what we take ourselves to be, that is, capable of reason and affected but not causally determined by our desires, *then*, if the argument of Chapter II is sound, we are subject to the standards of consistent willing that are spelt out in the various formulations of the Categorical Imperative, and to their specific implications in various determinate circumstances. If we are not what we take ourselves to be, and our supposed free agency is illusory, then the whole metaphysic of morals, the argument of Chapter II, and all the supposed illustrations in terms of human duties have not established practical implications for us.

The metaphysic of morals has left Kant with an acute but apparently insoluble problem. He cannot appeal to introspection or to other empirical evidence to determine whether human beings are free agents. Anthropology is doubly incompetent here. We cannot penetrate the opacity of self and other knowledge, nor resolve debates between those who think that we are naturally selfish and those who think that we are naturally altruistic. Even if we were granted insight into human nature, and knew whether we are naturally benign or malignant, the discovery would be beside the point. We could know that we were *naturally* one or the other, yet not know whether we are free agents who can deny our nature.

Nor, on the other hand, can Kant take the line (adopted in much modern ethical and social inquiry) of viewing what agents do as criterial for their desires and preferences. That move does indeed "settle" the question of whether any human action is independent of desires: but at the cost of

---

thought experiment of a being in whom desire never trumps reason would be empty, since there would be no content to the thought that such a being had desires.

trivializing the claim. If, by definition, preferences are revealed by action, then we can know that action never fails to reflect preferences. What we still will not know is whether the preferences so revealed must be as they are because human nature is causally determined, or whether they can be altered by reason. The opacity of self and other knowledge leaves open the possibility that, whatever the natural character of human beings, they may be free to act in ways not fully determined by that character.

6. The Practical Standpoint and the Extreme Limit

Chapter III of the *Groundwork* makes the transition to a Critique of Practical Reason. It is here, in the passages from 450 onwards, that the crucial arguments to show that human beings actually are free agents, in a sense that makes their actions imputable and the Categorical Imperative relevant to them, are undertaken. Neither Kant's articulation of our common moral consciousness nor his more abstract analysis of principles of obligation for rational beings as such showed, *or could have shown*, that *we* are agents of the required sort. Can we expect a Critique of Practical Reason to succeed where a Metaphysic of Morals fell short? If it cannot or does not, will Kant's whole moral theory be only of hypothetical importance? In particular, what importance will it have for human beings?

We would certainly have no reason to expect success in this task if a Critique of Practical Reason differed from a Metaphysic of Morals only by being *more abstract*. However, this is not the difference between metaphysics and critique, or between the last two chapters of the *Groundwork*. A Critique of Reason is a critique of *reasoning*, that is, of capacities of actual reasoners. It is undertaken from the standpoint of those who find themselves able to reason, led into antinomies in their reasoning, yet able to discipline their reasoning by its own standards. Kant offers a discursive account of the grounding of (unrestricted) reason in the methodology of the first *Critique*: the principles and standards of human reasoning are guaranteed by their sustained success, including their reflexive success, in human reasoning. In a post-Copernican world there is no absolute *up* or *down* and we cannot expect a foundationalist account of the grounds of reason (whatever that might be). A critical grounding of reason works by showing why we cannot do without certain interwoven and mutually supporting principles, which we term the principles of reason. Their authority is established by their indispensability: the fabric of our experience and practice unravels if these threads are pulled.

Although Chapter III contains few detailed anthropological discussions its standpoint is fundamentally that of a practical reasoner, and at times specifically the anthropological standpoint of a human practical reasoner. There is a difference between arguments whose *standpoint* is anthropological and arguments whose *subject matter* is (empirical) anthropology. Kant does not go back on his view that human self understanding is fragmentary and opaque, so that a critical perspective on human agency and practical reasoning cannot invoke privileged or scientific access to agents' mental states. He therefore faces a delicate and complicated task, which depends on subtle deliberations about the allocation of the burden of proof.

Chapter III has two closely linked aspects. Kant holds that we cannot grasp action at all if we try to do so without a conception of agency which entails subjection to the Categorical Imperative. Our grasp of human experience and activity requires that we be free agents, and if we are free agents we must be subject to the Categorical Imperative. Considerations in favour of each of these claims are interwoven in the text, but can be separated. For the present I shall consider only Kant's discussion of agency; his discussion of morality and of the relation between agency and morality remain bracketed.

The chapter begins with an analytical move linking the notions of freedom and reason. If there are beings in whom reason can be practical, in the sense that what they do is not simply determined by what they naturally desire, then such beings are free, in the sense that they are "able to work independently of alien causes" (G 4: 446). This analytical move cannot tell us whether human beings are free. We know from Kant's insistence on the limits of our self knowledge that we can no more have direct insight into human freedom than into human nature. The opacity of self and other knowledge means that no impression or conviction that we sometimes do other than we desire carries decisive weight. So it is no surprise to find Kant claiming that

we have been quite unable to demonstrate freedom as something actual in ourselves and in human nature. (G 4: 448)

He takes seriously the thought that what we think of as our experience of freedom may be illusory.

Still, he also holds that we cannot demonstrate that desire governs all action (unless, of course, we follow revealed preference theory and trivialize the issues by taking action as revelatory of desire). The opacity of self knowledge means that we can no more demonstrate that human beings are not free than that they are free. However, it will not suit Kant's purpose merely to assert that human beings may or may not be free agents. The whole enterprise of the *Groundwork* would be pointless for human beings if all we could reasonably think was that we do not know that we are not free agents. Kant did not aim to limit knowledge so that we could be impaled by doubt, but "to make room for faith" (B xxx; A745/B773). In the last chapter of the *Groundwork* as in the first *Critique*, his grounding of practical reason is closely linked to the limitation of theoretical reason.

The crucial contrast between a theoretical and a practical standpoint is introduced at an early stage of Chapter III (G 4:448), and discussed at some length in the later part of the chapter. Kant first observes that "from a practical point of view" we "cannot act except *under the Idea of freedom*" (G 4:448). Specifically, when we make judgments we must view ourselves as free. We cannot coherently view our own judging as due to impulsions. However, this consideration does not show that rational beings of any sort, or human beings in particular, *are* free, but only that they must think that they are when they act. Perhaps the truth is merely that in certain contexts we (and perhaps other rational beings) take ourselves for free agents. We may be incurably afflicted with a false view of ourselves as free, just as some optimists are incurably afflicted with falsely rosy views of their prospects.

Kant makes a series of moves that go beyond this initial claim about the practical standpoint. The *first* is that the practical and speculative standpoints form a pair:

a rational being... has two points of view from which he can regard himself... *first* — so far as he belongs to the sensible world — to be under laws of nature (heteronomy); and *secondly* — so far as he belongs to the intelligible world — to be under laws which, being independent of nature, are not empirical but have their ground in reason alone. (G 4:452)

The *second* is that rational, including human, beings not only can adopt each standpoint but must shift between them:

when we think of ourselves as free, we transfer ourselves into the intelligible world as members... when we think of ourselves as under obligation we look upon ourselves as belonging to the sensible world and the intelligible world at the same time. (G 4:453)

The *third* is that for rational, including human, beings neither standpoint is eliminable and that of the intelligible world is more fundamental:

the intelligible world contains the ground of the sensible world and therefore also of its laws... in spite of regarding myself from one point of view as a being that belongs to the sensible world, I shall have to recognize that qua intelligence I am subject to the law of the intelligible world. (G 4:453)

The *fourth* is that, despite appearances, the two standpoints are fully compatible:

both characteristics not merely *can* get on perfectly well together, but must be conceived as necessarily combined in the same subject. (G 4:456)

These claims can seem most puzzling.[8] In making use of a distinction between "intelligible" and "sensible" worlds Kant is said to avail himself of a transcendent vantage point which he otherwise repudiates. His views on self knowledge appear to undercut the possibility of knowledge of an intelligible world. From a Kantian perspective it seems that a two worlds story can neither be true nor knowable. And if the story were true, it would lead to a preposterous, metaphysically extravagant and psychologically implausible account of agency as atemporal.

These rebuttals may miss the point. It is true that the metaphors of the intelligible and the sensible world continually invite an ontological interpretation that fits their Platonic and Leibnizian heritage; but Kant repeatedly distances himself from such interpretations, and reminds us that he is discussing *two standpoints* and not *two worlds*. In the *Groundwork*, for example, he writes:

The concept of the intelligible world is thus only a *point of view* which reason finds itself constrained to adopt outside appearances *in order to conceive itself as practical* (G 4:458)

and warns reason against

flapping its wings impotently, without leaving the spot, in a space that for it is empty — the space of transcendent concepts known as "the intelligible world." (G 4:462, cf. A9/B5)

In the first *Critique* he reiterates that the concept of a noumenon is

a merely *limiting concept*, the function of which is to curb the pretensions of sensibility; and it is therefore only of negative employment. (A255/B310-11)

Although Kant nearly always uses the terms "sensible world" and "intelligible world" as the objects of propositional attitudes, there is no denying that he invited misunderstanding by using a "two worlds" metaphor. If that reading is firmly set aside, the first and second passages quoted from *Groundwork* III have to be read as claiming that we can see ourselves not merely as part of nature but also as free (so independent of nature) and also as free beings who are yet part of nature. The "two worlds" doctrine is a doctrine about two ways in which we see ourselves.

If we abandon the ontological reading of the "two worlds" idiom, and of

---

[8] Cf. discussions in J. Bennett, *Kant's Dialectic* (Cambridge University Press, 1974), p. 193; R.C.S. Walker, *Kant* (London: Routledge & Kegan Paul, 1982); Bernard Williams, "Morality and the Emotions," *Problems of the Self* (Cambridge University Press, 1973), p. 228; Allen W. Wood, "Kant's Compatibilism," in *Self and Nature in Kant's Philosophy*, ed. Allen W. Wood (Cornell University Press, 1984).

the closely related phenomenal and noumenal distinction, we discover that the controversial and exciting claims about agency in *Groundwork* III are *not* claims that we or other rational agents can be shown to be atemporal choosers, or members of other worlds. (Of course, such claims would be metaphysically exciting: it is just that Kant does not offer us that excitement.) The interesting claims are rather the metaphysically lower key ones: that these two ways of seeing ourselves are neither of them eliminable; that the practical one is more fundamental; that they are compatible.

There are various reasons why metaphysically flamboyant but philosophically implausible readings of *Groundwork* III persist despite good textual evidence against them. One may be this: if Kant's concern is only with ways in which agents conceive themselves, then he cannot (given his own misgivings about self and other knowledge) ground a theory of agency. All he can produce (it may be said) is the anthropological claim that human beings in fact see themselves under two ineliminable yet distinct sets of descriptions, but this anthropological fact would not tell us why we should take dualities in human self consciousness seriously. So since Kant does seek a theory of agency (it may be thought) he *must* be metaphysically more ambitious and so we should take an "ontological" reading of the "two worlds" seriously. The ontological readings can seem unavoidable if the tasks of Chapter III are understood in a certain way.

No doubt there are many dualities in human self consciousness which we should not take particularly seriously. But an *ineliminable* duality (if that is what we have) is a serious matter. Kant evidently did not think human cognition an infallible guide. Besides false empirical beliefs we have bogus concepts (A84/B117) and we cannot determine anything about things in themselves. However, the point of the Copernican turn is to see that objects must conform to whichever of our concepts are *indispensable*. The arguments of *Groundwork* III suggest that the two standpoints also are *ineliminable* features of human cognition and life. More specifically, I shall argue, Kant's claims about the two standpoints are a direct corollary of central claims about human knowledge and action in the first *Critique*.

The first *Critique* provides a revealing way of looking at *Groundwork* III because the *naturalistic* standpoint too is in question there. When we come to Chapter III of the *Groundwork* through Chapters I and II we are all agog to learn about agency. We are likely to take for granted that we must look upon ourselves as belonging to the sensible world. In the first *Critique* that is not taken for granted. On the contrary, the naturalistic standpoint both on ourselves and more generally is in question. The status of causal judgements is uncertain.

The central and serious reason why the naturalistic standpoint is in question in the first *Critique* is that it leads to antinomies when extended indefinitely. When we try to make it a sole and comprehensive viewpoint, it proves self undermining. We cannot form a coherent account of a spatio-temporal totality that is causally ordered. Although the empirical use of reason must strive for completeness in naturalistic understanding, the completeness is only a regulative ideal, and not attainable (A565/B593). A naturalistic account of the world lacks closure: it yields explanations of the natural world only on condition that naturalism is not the whole story. The only way to adopt the naturalistic standpoint without being led into antinomies is to acknowledge the restricted scope of naturalism. Naturalism provides the framework for understanding the world as it appears to us, but does nothing to explain why the world should so appear. Naturalism cannot claim to account for things as they are in themselves: if that were what it did, the antinomies would be fatal to the coherence of naturalism.

Consideration of the antinomies to which unrestricted naturalistic understanding leads shows why the ultimate grounds of "the sensible world" cannot lie within that world. Consideration of Kant's claims about the limits of human knowledge show us that he cannot mean that "the intelligible world" provides the ground of the sensible world and its laws (the fourth passage quoted above) as a (Platonic or Leibnizian) claim that we have a direct intellectual grasp of things as they are "in themselves," i.e. in abstraction from the naturalistic standpoint. On the contrary, we simply lack insight into and cannot seek out the "intelligible" grounds of nature.

Taken together these considerations may show us why Kant thought that those who view matters from a naturalistic standpoint must acknowledge *some other* standpoint. However, they are not enough to vindicate human freedom and agency. It may be the case that (as a matter of anthropological fact) we conceive ourselves from two standpoints and that (as a matter of necessity) the naturalistic standpoint presupposes a non naturalistic standpoint, without there being reasons to "transfer ourselves to the intelligible world" or to think of *ourselves* as able to act in independence of alien causes. Why should not the duality of *self* perception be a merely anthropological phenomenon, unconnected with the deeper reasons why dual standpoints are required? Why should we understand *ourselves* as part of the "intelligible world" that naturalistic understanding presupposes? Might not that "intelligible world" be not merely inaccessible to human cognition, but also irrelevant to human action, for which (despite our fragmented self understanding) we can best account in purely naturalistic terms?

Once again it may be helpful to look at the claims of *Groundwork* III in the light of the first *Critique*, where our claims to know that nature is causally ordered are themselves in question. The argument of the Second Analogy will be crucial here. In that argument the basis for claiming that events are causally ordered — that they have a necessary order — is that we can distinguish merely subjective from objective sequences in our perceptions. This distinction cannot be based on any direct apprehension of objective time, which we lack. Rather, the distinction between events, which are causally determined, and mere sequence which is not, must be one that we can draw *within* experience. Merely subjective sequences are those which could have been perceived in another order, as in Kant's example the parts of a house might be perceived in any order. Objective sequences are those in which the order of perception is (at least in part) outside the control of the perceiver, as in Kant's example a sequence of perceptions of a ship moving down stream cannot be (wholly) rearranged by the perceiver (A192-93/B237-38). We can know a sequence of perceptions as objective, and its parts as events, when it is beyond our control to vary their order. We understand what it means for the order of such perceptions to lie beyond our control when we contrast the situation with others where we have (some) control over the sequence of perceptions. Without the contrast we have no grasp of a distinction between empirical reality and fantasy. In a fantasy world, where "everything goes according to wish and whim," we cannot distinguish self from world, or our own doings from what happens, and the basis for naturalistic explanations of an objective world is lost. When our perception is objective, by contrast, "I cannot arrange the apprehension otherwise than in this very succession" (A193/B238); and we realize that "this compulsion is really what first makes possible the representation of succession in an object" (A197/B242).

The Second Analogy, in short, argues that the grounds of objective sequence, hence of naturalistic explanation, lie in the possibility of distinguishing what we control from what is beyond our control. Agency is presented as the presupposition of causal judgement. There is no claim that we can draw distinctions between subjective and objective sequences infallibly — given the limitations of our self knowledge we may sometimes think that we control what is in fact quite independent of us, or that we have no control over matters we can affect. Despite this qualification, the argument of the Second Analogy provides the additional move that explains why Kant maintains in *Groundwork* III not only that the sensible *world* has its ground in the intelligible *world*, but specifically that *we* cannot think of ourselves merely as members of the sensible world. The reason that we must "transfer" *ourselves* to the intelligible world is that if we are not agents, we will never have reasons to think of ourselves as confronting a natural world that is causally determined, so resists our control.[9] If we take the "speculative standpoint" for granted we will fail to see why we not merely may but must be free agents. For we will fail to note that the naturalistic view is a standpoint available only from the perspective of agency.

Of course, this argument by way of the first *Critique* must itself be undertaken from a standpoint. The standpoint of the Copernican turn is fundamentally the standpoint of *practical* reasoning which diagnoses the inconclusive battles of the metaphysical tradition as symptoms of a merely speculative approach. The disorientations of "nomadic" sceptics and the groundless certainties of "despotic" dogmatists both reflect failure to reason practically, and impose an appropriately "lawful" and bounded polity on our explorations. The "legislation of reason" has first to determine its own "jurisdiction," and so to secure an area for theoretical knowledge by limiting its scope. This limitation of human cognition is a real limitation; it is not one more horizon that we can shift by shifting our own perspective. Kant does not distinguish the sensible and intelligible "worlds" in order then to show us how we can after all have theoretical knowledge of the "intelligible world." Freedom is not something that we can explain theoretically (G 4: 459, 461-62). All that we are offered — Kant thinks it is all that we need in order to show that we are free agents — is the realization that if we reject the limitations of the causal principle, we will fail altogether to establish that principle. From the perspective of a (merely notional) comprehensive speculative standpoint this would be profoundly unsatisfactory. We, however, have only a (regulative) Idea of an intelligible world and no aquaintance with it. From the perspective of the practical standpoint, what we have allows us both a world which provides an arena for action and the realization that we would find no arena unless we were agents. Since all theoretical uses of reason — for example ordinary empirical judgments — themselves refer to some world, they presuppose the agency without which we find no world. This is why it turns out that

to argue freedom away is as impossible for the most abstruse philosophy as it is for the most ordinary human reason (G 4: 456)

[9] This suggests a serious defect in the thought experiment of the Holy Will. It may be stated as a dilemma. If Holy Wills are embodied beings, they too are part of nature and subject to alien causes, so (contrary to hypothesis) experience desire and temptation and must view moral principles as imperatives. If Holy Wills are not embodied beings, so not part of nature or subject to alien causes (as the text suggests), then it is not clear how they can distinguish those sequences that come about from those that they bring about. Mere conformity to their (disembodied) will cannot show that a change is their doing. Hence it does not seem that Holy Wills can view themselves as agents of any sort.

and also what lies behind Kant's otherwise incomprehensible aside at the beginning of the second *Critique*:

With the pure practical faculty of reason the reality of transcendental freedom is confirmed. Indeed it is substantiated in the absolute sense needed by speculative reason in its use of the concept of causality. (KpV 5:4/3)

and explains his comment that

theoretical reason had to assume at least the possibility of freedom in order to fill one of its own needs. (KpV 5:48/49)

When we accept that we must adopt both the practical and theoretical standpoints, one task that will remain for the latter is that of defusing the antinomies of freedom and determinism to which it is so naturally led (G 4:457). However, speculative reason does not have the impossible task of providing insight into human freedom (G 4:459). Nor are we required to establish the causal principle on the basis of a single standpoint. The distinctive mark of the critical philosophy is its commitment to questioning even our most fundamental commitments: such questioning is possible not because there is an Archimedean standpoint of reason on which we can base ourselves, but because we can shift between standpoints. The shifting frameworks of Kant's argument in the *Groundwork* is wholly appropriate to his conception of what critique requires.

Has agency in the sense of freedom from determination by alien causes then been established? This question can only be answered from a standpoint. From the standpoint of purely theoretical (speculative) reason agency has not been established. It could be established only by providing a theoretical insight into "the intelligible world," and it is one of Kant's most central claims that we can have no such insight. Commentators who hold that any such account of agency must be a shattering failure are correct. From the standpoint of practical reason we must give a different answer. Agency, in the sense in question, is lacking in beings who are determined only by alien causes. We can form a conception of beings who are determined only by alien causes only if we can vindicate a naturalistic outlook and the causal principle. But we cannot — because it leads to antinomies — vindicate an unrestricted naturalistic outlook. Such vindication as we can offer for a naturalistic outlook is available to us because we can distinguish events from our actions, and we can do this only from a practical standpoint. Hence our deployment of the naturalistic outlook depends on our being and taking ourselves to be agents who are not determined only by natural causes.

Double answers do not always satisfy. After considering Kant's account of agency we may ask: "But which standpoint is *really* fundamental?" Perhaps the only way to meet that question is to ask "From which standpoint is that question raised?"

University of Essex

Amihud Gilead

The Submission of our Sensuous Nature to the Moral Law in the Second *Critique*

1. According to Kant we are free to choose between two ways in which our will can be determined: either following our natural inclinations, desires and feelings — all of which are sensuous, given and pathological (passional) — or obeying solely the moral law from no other motive but respect for it. This freedom of choice is a fact of reason, which is necessarily presupposed (since without it morality is impossible) but not explicable. Were it possible to explain this fact, our choice would not be free at all but predictable, and, as such, subject to the deterministic laws of nature. No wonder, then, that Kant says that we cannot understand how our will is determined either pathologically or morally and rationally (KpV 5: 72). Neither rational explanation nor empirical example can make us understand the determination of our will (*Willkür*) which is capable of being independent both of sensuous impulses (A534/B562) and of the moral law, between the two of which it can freely choose. The two systems of determination — that of natural phenomena ("the causality of sensuous nature," KpV 5: 47) and that of free noumena ("the causality through freedom," ibid.) — are separate and independent, and the one cannot interfere with the other (A557-58/B585-86; KpV 5: 42-43). Following the one excludes the other. When following natural desires, our will is phenomenal, empirical and pathological; whereas when obeying the moral law from no sensuous motive, our will is noumenal. We can choose between enslaving ourselves to the deterministic, phenomenal system and setting ourselves, as noumena, free from it. In the latter case we reluctantly choose, *against* our natural inclinations, desires and interests, to obey the moral law, which is the most characteristic expression of our autonomy as self-legislative, rational beings.

In the second *Critique* Kant attempts to restrict his discussion of morality to the determination of our free will (5: 46). His main concern in this book is with our intention and decision to behave morally or not, rather than with our

Y. Yovel (ed.), *Kant's Practical Philosophy Reconsidered, 83-92.*

behaviour and actions in "the field of experience." His discussion is restricted to our intention to act morally as far as we can, whatever the results of that decision. The question is whether we really *wish* to act morally because we are constrained and obliged to do so by the categorical imperative, without feeling any pleasure and without promoting our profit. By doing so we may conceive or "feel" the "sublimity [*Erhabenheit*] of our own supersensuous existence" (KpV 5: 88/91), while remaining aware of our independence from our "pathologically affected nature" (ibid.) or "from everything empirical and hence from nature generally" (KpV 5: 97/100). Our sensuous (or psychological) nature is but a partial link of deterministic nature as a whole. All necessity of events in time (such as the internal concatenation of ideas in our mind) "according to natural law can be called the 'mechanism of nature'" (ibid.). Transcendental freedom, without which morality is impossible, means independence from that mechanism of (our sensuous) nature (suggested in 5: 87). Kant states that "there is in man a power of self-determination, independently of any coercion through sensuous impulses" (A534/B562).

At this point a decisive question must be asked: is such an independence possible? Can our will free itself from our sensuous nature, while the temptation to follow our desires and natural inclinations is so strong? Kant himself is well aware of the problematic nature of his theory concerning such independence and freedom. Indeed, an important chapter of the second *Critique*, entitled "The Incentives of Pure Practical Reason," deals not only with the required incentives for assisting (or promoting) our will in being morally determined, but also, of course, with the possible *obstacles* and *resistance* to such a determination. Let us take some examples:

Moral law, regarded as incentive, *weakens, strikes down* and *humiliates* such a natural inclination as self-conceit (KpV 5: 73). It removes a *resistance* (*Widerstand*) from the way and dislodges or lessens the *obstacle* (*Hinderniss*, 5: 75). As a matter of fact, sensibility, which is the expression of our finitude and limitation, is an obstacle to the practical reason (according to 5: 76). "We cannot know the force of the pure practical law as incentive but only the resistance to the incentives of sensibility" (5: 78/81). "The dissimilarity of rational and empirical grounds of determination is made recognizable through the resistance of a practically legislating reason to all interfering inclinations" (5: 92/95). A person does not obey the moral law willingly or out of love, because as a creature he is always dependent on satisfying his needs, and, consequently, "he can never be wholly free from desires and inclinations, which, because they rest on physical causes, do not of themselves agree with the moral law which has an entirely different source" (5: 84/86). Moreover, Kant describes *virtue* as a "moral disposition *in conflict*" ("moralische Gesinnung *im Kampfe*," 5: 84; here we may bear in mind the Latin word *virtus* which, beside virtue, goodness and moral perfection, also means manliness, manhood, strength and bravery, all of which have to do with *overcoming, overpowering* and *surmounting*). Indeed, even if before the moral law "all inclinations are dumb," still "they secretly work against it" ("ihm entgegen wirken," 5: 86/89).

Bearing these statements in mind, we may conclude that there is a *quarrel*, *conflict* or *competition* between the moral law (regarded as incentive) and the inclinations, feelings and desires of our sensuous nature over the determination of our will.

If there is such a conflict, on what basis can Kant expect a victory of the moral law over our passions in particular and our sensuous nature in general? Indeed, there is still another possibility for determining our will, namely, by our sensuous nature, which may gain the victory over the moral law. Kant actually speaks of the "will affected by the sensibility" (KpV 5: 76/78) and does not entirely exclude the possibility where "inclinations alone are the determining grounds of our will" (KpV 5: 81/84). Nevertheless he argues that

since the idea of the moral law deprives [*benimmt*] self-love of its influence and self-conceit of its delusion, it lessens the obstacle to pure practical reason, and the idea of the superiority of its objective law to the impulses of sensibility is produced, and, hence, so also is the idea of relatively increasing the weight of the moral law (on account of the will [*Wille*] affected by the sensibility) by removing, in the judgement of reason, the counterweight (KpV 5: 75-76/78, translation slightly modified)

and, moreover,

no other law precludes all inclinations from having a direct influence on the will. (5: 80/83)

How can Kant justify these ideas? Is there no possibility that our sensuous nature, rather than our moral law, will gain superiority, increase its own counterweight, resist pure practical reason and determine our will, which can be also affected by sensibility? Indeed, we can freely *choose* and *decide* to reject any influence of the sensuous nature on our will. However, what guarantees that choice against our passions and impulses? What can guarantee that reason will be capable of determining our will directly without being foiled by our sensuous, pathological nature? How is our free submission to the moral law possible? Does such a submission actually also constrain the "sensuously affected subject" (KpV 5: 80/83)?

Kant could be tempted to entertain the idea that the unpathological, a priori feeling of respect for the moral law gains an advantage by humiliating our sensuous inclinations. In comparison with the sublimity of obedience to the moral law, our desires may seem contemptible, as if we should be ashamed of them. Preferring them to moral freedom and elevation does not arouse any respect. Whereas respect, of which the moral law and the person obeying it are so deserving, "is a *tribute* we cannot refuse to pay to merit, whether we will or not [...] we cannot help feeling it inwardly" (KpV 5: 77/80). However, we cannot pay any respect to our "frail nature." On the other hand, *temptations* or pleasures of freedom, elevation, sublimity, etc., all of which are related to our transcending and overcoming any sensuous, natural drive and desire, can be considered as no less pathological than those of our most sensuous desires. Whenever we feel the *temptation* of being free — the *pleasure* of transcending our desires and circumstances of place and time, or the *displeasure* of shame and humiliation because of our sensuous nature — we are *pathologically* affected. Such temptations, pleasures and displeasures relate to *objects* of our desire or aversion. Affected by them, our will is not determined by the *form* of the moral law in an a priori manner, and, consequently, it is not morally determined. The pleasure conferred by the sublimity of obeying the law and the displeasure caused by shame at our sensuous nature are both a posteriori and sensuous. As such they are of a very different kind from that of the a priori feeling which is the legitimate incentive of the moral law. At this point let us bear in mind that there is no feeling prior to the moral law "as its basis" (KpV 5: 75/77). Kant, therefore, is justified in concluding that the "negative effect on feeling (unpleasantness) is, like all influences on feeling and every feeling itself, *pathological*" (KpV 5: 75/77-78). In saying so, Kant is not tempted to entertain the idea that the displeasure (i.e., the contempt), involved in our being enslaved to our sensuous nature, can determine our will morally or a priori. However, it seems that he is sometimes less prudent (for instance in KpV 5: 78-79). Nevertheless, I do not believe that Kantian morality can gain any real profit from humiliation, shame or other displeasures of this kind, as long as they are pathological. The same holds for any kind of pleasure. Indeed, Kant is more persuasive when speaking of respect for the moral law in the following manner:

> If this feeling of respect were pathological and thus a feeling of pleasure grounded on the inner *sense*, it would be futile to try to discover a connection of the feeling with any idea *a priori*. But it is a feeling which is concerned only with the practical, and with the idea of a law simply as to its form and not on account of any object of the law; thus it cannot be reckoned either as enjoyment or as pain, yet it produces an *interest* in obedience to the law. (KpV 5: 80/82-83)

However, how can *form* as such determine the will without arousing desire for an object? The answer is perhaps hidden in the awareness and even feeling of the confinement and limitation of our sensuous nature, which shares nothing of the absoluteness and categoricality of the formal law of morality, since it is entirely conditioned and relative in comparison with the categorical form of morality. Such feeling or awareness demands transcendence beyond the scope and limitation of our sensuous nature, and therefore it is not pathological. Indeed, it is not confined to any particular object but is related to the comparison between the sensuous nature in general and the form of morality, i.e., the moral law.

Being aware of our absolute dimension, we perhaps refuse to listen to the voice of our given, sensuous nature, which does not deserve any moral respect. Thus, we perhaps remove some obstacle and resistance to the moral determination of our will and assist it. However, awareness of our sublimity and absoluteness does not necessarily mean humiliating our sensuous nature, but only refusing to pay it respect.

As finite beings we have interests and needs. However, being rational as well we have a particular interest concerning our self-realization as regards our freedom, spontaneity and autonomy. Such a self-realization requires hard toil without pleasure, satisfaction and happiness of the sensuous, pathological kind. Moreover, it does not refer to any object, but concerns us as subjects transcending our phenomenal sensuous nature. We wish (will) to turn our self-realization into reality, therefore, we must obey the moral law as the most authentic expression of our self-legislative (autonomous) character. Nevertheless, being finite, we also have desires and needs which, by participating in the heteronomy of our sensuous nature, are not compatible with that wish. Is there any guarantee, then, that our wish for self-realization may not be defeated or overpowered by our sensuous nature?

We must find another way to explain how the determination of our will by the moral law can be guaranteed, in spite of the resistance of our sensuous nature. Finally, we have to show how sensuous nature itself submits to that law.

To do this, I shall proceed by arguing, in three stages, that (a) our sensuous nature cannot foil the submission of our will to the moral law by means of the counter-legislation of nature itself, because such a legislation is in fact impossible; (b) spontaneity, i.e., the ability to start a series of events of itself, can appertain only to rational beings; whereas the mechanism of our sensuous, conditioned nature cannot interfere with this spontaneity of absolute freedom and self-legislation, nor can it obstruct submission to this rational legislation (autonomy); and (c) reason is capable of confining our sensuous nature by not allowing it to determine our will; moreover, we can create another nature, a supersensuous one, in which, following our choice, our will is determined by the moral law alone and in which there is no possibility of any interference from our sensuous nature. Consequently, whenever we choose to determine our will morally, no sensuous, natural inclination can prevent us from doing so. Yet, we are always free to choose otherwise. Our freedom of choice is a well-founded fact which no deterministic law of nature or, obviously, the free law of our practical reason, can undermine.

2. No a posteriori feeling, no "moral desire," can replace the legislation of our practical reason. Just as the strict universal laws of nature are not a matter of induction (they are not given), but indicate the spontaneous *act* of synthesis made by our understanding, so the moral law too is not given to us by nature. Morality, according to Kant, is not a matter of given instincts and desires, nor of natural inclination, but is the fruit of education (*Bildung*), culture (*Kultur*) and enlightenment (*Aufklärung*), a fruit which can be produced only by human labour. There is no "natural," given legislation of morality and no natural inclination of ours can morally legislate. Legislation is based on principles (*ex principiis*) and not on given facts (*ex datis*). The possibility of moral metaphysics (namely, the possibility of practical reason), just as that of theoretical, of the first *Critique*, is solely dependant on the reality of the spontaneous, universal, indispensable legislation of our reason. Just as the metaphysics of nature is possible, because the laws of nature are not inductive, so moral metaphysics is possible, because the moral law is not produced by our sensuous nature. No counter-legislation of the given nature itself is possible. Nature, whether in the domain of theory or of praxis, is not self-legislative, neither can it subsume itself under universal law. The way is thus open for the legislation of reason alone in both domains. Given nature has no alternative but to submit to the laws of reason, whenever our reason prescribes them. In the practical domain we must first choose to obey them.

Speaking of the spontaneous character of reason's legislation (concerning both natural necessity and freedom), Kant remarks that when he explained freedom as the faculty of spontaneously initiating a series of events, he "exactly hit the concept which is the problem of metaphysics" (Prol. 4: 344). In other words,

The moral law is, in fact, a law of the causality through freedom and thus a law of the possibility of a supersensuous nature, just as the metaphysical law of events in the world of sense was a law of the causality of sensuous nature. (KpV 5: 47/49)

In these extracts Kant indicates the way that leads us to the next two stages of our discussion. Moral legislation and practical metaphysics are possible because our reason is *spontaneous* (whereas our sensuous nature is receptive) and because we are endowed with the capacity to create a *supersensuous* nature, under which our sensuous nature is subsumed by blocking and restricting its influence on our will.

Kant relates our absolute spontaneity to transcendental freedom

(A446/B474; cf. KpV 5: 48) in general and to the determination of our will (*Willkür*) in particular (A534/B562; A553-54/B581-82). The freedom of reason is its independence of sensibility, and in the moral domain freedom is our will's independence of "*coercion* through sensuous impulses" (sensuous will is a pathologically affected will, A534/B562). Again, Kant assumes that sensibility does not necessitate the actions of our will and that "there is in man a power of self-determination, independently of any coercion through sensuous impulses" (ibid.). Indeed, spontaneity is the power of originating a series of events of itself (A554/B582; cf. Prol. Sec. 53, 4: 344), and reason "frames for itself with perfect spontaneity an order of its own according to ideas, to which it adapts the empirical conditions" (A548/B576). Because of its freedom and spontaneity, reason determines nature and is not determined by it. Reason thus guarantees the freedom of our will from empirical, sensuous conditions, whenever we choose to follow the moral law of reason. We enjoy a capacity to break through the chain of conditions into the absolute domain of the "causality which is entirely self-determining" (KpV 5: 48/49). Only a rational being enjoys such a capacity. No phenomenal being as such can be self-determining. Conditioned, it must be subject either to other phenomena or to reason's legislation. Whereas, human beings, regarded as moral persons, have an absolute and unconditioned freedom of self-determination, which is entirely compatible with their finitude, as long as the clear distinction between absoluteness (categoricality) and totality (infinity) is maintained, as it is in the domain of praxis. No sensuous, phenomenal fact can confine our absolute, unconditioned freedom and spontaneity. Whenever we decide to employ them, no sensuous, conditioned inclination can prevent us from doing so. Each sensuous motive is receptive and cannot be autonomous and spontaneous, that is, it cannot initiate a series of events of itself. As such it is dependent on the unconditioned beginning which is solely caused by autonomous rational beings. Moral decision (choice) means entirely transcending the mechanism of nature, and, consequently, the latter cannot prevent the former, neither interfere with it, nor obstruct or foil it in any manner. Consequently, as long as we choose morally, our sensuous nature "submits" to the moral law by not foiling the determination of our will by this law alone.

3. Kant differentiates between the two objects of the legislation of human reason, namely, nature and freedom (A840/B868). There are respectively two kinds of laws, i.e., the law of nature and the moral law. Kant believes that these two distinct systems of law can be combined after all into "one single philosophical system" (ibid.), but we may doubt whether he actually succeeds in doing so. However, I should like to show that our sensuous nature is, in

some sense, subject to our moral legislation of freedom and must submit to it.

Discussing the free employment of our imagination in the third *Critique*, Kant says that "the material can be borrowed by us from nature [...] but be worked up by us into something else — namely, what surpasses nature" (KU 5: 314/176). Moreover, in the second *Critique* he says that the moral law

gives to the sensible world, as *sensuous nature* [...], the form of an intelligible world, i.e., the form of *supersensuous nature*, without interrupting the mechanism of the former. Nature, in the widest sense of the word, is the existence of things under law. The sensuous nature of rational beings in general is their existence under empirically conditioned laws, and therefore it is, from the point of view of reason, *heteronomy*. The supersensuous nature of the same beings, on the other hand, is their existence accord- ing to laws which are independent of all empirical conditions and which therefore belong to the *autonomy* of pure reason [...]. Supersensuous nature [...] is nothing else than *nature under [unter] the autonomy of the pure practical reason*. The law of this autonomy is the moral law, and it, therefore, is the fundamental law of supersensuous nature and of a pure world of understanding. (5: 43/44)

Nevertheless, he makes some reservations:

We are conscious of a law to which all our maxims are subject *as though [als ob]* through our will a natural order must arise [...] this law must be the idea of a supersensuous nature, a nature *not empirically given* yet *possible* through freedom. (KpV 5: 44/45, italics mine)

Kant then speaks of a law of a possible order of nature which is empirically quite unknowable. Supersensuous nature is one "which is subject to a will [*Wille*]" (ibid.). However, in the second *Critique* Kant also restricts his concern to

the determination of the will [*Wille*] and with the determining ground of its maxim as a free will, not with its result. For if the *will* be only in accord with the law of pure reason, the will's *power* in execution may be what it may; and a system of a possible nature may or may not actually arise according to these maxims of the legislation of a possible nature — all this does not trouble us in this *Critique*, which only concerns itself with whether and how reason can be practical, i.e., how it can directly determine the will. (5: 45-46/47)

Indeed, this is our concern too: How can the will be directly determined by the moral law without being interrupted by our sensuous nature? In other words, to what extent may our nature submit to the moral law or be subject to it? Without such a submission of our sensuous nature to the moral law, no determination of the will by the moral law alone is ensured, because our *natural*, "innate" inclination is to follow our desires and passions and not to obey moral *duty*. It is not "natural" to choose (or to act) reluctantly, unwill- ingly, under constraint and against our given desires and passions. Our mechanical, automatic and given reaction consists of following our sensuous, natural desires, even though we can choose otherwise; whereas, by creating the supersensuous nature, our will is free from the deterministic laws of the mechanism of sensuous nature. As such, our will is subject to quite a different law, namely, one that transcends and surpasses any empirical limitation and which is more *universal* than the law of sensuous nature, because the former is not restricted by any conditioning of our sensibility (concerning empirical data and circumstances), nor is it schematized in time. Supersensuous nature means, then, an absolute submission to one of the most universal principles of our reason, the categorical imperative. In this context, 'nature' means 'unconditioned (absolute) conformity to law'. It is *natura formaliter spectata* (following B165 with some reservations), which, moreover, is not restricted to objects (i.e., to "all appearances in space and time") but absolutely conforms to the *form* of the law. Supersensuous nature is more formal and conforms better to the law of reason than sensuous nature, because morality is solely based on form and does not require any given object of desire. Such an absolutely formal submission to the moral law means its unconditioned and unrestricted acceptance by our will. In creating the supersensuous nature, our will is absolutely not determined by the deterministic, heteronomic causality of our sensuous nature, but only by causality through freedom, which is an essential character of our spontaneous and autonomous reason.

Creating the supersensuous nature gives rise to two important effects: (a) transforming the determination of our will from deterministic causation (heteronomy) into causality through freedom (autonomy); (b) confining the application of sensuous nature and its deterministic laws, namely, preventing our natural inclinations from determining our will. This means giving form to, and restraining, moulding or *educating*[1] (KpV 5: 85) our sensuous nature according to the categorical imperative. This imperative commands our will *not* to follow that nature "mechanically," automatically, even though we are inclined to do so "by nature." In such a way the legislation of freedom is also a legislation of nature, namely, of confining the sensuous nature and also of transcending it.

Whenever we choose to obey the moral law unconditionally and to deter-

---

[1] Which is also our *enlightenment (Aufklärung)*, namely, our release from the self-incurred tutelage (*Unmündigkeit*) for which only we ourselves are responsible (according to the beginning of *What is Enlightenment*). To use this concept for my present purpose, our self-incurred tutelage is our (explicit or implicit) choice or preference to follow our sensuous nature, that is, to remain in a state of heteronomy and dependence, i.e., tutelage, instead of obeying our autonomous, moral law.

mine our will accordingly, we confine our sensuous nature by preventing it from determining our will. We give our sensuous nature a new "form" by drawing a borderline which is obliterated whenever we choose and prefer to let our will to react pathologically and to be determined by our sensuous nature, but which cannot be encroached upon by this nature whenever we make a moral and free choice. In the latter case, no natural inclination and desire can have an influence on our will, because as free, spontaneous and autonomous, we unconditionally obey the moral law which forbids us to act from any motive of sensibility. This law instructs our will to *transcend* any possible obstacle of our sensuous nature and to overcome such a resistance. That transcendence means freedom from sensuous nature, on the one hand, and, on the other, creating another order of law and causality (supersensuous nature, causality through freedom), to which "the entire world of sense, including the empirically determinable existence of man in time" (KpV 5: 86-87/89) is subordinated. In this other order of determination, our will entirely conforms to the form of the moral law.

Supersensuous nature actually draws the borderline for the influence of sensuous nature and, hence, transcends it. Drawing such a line according to the instruction of the moral law means giving sensuous nature another, new *form* or *restriction* by preventing it from determining our will whenever we choose to obey the moral law. In such a case, we exclude any sensuous motive from the domain of the determination of the will. This restriction or exclusion has a common denominator, namely, the *submission* of our sensuous nature to the moral law. It has no alternative but to submit, because being blocked or confined, it has a border which is a restrictive form. However, not being self-legislative, it cannot give itself that form but must receive it from the unconditioned, supersensuous nature on which the sensuous one, as conditioned and determined, is dependent. Nor can the latter prevent our will from transcending the confined domain of sensuous determination. Consequently, whenever we make up our mind to obey the moral law unconditionally, no desire or natural inclination can foil, obstruct or interfere with the moral, free determination of our will.

The University of Haifa

Gerold Prauss

Theory as Praxis in Kant

This title is meant to indicate the doctrine which Kant's "Copernican turn" in epistemology actually amounts to: knowledge cannot simply consist in the objectification of something that is always already actual, as presumed by pre-Kantian epistemology, which was a theory of natural consciousness. Rather, our knowing must consist precisely in the attempt to actualize for the first time something that is always already objective, and ultimately, to do this in action. For in fact when we have a concept of something in action, this something is, as such, always already an object, though not one which is thereby already actual, but that which we are trying to actualize for the first time through our action. In principle, only that which is not yet actual can meaningfully become an object for action, because were it already actual, action would be meaningless, that is, superfluous.

There is no question that Kant did not himself think through his "Copernican turn" to this "practicism," that is, he did not think it through to its conclusion. Yet there is also no question but that more than once in his reflections he faces such a practicism as the ultimate consequence of his "turn"; however, he was unable to fully appreciate this conclusion. For Kant, prior tradition, which understands "theory" in terms of a systematic distinction between theory and praxis, was still too strong. This makes it all the more urgent to pursue this practicism still further along the Kantian path, that is, within the foundation of transcendental idealism, and not to fall prey to an absolute and hence foundationless idealism. Hence, all the passages where Kant hints at taking this path are worthy of examination.

Kant engages in such reflections on the relation between "representation" and its "object" in the middle of the *Critique of Pure Reason*, indeed at the juncture designated for the "Transition to the Transcendental Deduction of the Categories" in section 14 (A 92/B 124-25). Here he proceeds on the assumption that for such a relation there are "only two cases possible," namely, "either it is the object which alone makes the representation possible, or the latter is what alone makes the object possible." Kant characterizes the

93

Y. Yovel (ed.), Kant's Practical Philosophy Reconsidered, 93-105.

former option as one in which the relation is "only empirical, and the representation... can never be a priori." Then he turns to the second option, that which is of special interest to him and concerns a priori representation. On this assumption, this must be a relation of object and representation in which "the representation alone makes the object possible." But in the context of the alternatives allowed by his assumption, "possible" here must mean "really possible," which ultimately means the same as "actual." This is the kind of formulation Kant frequently favours as, for example, when he says of the "categories" that they have the function, as it were, "of prescribing a law to nature and even making it possible" (B 159). He also makes it clear that when we ask whether the object is responsible for the representation, or the representation for the object, his true concern is the question of which is responsible for bringing about "the existence" of the other. Hence it is only consistent that the latter alternative amounts to saying that a representation a priori "is what alone makes the object actual."

However, at this point Kant suddenly shrinks from precisely this conclusion, although it can be shown that in other places he does entertain it, at least verbally. The justification he cites for this conclusion shows clearly why he does this. As soon as he begins to draw this conclusion ("but if it is the second option"), he immediately shifts in word and content to exactly the opposite claim, using a "because" to say that "representation in itself... does not bring about *the existence* of its object"; he then inserts this revealing justification: "For here we are not speaking at all of a causality of the will."[1]

In my view the total evidence invites the following interpretation. Kant suddenly retreats here from a conception that he always holds elsewhere, and must hold, given the sense of his "Copernican turn." The reason he does so is simply that this turn gives rise to a special problem for him here, one for which he is clearly not prepared: the question of the delimitation of spontaneity as theoretical in thinking or knowing and as practical in willing or acting. For, if thinking or knowing consisted in already bringing about "the existence" of an object, thus in always effecting its actuality for the first time, how could it be distinguished from willing or acting?

Kant is clearly so struck by this question that he goes so far as to directly deny his own conception, even to invert it, for he dismantles the second option by saying that it means "representation determines an object a priori when it

---

[1] See also: "practical reason is concerned not with knowing objects but with its own faculty to *make them actual* (in accord with knowledge of them), i.e., it is concerned with the will" (KpV 5:89).

alone makes it possible to know something as an object" (A 92/B 125). This undoubtedly constitutes a retreat from his real conception: Kant is asserting that from the perspective of its a priori contribution, cognition consists simply in the elevation of something already actual to the status of an object. But of course in truth, in the context of his classical critical philosophy, he holds the opposite, namely, a critical concept of actuality. According to this concept, actuality is not a "being in itself" that is always already "pregiven" to cognition as something objective, but rather, as an "appearance" for cognition, it is always an actualization and thus from the first a "product" of cognition.

In a similar way it can easily be shown that in the above quoted passage Kant not only turns away from his classical critical position but ultimately deserts it altogether and falls back upon a precritical one with a concept of actuality that is also still precritical, one that can even be found in the letter to Marcus Herz of 21 February 1772. In a way that is directly comparable with the former passage from the *Critique of Pure Reason* of 1781, here too Kant considers the relation of "representation" and "object," asking on what basis something can represent an object at all, or be the object of a representation. And as in the other passage, he says here too that this is "easy to comprehend" if the object brings about the representation as an *intellectus ectypus* in an empirical way through "affection," or if, contrariwise, the representation as an *intellectus archetypus* "brings about" the object (GS 10: 130).

However, neither of these options apply to our understanding in so far as it possesses "intellectual representations" or "pure concepts of the understanding" for objects, which "rest on its inner activity." And it also appears to be certain that for Kant here, these objects "are not to be somehow brought about through this activity." This is a certainty which, to the extent that it is really genuine, is characteristic of Kant's precritical stage, on the one hand, and, on the other, is about to be shaken by critique, namely, through a question which is already posed here quite clearly: "If such intellectual representations rest on our inner activity," how can they have any reference to objects, "which still are not to be somehow brought about through it?" (ibid.).

In any case, one can use *Reflexionen* to show that Kant reaches his later critical standpoint through a change of opinion on exactly this point. Thus, in a text of 1783/84, in a kind of retrospective reflection on his *Critique of Pure Reason*, he again takes up the contrast between *intellectus ectypus* and *archetypus* and says: "finite beings cannot by themselves know other things, for they are not the producers of those things." If Kant had broken off his *Reflexion* at this point, one would have received the impression that this was something from the precritical period. But he continues as follows: "finite beings cannot by themselves know other things, for they are not the producers of those things, unless these are mere appearances which they *can* know a priori," which in this context means they *are* their producers. By "appearances" here Kant refers specifically to empirical things of the external world, as he goes on to clarify in a remark added later which he formulates as follows: "It is said that all a priori knowledge is knowledge of things in themselves; but the truth is precisely the opposite, knowlege is rather always of things as appearances, that is, as objects of experience" (R 6048, 18: 433f).

The second *Reflexion* after this provides further support for the thought that our production of the things of the external world is now also to be taken literally from Kant's critical standpoint. Here too he proceeds from consideration of how the relation of representation to an object, or of an object to a representation, can be possible at all, taking the following position: "For our representation to agree with an object," it must be thought of as "either brought about by the object or as bringing about the object... In the latter case, it would be an original representation (*idea archetypa*), which we humans are not capable of, if it is supposed to be original in *all* respects" (R 6050, 18: 434; my emphasis).

Taking these two *Reflexionen* together, one reaches the following conclusion: in contrast to his precritical approach, Kant's critical standpoint is characterized by the fact that now it is no longer the case that our understanding is *neither* an "intellectus ectypus" *nor* an "intellectus archetypus"; on the contrary, in a certain sense it is the one *as well as* the other. For according to this view, in our "a priori knowledge" in experiencing empirical objects, we are without doubt the "producers" of these objects, since it is through such knowledge that we "bring about" the external world of empirical things as "appearances." In doing so, we are in fact something like an *intellectus archetypus* of these appearances, although not "in all respects," which is to say that in at least "one respect" we are also an *intellectus ectypus*. There can be just as little doubt as to *what* this respect is, according to Kant, for it lies precisely in that which is *not* "brought about" spontaneously by us as "producers" in the experiences constituting our empirical knowledge but which is, on the contrary, something we are "receptive" to or just "receive," namely, in "sensation" as a "sense impression" or "sense datum" for us.

From a historical perspective we can therefore say that it is this revision of the duality of *intellectus ectypus* and *archetypus* by which Kant moves from his precritical to his critical standpoint. And from this perspective it is also immediately comprehensible that thereafter in his critical writings he is of the opinion that the "genuinely empirical" feature in what is empirical is always such sensation.[2] From the systematic perspective of his new critical conception, however, this opinion must remain incomprehensible and possibly misleading.

In order to see this, one need only try to take literally the remark about sensation as that which is "genuinely empirical." This sense of "empirical" implies that there could also be something that is "empirical" in another way, which of course would not be "genuinely empirical" but would be characterized as "non-genuinely empirical." Two candidates come into consideration here, namely, experience as "empirical" knowledge and that which is experienced as its "empirical" object; but in the sense of "empirical" presupposed here, not only must these be excluded, but in principle they would not even be something "non-genuinely empirical."

According to Kant, if we abstract from given sensation, not only knowledge but also its object must be described as "brought about" by us "spontaneously," and so knowledge as well as its object can never be "received" by us in a "non-genuine" way. This is true of knowledge, because in no instance does it simply befall us without any contribution from us, and it is even truer of its object, for as Kant himself stresses, this can never "wander over" into us (Prol. 4: 282) to be received, that is, to be used in experience as what thereby constitutes empirical knowledge. Accordingly, if the criterion of the empirical was something's being received rather than brought about by us, then not only would sensation be "genuinely empirical," it would also be the *sole empirical* item, and consequently empirical knowledge, like its empirical object, would turn out to be not empirical at all, as it is not received but rather entirely brought about by us.

Since this conclusion is absolutely unacceptable, the misleading idea that Kant allows knowledge and its objects, in so far as they are empirical, to be merely received by us, is frequently suggested as a way out, but this conclusion is equally unacceptable.

One can hardly escape this persistent confusion by simply acquiescing in it; on the contrary, one must confront it and try to dissolve the confusion and in this way mastering it. A decisive step in this direction is taken as soon as one attains this insight: in characterizing sensation as the "genuinely empirical," Kant is not yet working within his new critical conception. On the contrary, he still remains totally outside it in a tradition both empiricist and Cartesian which, it appears, he had not even begun to shake off, for he is clearly unaware of its inconsistency with his developing critical view. And this is no mere

---

[2] Cf. Prol. 4: 284, 303; R LX, 23: 27; "Preisschrift," 20: 266.

coincidence, because within his critical view this conception of sensation is not simply a mere impurity which should be ignored if one is to achieve proper critical purity. Rather, though Kant himself may not have been clear about this, it plays the role of a stopgap. This appears, at least to some extent, to prevent us from seeing that precisely at this juncture there is an important gap in Kant's critical conception which has not been systematically worked out.

If one drops the thesis about sensation being that which is "genuinely empirical," one can immediately see that Kant had not developed his critical conception far enough for it to clearly specify a new sense of what is "empirical," in a way that would suggest other possible candidates for the "genuinely empirical." It must be kept in mind that in the framework of the critical conception it is not undeniable that sensation is always something merely receptive, something "received" by us (this point remains completely valid here); what is given up is the claim that it provides the criterion for what is "genuinely empirical." But the only other possible candidate is that which is spontaneously "brought about" by ourselves through our "a priori knowledge." Of course, in one sense this is immediately comprehensible, in so far as it makes what is empirical coincide with the actual things of the external world. But in this context how can it be made comprehensible, with respect to the empirical and actual things of the external world, that now their very empiricality and actuality constitute that which is to be brought about spontaneously by us? What is the critical concept of actuality here, which will have to serve as the critical concept of empiricality as well?

It is no accident that neither sense of the concept can be understood merely by quoting from Kantian writings, as is also the case regarding the question of the sense in which that which is genuinely empirical and actual in the external world is to be regarded as something brought about spontaneously by ourselves. These questions are not only interconnected, but also stem from the same shortcoming: Kant was never able to reach the point of clarifying in all its consequences the fact that on his new conception, that which is empirical and actual in the external world must be regarded as something that "in its existence" is brought about by our spontaneity. On the contrary, on this issue he made no progress.

The passage cited at the beginning of this paper, in which Kant shrinks from these consequences, provides further confirmation of this, if one goes back to it with a view to the broader context in which it stands. According to the passage, our practical spontaneity in will or action, though not our theoretical spontaneity in thinking or knowing, can bring about an object "in its existence." But in the context of the discussion of the *Reflexionen* concerning the distinction between *intellectus ectypus* and *archetypus*, this concession would mean that for the case of praxis but not that of theory in our spontaneity we are always clearly *intellectus archetypus* in the full sense.

This, however, is absolutely incorrect. Even through our will in praxis we in no way bring about objects "in all respects," for even in this case we are, at least "in one respect," dependent on something that is not brought about by us but is provided for us, namely "material," from which alone we can bring about objects. For this reason, it could be said with the same, or inded, even greater right, that our will in action "does not bring about the existence of its object," since the material has already been there for a long time and is simply being brought into a new form.

This implies more than just the collapse of the (prior) distinction between theory and praxis, because in both we are equally *intellectus ectypus* and *archetypus*; it also implies that the problem Kant tried to shift from theory onto praxis falls back squarely on the former. For it follows that if it is true of anything that it "brings about" its object "in its existence," then this is true of our thinking in knowledge, especially in the case of Kant, who is convinced that this cannot consist in simply objectifying something actual that is always already given as a "being in itself," but on the contrary consists in actualizing something that is always already objectified. And where else is what is actual as well as "material" for praxis to be found, if not in such a theory, which itself is already praxis?

The reason why Kant was unable to develop this practical view of knowledge completely might be that in spite of a series of passages implying this, Kant never makes it sufficiently explicit that he ultimately presupposes intentionality in the spontaneity of subjectivity as it operates in the synthesis of knowledge. It was never completely clear to him that in the structure of intentionality he had a sure guide for the construction of this synthesis. Analysis of intentionality readily reveals that in its normal sense intending is always the intending of something else, indeed of something other than this intending itself, for its meaning also comprises the intending of success and not failure. But just because it is at first merely intended, success can either occur or fail to occur, and so such intending always has both failure and success as something other than itself, outside itself. For in no case, whether successful or not, can intending itself fail to occur; for one can speak of success or failure only with respect to an intending that is already taking place.

It is precisely by this success that the object of the intending subject is constituted as something which is other than itself, and which is also actual and not merely objective, rather than contrariwise, as something which is also objective and not merely actual, as was the pre-Kantian tradition. What subjectivity as intentionality intends is not the objectification of something that is already actual, but rather the actualization of something that is already objective, and thus it intends the actuality of an object as something that is to be actualized for the first time. It is only as intention in this sense that it can succeed or fail, as in the familiar case of sensory illusion, hallucination, or dreaming. Whenever something is an instance of "falsity" or failure it is not because nothing is objective for us, but rather because that which we very much do have as an object is not also actual. Similarly, as long as we are caught up in this falsity, it will be held to be actual by us, because what we are concerned with is solely its actuality and not its mere objectivity. As subjects, what we ultimately intend in this way is thus to successfully actualize an object, which will always be attained only as something other than intention, thus as an actuality that is to be actualized for the first time. It is for this reason alone that intentionality can succeed or fail, as in the case of sensory illusion, hallucination, or dreaming noted above, where objectification of something is indeed present, but where there is a failure of the actualization of the object that is genuinely intended. Its mere objectivity is not what is intended, is not that in which the intending culminates, and thus is not a possible success or failure apart from the intending. On the contrary, its objectification is rather just the intending itself, in that already in its intention, that is, a priori, a subject intends something other than itself, and thus already projects it a priori as an object in general.[3] It is also for this reason that if a subject is at all capable of actualizing something, this must be an object of so-called "true" knowledge of it.

There is an integral connection between this conception and other passages according to which in the synthesis of knowledge the subject forms categories "which apply a priori to objects" or "apply a priori to objects of intuition in general" (A 79/B 105). Here not only is the term "apply" in the sense of "intend" to be taken literally, but so also the term "objects" is to be taken in the sense of "objects in general." For it follows from the above that in the context of this synthesis the spontaneity of subjectivity operating through a priori categories is its intentionality, because for the term "a priori" in the sense of "from the outset" or "always already," the phrase "already in its intention" can be substituted as equivalent in meaning. Then the fact that subjectivity through its categories applies a priori to objects in general becomes more comprehensible, because as intentionality it really is already a priori, that is, already in its intention of success alone it intends something other than itself, namely, an object whose actualization can thereby succeed or fail.

[3] Cf. B xii and B xvi; also Prol. 4: 318f; KpV 5: 68f.

But as such an intentionality it can intend objects as something other than itself only in the sense of objects in general, as something other in general, for it is precisely a priori or in its mere intention that subjectivity cannot know whether there is such an other in general, and if there is, whether it is like this or like that, i.e., is empirically like this or like that. What is other for subjectivity can be given, in its existence as well as in its nature, only in so far as it in fact arises for this subjectivity as intentionality in a way that is always contingent, namely, as a success. This success is other than subjectivity because it is an empirical as well as an actual item, and thus is something that is pure contingency or facticity.

Because Kant has this intentionality in view as, on the one hand, a priori, and, on the other, in its success a posteriori, he is in fact a transcendental idealist at the same time as he is an empirical realist. Something that is actual or empirical becomes comprehensible only in so far as it is something that can succeed or fail, and as success, coincides with the contingent and factual. Precisely because the empirical-actual is something other than subjectivity that is always attainable only through intention, it follows that when the empirical-actual really is attained, it must be regarded as that which is made actual and empirical through precisely such intention.

According to Kant there should be a lesson for us in the fact that we are initially taken aback by the idea of something which is made empirical in this way or is, so to speak, empirically dynamized. For Kant, it is precisely at this systematic juncture that the original and genuinely spontaneous, indeed intentional, sense of the empirical as *empeiria*, that is, "attempting" or "trying out," arises. This sense is based on the Greek *peir* which only later degenerated from the no-longer understood Latin term *empiricus* to the sense of a mere receiving.

In the genuine Kantian sense of "empirical," which for the reasons just given was not yet fully available to Kant himself, a merely receptive sensation is not only not "the genuinely empirical," but is rather not anything empirical at all, for it is not something that is first actualized through knowledge, something which could succeed or fail. Rather, sensation should be understood as something that is already an instance of self-consciousness. For this however no special sense of the term "empirical" is needed: in order for it to be plausible that a special sense of "empirical" is involved, it would have to share the decisive characteristic of the empirical. But how can that be possible? On the contrary, what is actual in the external world is not "the genuinely empirical," but it is, rather, the sole thing that is empirical, for it is the only thing that is always solely something to be actualized by us, and thus it is the only thing that is factual and contingent.

It is precisely in this way that Kant's full "practicism" comes into view: his conception of theory and praxis, which reveals the truth or falsity of knowledge as its ultimate success or failure. Accordingly, knowledge can have success (or failure) only as something outside itself, as the actuality or non-actuality of its object, and in no way as "truth" or "falsity" in itself. These are nothing more than mere *words*, and misleading ones at that, because from the beginning of Western philosophy they have led us astray to a false "theoreticism" of knowledge. To reconstruct the genuine practicism of knowledge leads to a kind of nominalism, a nominalism which is more radical and at the same time more interesting than almost any other that can be imagined. For in a radical way it bypasses the remains of Platonism in the "ideal being" of the "truth" or "falsity" of a "thought," of "noema," "proposition," "meaning," "state of affairs" or "fact." But in place of these, it in no way proffers, as prior nominalisms did, something like mere naturalism or materialism. Quite to the contrary, this Kantian nominalism negates any naturalism or materialism, because it is the first to oppose the things and events of material nature by bringing to the fore something like ideal being, namely, arguments. It is only in showing itself as the absolute accomplishment of the free, autonomous self-actualization of subjectivity as intentionality that it is possible to bring out the genuine worth of something like ideal being, a worth in principle not allowed by Platonism, which is a hypostatization of that worth. Precisely because of its development as intentionality, subjectivity is incapable of being reduced to things and events of a material nature, and the actuality of the latter turns out instead to be dependent on such subjectivity, yielding a full transcendental idealism in the context of which the dualism of nature and freedom proves to be irreducible.

But in view of the radical practicism which is ultimately at the base of this idealism, it is no longer surprising that a tormenting question forces itself upon Kant in the text quoted at the beginning of this paper: how is it possible within the critical conception to distinguish between spontaneity as theoretical and as practical, especially, as can be proven in many ways, when this spontaneity is at work in synthesis as intentionality, and intends nothing other than the actuality of objects, that is, success as the actualization of something other than itself? Indeed, in the earlier text Kant had simply repressed the will as the genuine essence of this spontaneity as intentionality, and even in this context there is a repetition of this response.

It appears relatively clear to me that this happens in a passage of "The Postulates of Empirical Thought" (A 221/B 268-69, cf. A 729/B 757) where Kant returns to discussion of the categories of relation, namely, those within the "dynamic" group that originally "are directed" at the "existence" of objects (cf. B 110). Here these categories are spoken of as schematized, that is, in terms of the synthesis which subjectivity carries out through their schematization. But although subjectivity, through this synthesis with the help of all its categories, intends the actuality of objects, Kant insists concerning each of the individual categories that the synthesis of permanence, causality, or reciprocity still by no means guarantees "that such a thing is possible" or "whether such a property... is to be met in any possible thing," "or whether such a relation can apply to any things." But this can only mean that through the schematization of the rational categories subjectivity successfully intends but can in no way guarantee the actuality of something permanent, causally effected and standing in reciprocal influence, because it is dealing with "a merely arbitrary synthesis."

In this way arbitrariness (*Willkür*) or will as the genuine essence of spontaneity as intentionality forces itself in again. For it would be impossible in this context to understand the expression "arbitrary" solely in its ordinary language, everyday sense, according to which subjectivity carries out its synthesis in an "ungoverned" or "unlawful" way. For like the schematization of the categories, it completes its synthesis in just the opposite fashion as a sum of rules or legislation regarding what can count as an actual object in the external world. Accordingly, the expression "arbitrary" is to be understood in a philosophical-terminological sense, and for Kant, this is indeed the most appropriate characterization of the fact that subjectivity in this synthesis is spontaneous precisely in the sense of intentional. Although it is totally law-governed, it ensues as intentional in an arbitrary way in so far as whatever this synthesis may intend, it is always intended in a haphazard way without a guarantee, for example, as to whether something quite specific, which it intends a priori to actualize as permanent, will in fact thereby become factual, contingent, and a posteriori actual.

From here on, then, the expression "arbitrary" is to be taken in a philosophical-terminological way, so that spontaneity as intentionality is no longer to be distinguished from arbitrariness or will. As such it is so fundamentally practical that for the first time the question of how it can become anything like "theoretical" arises. Instead of simply accepting, of dogmatically presupposing from tradition a sense of "theory" and "theoretical," from the start Kant should have derived a contrast between this sense and that of "praxis" or "practical." In fact, although he did not notice this, at the base of his new conception he already had at his disposal a new sense of "theory" and "theoretical" after the adoption of which there would be no question of using the old sense of a receptive "theory."

The fact that Kant did not develop this sense, indeed did not once bring it into view, hardly signifies that he had no solution to the problem. On the contrary, a specifically Kantian solution appears to me to be close at hand.[4] To obtain it, we merely have to further develop the fundamental practicality of spontaneity as intentionality, a point Kant probably was aware of only as something to fend off.

This immediately leads to an important inference: it is not only subjectivity's relation to something other than itself in the context of its intentionality that cannot be considered simply as a "theoretical" matter of mere "self-consciousness"; the same is also true of its relation to itself, that out of which subjectivity steps for the first time in order to enter into a relation to something other. It must likewise be understood at first as practical, as Kant originally attempted to conceive of it in his concept of subjectivity as an "end in itself." Accordingly, every relation to something other than itself would be a relation of an *intention* of this other only in so far as subjectivity thereby intends something other than itself precisely *for itself*, as it strives to actualize it for the "final purpose" (*Endzweck*) of its own self-actualization.

But if this is true, it is immediately possible to infer the following: even when subjectivity succeeds in the actualization of something other than itself, this does not guarantee that subjectivity is thereby already successful in its self-actualization. For the very meaning of actuality as the contingent or factual actualization of something other implies that whether subjectivity attains self-actualization through such actuality is a matter of the same contingency or facticity. This is so since it also experiences this actuality as self-satisfaction, namely, satisfaction of the need due to which it intentionally directs itself to something other than itself in order to move from self-dissatisfaction to satisfaction.

From this it also follows that on the basis of this same contingency and facticity, subjectivity must learn that in the great majority of cases, regarding the actuality of something other than itself, whatever it actualizes is not thereby also satisfying for it, and, on the contrary, as a rule it always remains unsatisfied. But in experiencing in this way disappointment with what is actual, something like "theory," as the consciousness of this actuality as something fundamentally disappointing, comes into view for subjectivity as practical. In precisely this way it becomes aware of the actual as the only thing through which it can gain the satisfaction it was striving for, namely, when actualization proceeds beyond what is originally and immediately actual to something derived from it and mediate, that is, through "change" as a

[4] See here, as throughout, my *Kant über Freiheit als Autonomie* (Frankfurt: Klostermann, 1983).

restructuring of the actual. In this way that which is alleged to essentially differ for "theory" and "praxis," namely, that they appear to give rise to a priori different kinds of intentionality, proves instead to be the same practicism of intentionality in the genuine Kantian sense in both cases: on every factual and contingent occasion, after its original and immediate actualization of the actual, it must simply repeat its activity in a derived and mediate change of this actuality, and thus it need only differentiate itself in a manner entirely free of the distinction.

Albert-Ludwigs-Universität
Freiburg i. Br.

Carl J. Posy

Autonomy, Omniscience and the Ethical Imagination: From Theoretical to Practical Philosophy in Kant

We all know that Kant held ethics and empirical science to be separate, incommensurable disciplines. He also claimed that his views about ethical and empirical knowledge fit together in a single "Critical" system. In the essay that follows I want to sketch a modern, "semantic," interpretation of Kant's philosophy which explains both the unity of the critical system and the unbridgeable gap between ethical and empirical knowledge. I believe that this interpretation can help resolve some exegetical problems that appear to plague Kant's theories about ethics and empirical science. And I believe that it can also focus attention in a new way on some aspects of Kant's moral theory that seem most troubling today.

But before sketching my interpretation I would like to preface the essay with a small, familiar piece of Kantian analysis. Consider Macbeth, the Shakespearian villain, whose self-confessed ambition leads him to murder his king, and who then — in a pattern that has become all too familiar to us nowadays — is sucked into a whirlpool of intrigue, cover-up, more murder and finally war, in order to protect his usurped crown. Macbeth, as we will see, is quite a Kantian character. He is obsessed by the notion of a good will ("What thou wouldst highly," says Lady Macbeth, "That wouldst thou holily" i.5); and I will suggest that he even universalizes. But in this essay I am specially interested in Macbeth because he has a hyperactive imagination; and imagination, I shall argue, is an essential component in the Kantian theory about how we assess such matters as goodness and villainy. Indeed, I shall want to claim that a general notion derived from Kant's theory of imagination is one of the links that unites the "theoretical" philosophy of the *Critique of Pure Reason* with the notions of autonomy, universalization and the ethical self that lie at the core of Kant's moral philosophy. I shall make this claim in spite of the fact that in the *Critique of Practical Reason* Kant himself denies that imagination can play a role in ethics.

106

Y. Yovel (ed.), *Kant's Practical Philosophy Reconsidered, 106-134.*
© *1989 Kluwer Academic Publishers.*

Turning to the Kantian analysis that I promised, let us focus for a moment on Macbeth as he draws his dagger, at the very instant he embarks upon his bloody career. Kant suggests two ways to look upon Macbeth and this deed. First, we might take the "empirical" perspective and view the dagger-drawing as an *event* which is part of the natural order of things. If we do this, then, Kant says, we must assume that this event is inescapably determined by its natural causes.[1] And so from this point of view we are enjoined to search for the physical or psychological causes — the feelings, inclinations or passions[2] — that drive Macbeth and his dagger to this deed.

Kant's second way is to adopt the "ethical" perspective, and view Macbeth's deed not as a lifeless event but as a morally weighted *act.* Since Kant holds that all such acts are purposive, we must now suppose Macbeth to have drawn his dagger with the intention of using it to accomplish a particular goal (which Kant calls an "end"). We must also suppose that Macbeth can articulate a principle (Kant calls it a "maxim") announcing his intention to pursue this end. (Falling under a maxim is one mark of a purposive act.) To be sure, we need not ignore Macbeth's psychological drives; a perfectly conceivable maxim is the principle which says "I shall act in such a way as to satisfy this or that desire." But, says Kant, from the ethical perspective we assume that Macbeth has the ability to overcome these drives; and so we must hold him responsible for his crimes and for all their natural consequences.

Now Kant tells us that if we adopt his famous transcendental idealism (his doctrine that ordinary objects are mere appearances) then we are free to assume that both perspectives — the empirical and the ethical — are equivalid, and that the ethical perspective will not conflict with the empirical one. Indeed, this is part of his elaborate *reductio* of the rival transcendental realism (the view that these ordinary objects are independent things in themselves). For in the third antinomy we learn that the transcendental realist is logically bound to assume that either Macbeth acted freely (this is the thrust of the "thesis" claim) or that he was forced by natural causes (the "antithesis" claim) *and not both.* Kant then shows that the transcendental realist must also accept arguments which refute the antithesis and the thesis respectively. And so the realistic position proves to be untenable.

Unfortunately this neat little picture of transcendental idealism's triumph,

---

[1] Kant says: "In its empirical character, therefore, this subject, as appearance, would have to conform to all the laws of causal determination. To this extent it could be nothing more than a part of the world of sense, and its effects, like all other appearances, must be the inevitable outcome of nature" (A540/B568).

[2] Compare A55/B79.

and the door it opens to the ethical perspective, is the source of the problems I mentioned above. So the victory may well be a hollow one.

There are first of all the famous problems of phenomenalism, the self-in-itself and circularity that plague the first *Critique*: to make all of this work we have to equate causally determined empirical objects with mental appearances (that is phenomenalism); and to escape the grip of empirical causality we have to assume that moral agents are unknowable, supersensible things-in-themselves.[3] Neither of these is an acceptable assumption. Moreover the allegedly realistic arguments that refute the thesis and antithesis of the third antinomy reek of transcendental idealism. The realist supposedly rejects the thesis (the claim that Macbeth acted freely) because it conflicts with Kantian doctrines about the "unity of experience," and he supposedly denies the antithesis because it lacks epistemological completeness (see A444-47/B472-75). No self-respecting realist would offer either of these subjectivist arguments.

But there are problems for Kantian ethics as well. I call them the problems of ethical omniscience and ethical imagination.

Ethical omniscience: at A476f/B504f Kant says a most amazing thing: he tells us that ethics along with mathematics and something he calls "transcendental philosophy" are disciplines in which there can be no unanswered questions, no possibility of ignorance. Of ethics in particular he claims that "we must be able in every possible case, in accordance with a rule, to know what is *right* and what is *wrong*." This doctrine of omniscience, this view that there can be no unresolvable ethical issues, contradicts much of our ordinary experience, and conflicts with several of Kant's own remarks about morality and decision making.

Ethical imagination: when we look carefully at the role Kant attributes to imagination in theoretical knowledge (and particularly in mathematics and transcendental philosophy) and when we then look at his foundation for

---

[3] Strawson's *The Bounds of Sense* (Methuen, 1966) vigorously defends the interpretation of transcendental idealism as phenomenalism. Regarding the self as an ethical agent Kant himself says: "In its intelligible character... this same subject must be considered to be free from all influence of sensibility and from all determination through appearances. ... And consequently, since natural necessity is to be met with only in the sensible world, this active being must in its actions be independent of, and free from all such necessity" (A541/B569). There have been many objections to this doctrine of the self-in-itself from Pistorious (in *Allgemeine deutsche Bibliothek* 66) in Kant's own time to Ross (*Kant's Ethical Theory*, Oxford, 1954) and Bennett ("Kant's Theory of Freedom," in *Self and Nature in Kant's Philosophy*, ed. A. Wood, Cornell, 1984) in our century.

ethics, it becomes clear that this faculty of imagination ought to play the same role in ethics as it does in the theoretical disciplines. Yet, as I mentioned above, Kant curtly denies any place for imagination in ethics.

I do not propose to resolve these problems in detail here. But I do want to show in outline how the interpretation which I shall sketch connects the theoretical and practical sides of Kant's philosophy in the way I promised above; how it proves that Kant's claim about ethical omniscience is not an isolated remark but is in fact part of that tightly knit web of "Critical" doctrines; and how it provides the machinery to answer the charges against the first *Critique* and the problem about imagination.

I shall begin by elaborating the final problem — the claim that Kant ought not to have banned imagination from ethics — for as far as I can tell it is not well developed in the Kant literature.[4] Thus in the first two sections of the essay I will outline the Kantian roles of imagination in theoretical knowledge, and I will show why these roles ought to carry over to Kantian ethics. Then in the last two sections I will introduce my semantic reading of Kant's critical philosophy (specifically a version of the currently popular "assertabilist" theory of truth), and I will show how this can solve the problems of pheno-menalism and circularity and can explain Kant's ban of imagination from ethics. This ban turns out to be a semantic decision that leads us to refine our initial understanding of Kantian imagination. I will also use the semantic interpretation to demonstrate that Kant's noumenal view of the ethical self is simply his way of contrasting the belief that empirical questions are not all decidable with his claim of ethical omniscience, and I will show the systematic origins of this latter claim.

But even knowing its place in the critical system cannot change the fact that

---

[4] Indeed, the discussion (from various perspectives) of the role of imagination in Kant's ethics often simply endorses Kant's dismissal. See, for instance, G. Deleuze, *La philosophie critique de Kant* (Presses Universitaires de France, 1963, chs. 1 and 2). Hannah Arendt in her *Lectures on Kant's Political Philosophy* (Chicago, 1982) as well as Paul Guyer in *Kant and the Claims of Taste* (Harvard, 1979), Mary Warnock in *Imagination* (University of California Press, 1976) and Donald Crawford in "Kant's Theory of Creative Imagination" (Chapter 5 of Ted Cohen and Paul Guyer [eds.], *Essays in Kant's Aesthetics*, Chicago, 1982) all discuss the analogies and disanalogies governing the roles assigned to imagination by the first and third *Critiques*, but they do not compare these with Kant's treatment of imagination in the second *Critique*. Finally, L. W. Beck, in his *Commentary on the Critique of Practical Reason* (Chicago, 1960, p. 67), does suggest that there is an element in Kant's ethics that is parallel to the role of pure imagination in the *Critique of Pure Reason*; but Beck does not develop this point nor take up the question of why Kant refused the title of imagination to this parallel faculty.

the doctrine of ethical omniscience seems counter-intuitive and *prima facie* unKantian. So at the end I will briefly consider how to reconcile this doctrine with opposing Kantian texts, and I will speculate about the origins of our own skepticism towards it.

I. Imagination in Theoretical Knowledge

To begin our quick study of the role of imagination in theoretical knowledge, let me remind you of Kant's famous remark in the A-Deduction that "imagination is a necessary ingredient of perception itself" (A120n.). So our first task will be to see why, according to Kant, imagination — "the faculty of representing in intuition an object which is not present" (B151) — is part of empirical perception, which is after all representation of an object that *is* present. Later I will expand this analysis of the role of imagination in perception to cover its analogues in the theoretical disciplines of transcendental philosophy and mathematics. I will then, in section II, discuss its role in ethics.

A. *Empirical Perception.* Turning to simple perception, suppose we stop the action again and eavesdrop on Macbeth's empirical perceptions as he lifts his dagger from its sheath and remarks to himself, "this is a dagger I see before me." When we do this, according to Kant, we will find two separable elements in Macbeth's perception of this event. There are on the one hand the passively received sensations, which are supposed to be wholly subjective and which come into his mind in a generally haphazard order. On the other hand, there is Macbeth's conceptual activity (contributed by his faculty of understanding) which organizes the sensory data and arranges them into distinct groups, each of which purports to represent a single object. Kant uses the term "objective synthesis" to describe that organizing and arranging. Without this synthesis there would be sensory confusion and no representation of an object. In that famous "A-Deduction" remark Kant is saying that imagination is a component of this objective synthesis.

Kant's point is that Macbeth may have noticed the sheath and the handle of his dagger simultaneously and the blade only later. Nevertheless he will ignore that subjective ordering in his objective synthesis. He will link the handle and blade as parts of one object (the dagger) and will distinguish them from the sheath.

The reason this synthesis — this linking of handle data with blade data and this exclusion of sheath data — requires imagination is because it is governed by a concept, in this case the concept of a dagger.[5] (For Kant, subsumption under a concept is the mark of objectivity. It provides what Kant calls the "objective unity" (B142) that characterizes the experience of an object and makes that experience intersubjectively communicable.) But a concept, Kant tells us, is a "rule" for the "reproduction of the manifold" (A105) — a rule with repeated instances. And the instances have to be imagined. Thus, specifically, to say that Macbeth has combined the blade perceptions with those of the handle in a rule-like way is to say that he has projected beyond his present conscious episode and imagined future conscious moments in which the same connection is made. He might, for instance, imagine viewing the dagger from a different angle or noting its features (the blade, the handle and the sheath) in some different order. But if these flights of imagination are part of the objective synthesis of handle with blade, then in all these thought experiments Macbeth must imagine himself linking the perception of the blade and that of the handle, and excluding the perception of the sheath from that union. According to Kant, then, perceiving the dagger *qua* dagger means calling up all these non-actual perceptions, surveying them with the mind's eye, and noting that the handle and the blade are linked in all of them.

I like to use *Figure* 1 to picture a conscious episode with some of its attendant projections made explicit.

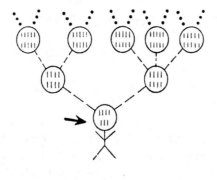

Figure 1

The important features of this tree-like diagram are (a) its single root or "origin" (designated by the arrow in *Figure* 1), (b) the attenuated paths (the strings of nodes, each representing a possible conscious episode) that stem

---

[5] Perception always comes in service of a judgment, which in turn provides the governing concept for the synthesis.

from the origin, and (c) the fact that each path branches at each of the upper nodes. The origin represents the only actual perceptual episode. The others have to be imagined projections, presentations to the mind of objects (or aspects) which are not actually perceived. It is important to allow the paths in this figure to extend in principle *ad infinitum*: our conscious episodes, be they real or imagined, are of limited finite duration. There are always more details to be learned as time goes on, so we must allow that perceptual experience grows in temporal stages. The branching in this diagram captures the fact that imaginative description is incomplete, or (to use Kant's term) "schematic": no matter what temporal stage of perception we may be imagining, some detail or other which could be learnable at that stage, will in fact be left out. At each stage according to Kant we have "a kind of *monogram*, a mere set of particular qualities" (A570/B598). So each imagined stage must include multiple possibilities. Indeed, there is no limit to the imaginable variations. So there are infinitely many possibilities, and were the diagram fully accurate it would have infinite branchings.[6]

This tree is an idealization of perceptual experience, an artificial construct designed to show why according to Kant imagination is an element of objective synthesis, indeed a "blind but indispensable" one (A78/B103; see also A141/B180-81). It is "indispensable" because perceptions cannot be objective unless they are subsumed under concepts; and we must appeal to schematic projection in order to explain how finite beings like Macbeth and us with our limited perceptual scopes can do this rule-governed subsuming.

It is "blind" because Macbeth cannot be aware of any of this elaborate structure. He certainly cannot survey all the details (all the branches) which are present only "schematically" in these projections. At best he might be conscious of what Husserl calls a "horizon," a vague projection, or as Kant describes it, "a blurred sketch or shadow image [*Schattenbild*]" (A571/B598), something that is felt explicitly only when the expectations it depicts are violated. So imagination, for Kant, is more a theoretical than an introspective notion. Like contemporary phenomenologists, he starts with a kernel of introspected experience (in this case a perception and its hazy penumbra) and builds upon it an elaborate structure which is designed to explain certain theoretical properties (in this case the property of objectivity).

Adopting the faculty metaphor which Kant so often uses, we can view the

---

[6] See KU 5: 316, where Kant speaks of the aesthetic imagination as producing a "multiplicity of partial representations." Interestingly, in the aesthetic case Kant drops the assumption that all the elements of this multiplicity already fall under a recognized concept.

Kantian imagination as this theoretically posited faculty which schematically projects non-actual mental states. When these projections are designed to flesh out a judgment that some aspect or other of the actual state is objective I shall speak of them as made by the "anchored imagination." For we have seen that objectivity demands that the imaginative projections be continuations which are anchored in an actual perceptual experience. As we expand this analysis to cover the roles of imagination in transcendental philosophy and mathematics we shall find a second, "unanchored," Kantian use of imagination as well.

B. *Transcendental Philosophy.* Transcendental philosophy, which studies the scope and limits of human knowledge, is based on phenomenological analyses precisely like the analysis of perception we just carried out. So for the present essay I will equate transcendental philosophy with phenomenology. Let us, then, suppose that Macbeth is now observing his dagger *qua* phenomenologist. Thus he is now observing his own conscious perception of the dagger. This is a special sort of observation. As a phenomenologist Macbeth concentrates only on the *universal* aspects of that perception: the aspects we philosophers call sensation, understanding, synthesis and the like, aspects which are supposed to be parts of every perceptual act.

Now Macbeth's self-perception is still a perception. It too is of finite duration, so it too will need syntheses, a horizon and rules as marks of its objectivity. In particular, a phenomenological observation of some sample conscious act — my perception of my perception of this hand-wave, for instance — will itself have to include projections about additional introspective observations of that original perception. Thus the anchored imagination that was a constituent of ordinary external perception must be present in phenomenological (internal) observation as well.

But, as I said, there is also a second use of imagination in transcendental philosophy. I call it the "exploratory imagination." For in order to capture the universal aspects of perception that concern the phenomenologist (in order to characterize the experience of perception in its most general form), Macbeth needs to go beyond his present self-observation. He needs to consider his observed perception as merely a paradigm. Thus he must imagine all sorts of other sample perceptual experiences and must explore them for the elements that they all have in common.

Now this exploratory imagination differs in two ways from the anchored imagination we met in Kant's analysis of perception. First of all, to do phenomenology we do not have to start with actual perceptions. An imagined one will do just as well. So Macbeth as a phenomenologist can use his famous imaginary dagger ("A dagger of the mind / A false creation" ii.1) just as easily as a real one, and we can use Macbeth's (imaginary) arm-sweep just as easily as a real one as examples at the base of a phenomenological analysis. Secondly, the projected comparisons need not be connected with the initial (real or imagined) sample perception. In Macbeth's dagger-perception the weight of *objectivity* was carried by assuming that the imagined perceptions were extensions of his present state of mind. But now if Macbeth wants to use this perception for phenomenology, if he wants to glean from it the essential character of perception *per se*, then he must imagine arbitrary perceptions of different subject matters made on disconnected occasions, and he must distinguish the features common to all of these imagined perceptions.

However, in spite of these differences, this exploratory use of imagination easily fits into the general definition of imagination I gave above. Once again imagination presents to the mind objects which are not actually perceived. (In this case the objects are themselves acts of perception.) Once again, because of his finitude, the subject must assume that his knowledge of these imagined objects will grow over time. (Thus, for instance, he might not initially recognize that the imagined perception has sensory and conceptual components.) And, once again, the imagined object will lack some relevant details. So this unanchored imagination is "schematic" in precisely the way I outlined above.[7]

C. *Mathematics.* Next let's look at the imagination associated with mathematics. So, our man Macbeth is now a mathematician, concerned with the geometric aspects of spatial objects like daggers. Once again, what he is really doing, Kant says, is studying certain selected aspects of his ordinary perceptual episodes. For according to Kant, mathematics is a special sort of phenomenology.[8] The mathematician, however, concentrates on particular rarified features of these episodes ("pure intuitions" in Kant's terms), and he introduces mathematical concepts to describe these features. Thus according to Kant he might attend to the process of physically measuring or tracing out the dagger, or perhaps to observing the actual motion of the dagger. To make his observations "pure," he then "abstracts" from the special medium of drawing and from the particulars of the motion. (See A714/B742.) But, still, the mathematical introspection, like the other types of perception, is finite

---

[7] Thus something like *Figure* 1 can also be used to depict the exploratory imagination. We would, however, no longer assume that the nodes in the first level projections represent extensions of the conscious state which is at the origin. And we do not even assume that the node at the base of the diagram represents an actual perception.

[8] Kant is what I call (in "Brouwer's Constructivism" *Synthese* 27, 1974) a "constructivist of the left."

and limited. So it too must have a horizon of possible extensions, and it too is governed by its own structured thought-experiments, as sketched in *Figure* 1.

Once again, however, the mathematician, like the phenomenologist, achieves generality because he implicitly compares his present perception with an array of similar but disconnected perceptions. That is the effect of his "abstraction": the elements of his hypothetical survey may differ from his initial perception on any of the abstracted details. And once again he can "construct" or create his own initial observation at will. Here too an imagined dagger will do just as well as a real one ("an air-drawn dagger," says Lady Macbeth, iii. 4), or an imagined line or artificial motion.

Thus mathematics, like ordinary phenomenology, has an unanchored, exploratory as well as an anchored imagination. The special nature of the exploratory imagination makes these into what Kant calls "formal" sciences. Since the individual examples considered in mathematics and phenomenology serve only as paradigms for an entire class of mental experiences, they can be, and often are, freely imagined. And when we actually do perceive the paradigm, we consider it, Kant says, only schematically, only as "a rule of synthesis of the imagination" (A141/B180): a rule, we may say, for the production of the elements of the accompanying comparative survey.

I hope you can see the element of *necessity* in all these different uses of imagination. Subsumption under a concept and objective synthesis provide a "necessary" unity to a manifold of intuition (A105). Phenomenology uncovers the properties that a perception *necessarily* has simply in virtue of being a perception. Geometry explores the properties that objects *necessarily* have *qua* spatial objects. And for Kant each of these cases, each of these judgments about necessity, requires a survey of infinitely many (actual and non-actual) possibilities. So for Kant these judgments are always problematic when attributed to finite beings. He uses the notion of a rule to replace that infinite survey. And he introduces the notion of imaginative (and thus schematic) projection to explain how we humans handle these infinite rules in actual thought. Imagination, then, is the Kantian device for combining finitude with necessity.[9]

II. Imagination in Ethics

Finally, let's turn to ethics. As ethicists we now want to evaluate the morality of Macbeth's deed. So let's assume that our man Macbeth is viewing the

---

[9] A non-finite being, who could survey all that is actual and possible, would have no need for the Kantian imagination.

motion of his dagger as part of an *act*: a purposeful happening, aimed at achieving a specific end. And let us assume that he has honestly evaluated his motive and has articulated his intention to achieve this end in his maxim.

According to Kant, only an appropriately good maxim will qualify an act as morally worthy. (The truly good acts are those which are done for the right reasons.) And this provides an important parallel between Kant's theoretical concern with objectivity and his ethical concerns. For Kant is quite insistent that objectivity — even intersubjectivity — is a condition *sine qua non* for the moral worthiness of a maxim (and hence of the corresponding act).

A maxim, he tells us, is by its nature a "*subjective* principle of action... [which] contains a practical *rule*... and is thus a principle on which the subject acts" (G 4:420n; see also KpV 5:19). But, he says, only those acts can be morally worthy whose maxim can be raised to the level of an "objective principle... valid for every rational being." Only this intersubjectivity can give a "principle on which he *ought to act* — that is an imperative" (*ibid.*).

Now it is sometimes easy to forget that this familiar basis for Kant's ethics has to seem strange to a reader coming fresh from the first *Critique*. For this reader will ask how a maxim could ever be subjective to start with. Inclinations and desires — the ethical parallels of sensory intuitions — these are clearly subjective. But a maxim, even one indicating that my goal is to satisfy some desire or other, is after all a publicly communicable principle. It is a rule; it is conceptual; it involves normative necessity. And thus it has a firm place in the understanding. Yet are not rule-likeness, necessity and a lineage from the understanding precisely the Kantian criteria for objectivity?

Indeed, our friend, the anchored imagination, is at work in applying a maxim to its act.[10] If Macbeth's maxim is *"Act so as to satisfy your ambition,"* then he must imagine (schematically, to be sure) continuations of his current state which include his being king and his ambition achieved. So how can we speak of this or that maxim as "subjective"?

But the relation between a maxim and its act — this is really the relation of subsumption that holds in the first *Critique* between a concept and an empirical perception. It does not provide the sort of objectivity that Kant wants here (see KpV 5:68).

Kant is concerned here with a different sort of objectivity: the objectivity of the goal or "end" that is announced in the maxim. Ambition, pride, and for that matter generosity, sympathy, love and all the other passions which stem from man's "sensuous nature" are radically personal. So an act designed to

---

[10] In *Anth.* 7:251 Kant tells us that "Appetite is the self-determination of a subject's power through the idea of some future thing as an effect of this power."

satisfy one or another of these desires is directed at the actor's own subjective state, no matter how vividly describable that desire might be. And — no matter how clearly articulated it might be — the maxim governing that act must count as ethically *subjective*. In Kant's view, such a maxim can never be morally worthy. Acting simply to satisfy a need can never be morally noble, even if it is a need to do noble things. By contrast, a maxim will be ethically *objective* only if its end has no taint of personal (sensuous) motivation.

There is, to be sure, a notion of subsumption involved here. The truly objective maxim is one whose end can be subsumed under the concept of rule or law *per se*, the concept that remains when we eliminate sensory goals from the notion of purposive action (see KpV 5: 68). Such a maxim will relate the act to an end which has been produced entirely intellectually, and this, says Kant, is the only truly "obligatory end" (TL 6: 388), the only "duty." Maxims which posit such ends have two distinctions.

(1) Since in this case the maxim and the end are both produced entirely intellectually (i.e., by reason) the intellectual faculty is acting "autonomously" in formulating such maxims. (Maxims which posit subjective ends are "heteronomous" because, even though they themselves are intellectual, they point to goals which are generated by the sensory faculty.)

(2) Since, according to Kant, all rational beings are united by a common rationality,[11] these ends are "valid for all rational beings." That is why the corresponding maxims are truly objective.

And so, when faced with an ethical choice, having sorted out my options and formulated potential ends and corresponding maxims, the next step in my deliberation is to weed out my subjective maxims and isolate only those maxims which direct me to achieve an end generated by pure reason. Only those are legitimately *objective* (see TL 6: 224).

Under this definition Macbeth himself testifies to the subjectivity of the maxim governing his dagger-drawing and his stabbing of Duncan: "Stars hide your fires," he says, "let not the light see my black and deep *desires*" (i. 4). And, even more specifically, he is driven, he tells us, by a "vaulting ambition" (i.7).

Macbeth is, of course, an exception in these remarks. He makes it seem as if a simple introspective glance will determine whether a goal is ultimately based in reason or desire. But that is not true, and Kant is the first to admit it. We need to have a formal test that we can apply to determine whether or not any

---

[11] This is a constant theme in Kant. Insofar as he considers non-human rational beings, he characterizes them solely according to differences in their faculties of intuition. See for instance B148-49.

given maxim is ethically objective. This is not merely because most of us are more like Hamlet than Macbeth, struggling to determine which maxim is "nobler in the mind." But it is because the very distinction between intellect and sense, reason and desire, is not an introspective one. The concept of an intellectual faculty is itself introduced by Kant in these works in order to achieve a certain purpose: he wants to found morality on intersubjectively valid principles of action. And we can attribute a maxim to that faculty only if it lives up to that purpose, only if it is truly intersubjectively valid.

Thus a maxim can be said to be wholly rational and morally good only if it is possible without contradiction to assume (and indeed to will) that it be a law for all rational beings, only if it is "universalizable." So to test a maxim for objectivity you must imagine a universe in which every rational being will act under the same maxim in relevantly similar circumstances. You must then probe that imagined picture for contradictions. In Kant's famous example, no objective maxim could direct me to ignore a destitute acquaintance if helping him would not greatly inconvenience me (G 4: 424). For I could never will that such a maxim be universally accepted. As soon as I *imagine* the circumstances in which our places are reversed, I will recognize that I would then want this fellow to help me. And Macbeth's announced maxim is revealed to be subjective as soon as he *imagines* a situation in which anyone may act against his king to satisfy ambition. Once again, I may add, Macbeth appears to meet the Kantian test. While contemplating the murder not only does he consider the duties imposed by his special relationship with Duncan, but he also considers the general principle that can be learned from this deed, and says:

> ... But in these cases
> We still have judgment here; that we but teach
> Bloody instructions, which being taught, return
> To plague th' inventor. This even handed justice
> Commends the ingredients of our poison'd chalice
> To our own lips. [i.7]

So Shakespeare has given Macbeth just the sort of deliberation that Kant would require him to have in order to determine his own villainy.[12]

---

[12] As I interpret this soliloquy, Shakespeare here has transformed into a moral deliberation the following political and psychological observation that he found in Raphael Holingshed's *Chronicles of England, Scotland and Ireland*: "These and the like commendable lawes Makbeth caused to be put as then in vse, gouerning the realme for the space of ten yeares in equall iustice. But this was but a counterfet zeale of equitie shewed by him, partlie against his naturall inclination to purchase thereby the fauour of the people. Shortlie after, he began to shew what he was, in stead of equitie practicing crueltie. For the pricke of conscience (as it chanceth euer in tyrants, and

I will not for now probe more deeply into these examples, nor ask whether the contradictions (in concept or will) are always so obvious as they were in these two thought experiments. All I want to do for the present is emphasize how central this sort of thought experiment and the associated projection are to the whole enterprise of Kantian ethical deliberation. There is the same element of necessity (now a normative necessity) that we saw in the theoretical cases. There is the same need for an exhaustive survey of situations which are not actually present. Judgments about moral worthiness can come only after surveying an infinite array of such situations. And this survey must be contrasted with the same human finitude. So once again imagination, with its schematic representations, is the Kantian device for handling this sort of infinite survey. The imagination at work here is just the same *exploratory* faculty that we have been discussing in the theoretical sciences: it roams at will and schematically produces representations of those ethically relevant situations.[13]

I want to emphasize this centrality of imagination in ethical deliberation, because I want to stress how anomalous it must seem that Kant claims in the Typic that imagination plays no role in ethics: "the moral law," he says, "has no other cognitive faculty to mediate its application to objects of nature than the understanding (*not the imagination*)" (KpV 5: 69; my emphasis). The natural objects mentioned here are human actions. Our ethical deliberations must be action guiding, and ethical concepts like duty and goodness must be able to characterize human actions, if ethics is to have any value. Kant here is denying that this connection involves imagination. But we have just seen that in fact the process by which we test our maxims — and thus apply these concepts to our actions — must employ imagination.

As I suggested at the outset, the solution to this anomaly will come from our efforts to give a modern interpretation of transcendental idealism. So let us turn to those efforts now.

III. Transcendental Idealism and Imagination

Transcendental idealism, as it is traditionally understood, claims that synthesis, perception and the like are processes that actually produce empirical

---

such as atteine to anie estate by vnrighteous means) caused him euer to feare, lest he shoud be serued of the same cup, as he had ministred to his predecessor" (Second Edition, 1587, page 172).

[13] R.M. Hare's *Freedom and Reason* (Oxford, 1963, esp. pp. 94ff.) shows that even today imagination is recognized as a necessary constituent of universalization.

objects. That is why Kant's idealism is linked with phenomenalism. The modern twist that I have in mind is to speak of the *truth* of empirical judgments instead of the *being* of empirical objects. So I will equate transcendental philosophy with semantics: the study of truth conditions for various classes of judgments.[14] Transcendental idealism will be that style of semantics which makes empirical perception (together with its anchored imagination) the central factor in empirical truth, and *Figure* 1 will now characterize its formal semantics. By contrast, the transcendental realist will deny any role to synthesis and imagination in defining truth. For him *Figure* 1 can bear no semantic weight.

Now this move from ontology to semantics might not seem to be a very substantial change, and scarcely any defense against phenomenalism. For according to the standard (model theoretic) semantics that we all learned in logic class, truth rests on the relation of reference between the terms in our language and the objects in the domain of discourse. So the global properties of truth (the properties reflected in our formal semantics) are only mirrors of the most general properties of the objects in the domain. The formal semantics might well respect the role of synthesis and imagination, and might indeed be structured like *Figure* 1, it might do this however simply as a reflection of the belief that these processes and this structure characterize the production of empirical objects.[15]

But I propose to abandon the traditional model theoretic conception of truth altogether, even as an interpretation of transcendental realism. Instead, as I said at the outset, I shall use a version of the currently popular assertability semantics in order to interpret Kant's transcendental idealism and realism. Assertabilism — a theory championed at one of these Jerusalem Encounters

---

[14] This interpretation is not so anachronistic as it might at first seem. Its basic assumption is that transcendental philosophy is concerned with the nature of empirical judgments, rather than with the nature of empirical objects. That is not so radical a claim. Moreover, we need not construe these judgments as "linguistic" entities. Thought entities will do just as well, so long as we require (as Kant clearly did) that these judgments have grammatical form.

[15] The model theoretic reading also causes difficulties in interpreting transcendental realism. The realist, while admitting that imagination is a constituent in determining the objectivity of our empirical judgments, will deny that it has any role in the construction of empirical objects, and thus in the truth of those judgments. This is pictured in *Figure* 2. The right side of the diagram represents mind independent truth, and is the only side that has semantic weight. But this is precisely the understanding of transcendental realism that led to the accusation of circularity in the realist's "Antinomy" arguments.

some years ago by Michael Dummett[16] — holds that a judgment is true if and only if there is sufficient evidence justifying it. Justification (or in Dewey's phrase, "warranted assertability") plays the role that correspondence with objects played in the more standard theory. Thus, on this view, we must replace the correspondence notion of truth relative to a domain of objects with the idea of assessing a proposition at an "epistemic situation," a collection of basic pieces of evidence.

The connection of all this with Kantian phenomenology (and thus at least with transcendental idealism) seems clear enough. For Kant, empirical judgments must be justified by perceptions. So the Kantian theory of perceptual episodes that I sketched a few moments ago will be the backbone of a theory of epistemic situations. With each simple judgment we will associate the sort of perceptual situation that would corroborate that judgment. The judgment "Macbeth's dagger is bloodied" will be true at those (real and hypothetical) epistemic situations in which it is perceived to be dripping blood.

And imagination apparently comes in too: perceptual evidence, as we saw, is incomplete and comes in stages. This means that at any given stage some relevant judgments will be neither assertable nor deniable — the claim, for instance, that there is life on some distant galaxy — for we can imagine the evidence going either way. That is why assertabilism is often used to deny the principle of bivalence, the principle that every judgment is either true or false. Speaking assertabilistically, our astronomic claim is neither true nor false. But sometimes — and here imagination plays an even bigger role — sometimes the imaginative projections which are part of an objective perceptual

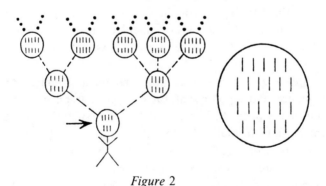

Figure 2

[16] See Dummett's contributions to A. Margalit (ed.), *Meaning and Use* — Papers Presented at the Second Jerusalem Philosophical Encounter, April 1976 (Reidel, 1979), pp. 123-135; 218-225.

experience can permit us to assert a judgment which is not strictly warranted by the perceptual evidence. Conditionals provide the standard example. Macbeth's judgemnt *"if I stab Duncan, my dagger will be bloodied"* is assertable, and thus true, even before the actual stabbing. For whenever Macbeth imagines having stabbed Duncan he perforce imagines having a bloody dagger. ("I see thee still," he says, "And on thy blade and dudgeon gouts of blood, / which was not so before" ii.1). Indeed there are a number of formal semantic systems which do employ tree-like structures depicting the potential growth of knowledge in order to model conditionals and to invalidate bivalence. So the assertabilist interpretation apparently does give semantic force to *Figure* 1 and imagination, and thus seems a natural candidate to interpret at least transcendental idealism.

But, as things turn out, we need to refine this apparently simple connection between assertability and imagination. The assertabilist needs to make an additional semantic decision and an epistemic one before he is entitled to take phenomenology as a constituent of truth and use the trees of *Figure* 1 as a basis for his semantics. The semantic decision concerns an issue that I call "Dummett versus Peirce." The epistemological one concerns something I call "optimism." I will explain them briefly.

The semantic decision. In Dummett's version of assertabilism the truth of judgment is simply equated with its warranted assertability *right now*. But this ignores the famous Peircean view according to which a proposition is true if it is *eventually* assertable — in the fullness of time. The Peircean theory does not change the definition of assertability, nor does it automatically make truth into an inhuman notion, independent of our epistemic achievements. But it does divorce truth from assertability right now, and thus makes it a tenseless notion. (For the Peircean, if mankind were to explore a planet in that distant galaxy some time in the next century and discover a recognizable and ancient life form there, it would simply be true, tenselessly, that that galaxy contains life.)[17]

The epistemic decision. Now suppose that the assertabilist does take the Peircean stance; and suppose that, for some given fragment of the language, he combines it with the brazenly "optimistic" assumption that every statement which can be formulated within that fragment is ultimately decidable. This optimism does not entail any relaxation of our strictest evidential methods. It is simply an extraordinarily sanguine attitude about the power of those methods. And it is perfectly consistent with basic assertabilism. But it is

---

[17] Crispin Wright has recently discussed a similar notion under the title of "superassertability." See *Realism, Meaning and Truth* (Blackwell, 1987).

easy to see that this combination of the Peircean semantics with epistemic optimism leads to bivalence, even for the assertabilist. For, no matter what is assertable at any given epistemic situation, the optimistic premise guarantees for any proposition A that in the long run either A will be assertable or its negation will be. For the Peircean that is enough to show that A is either true or false — tenselessly. But this means that the attenuated structure of imaginative exercises, which is depicted in *Figure* 1 and which is so crucial to our Kantian account of objectivity, is, from the semantic point of view, a mere empty flourish.

Once again, as assertabilists, we might well recognize that the truth of an empirical judgment about a distant life form depends on our perceiving the form or its traces. And we might also admit that when it occurs this perception will have to be encased in a network of imaginative projections in order to be objective. But the semantic bottom line is truth and falsity; and for the Peircean optimist these glances towards the future would play no effective role. Our optimism would guarantee that either we will have this perception or we will discover that no such perception is possible. In practice, to be sure, we do not know which of these possibilities will come to pass. But our Peirceanism tells us that this temporary ignorance is not semantically relevant. For the Peircean, only the possibility that there is some eternally undecided judgment or other can justify a formal semantics in which we need to employ the sort of imaginative projections that are sketched in *Figure* 1.

So if the assertabilist wants to incorporate phenomenology and *Figure* 1 in his account of truth, then he must either take the short-sighted Dummettian approach, and link the truth of each proposition to its assertability right now, or else he must somehow refute or constrain the optimistic premise. If he does neither, then there is no role in his semantics for the phenomenology of perception and for imagination.

Now, assuming as I said that Kant is an assertabilist, let us determine how he stands on each of these issues, Dummett versus Peirce and optimism. In fact, on the first issue there are texts which show him plainly to be a Peircean (A493/B521 for instance).[18]

What about optimism? Here Kant's views are more subtle. At A477/B505, speaking as a transcendental idealist, he tells us that in natural science, "much must remain uncertain and many questions insoluble." There is no optimism here. His reason for pessimism about empirical science is that empirical judgments must rest on sensory intuitions, perceptions, as their evidence; and

---

[18] I have explored this in more detail in "Kant's Mathematical Realism," *The Monist* 67 (1984): 115-134.

these states of mind are essentially "receptive." That means that they cannot be produced automatically or at will. Their "key," Kant says, "does not lie within us." We can, of course, search for these sensations, and can put ourselves in position to receive them. But we have no general guarantee that this search will be successful, will "converge," or even terminate. Nor can we fully systematize our empirical knowledge in a way that will predict our future perceptions with certainty (see A664/B692ff). Because of this "receptivity," the indeterminacy that comes from our perceptual (phenomenological) structures will characterize empirical truth. In other words, the imaginative projections of *Figure* 1 do give a *semantic* framework for empirical truth.

But what about the realist? If we now ask the same question about empirical optimism of Kant's transcendental realist, his answer will be different. Kant characterizes the transcendental realist as someone who "abstracts from the conditions of sensible intuition," and looks at empirical objects from the perspective of pure reason. Taking that God's eye view, officially, is what it means to view these objects as things-in-themselves. (See, for instance, A28/B44.) We can see from the third antinomy that this "abstraction" cannot amount to denying that the truth of empirical propositions rests on the possibility of perceptual confirmation. The realist must be an assertabilist too! What his "abstraction" must come to is ignoring the "receptive" aspect of our empirical evidence. Ignoring receptivity cancels Kant's official grounds for claiming that empirical knowledge may be incomplete. Thus ignoring receptivity is no more than embracing optimism. The point is that for the realist the epistemic structures based on the faculty of imagination are once again, from the semantic point of view, "mere flourishes." Pure reason engenders optimism, and thus cancels any semantic effect of imagination or of *Figure* 1.

Now we can begin to answer the traditional objections to Kant's theory. First and most simply the pitfall of phenomenalism: assertabilism is not phenomenalism, because semantics and ontology are separate topics for the assertabilist. Assertabilism is a theory about empirical *truth*; it says nothing about the *being* of empirical objects.[19]

Secondly, the problem of circularity in the third antinomy: the realist and the idealist will both share Kant's assertabilism. Both will ground truth on

[19] See my "Where Have All the Objects Gone?" *Southern Journal of Philosophy* 5, Supplement (1986). William James is struggling to make a similar point in several of his writings. Thus, for instance, in the Preface to *The Meaning of Truth* (Longmans, Green and Co., 1909) he says: "Most of the pragmatist and anti-pragmatist warfare is over what the word "truth" shall be held to signify, and not over any of the facts

evidence, and both will admit that epistemic situations are built on perceptual episodes. So the realist *will* agree that experience is relevant to truth, and the threat of freedom to the unity of experience *is* enough to render freedom impossible. But the realist, because he takes the perspective of pure reason, will add optimism to his assertabilism. This explains Kant's *reductio* of transcendental realism. The realist's optimistic assumption together with his assertabilism commits him to the semantics depicted in *Figure* 3, a single noded semantics which still equates truth with human assertability.

Figure 3

This semantics guarantees that exactly one of the propositions expressed by the thesis and antithesis in the third antinomy will be true. And so the realist can argue from the falsity of one to the truth of the other (which is exactly how Kant has him do it). But since his assertabilism tells him that both are false, he is in a fine fix!

Before turning to the remaining questions, let me point out that this talk of the realist's "abstracting from the receptivity of sensations" sounds like precisely the methodology that I have attributed to our friends the phenomenologist and the mathematician. These researchers, in attending only to the universal aspects of consciousness in general or perception in particular, will be able to call up their sample data at will ("spontaneously," in Kant's terms) from their own internal resources. And, for them it does not matter at all if

---

embodied in truth-situations; for both pragmatists and anti-pragmatists believe in existent objects, just as they believe in our ideas of them. The difference is that when the pragmatists speak of truth, they mean exclusively something about the ideas, namely their workableness; whereas when anti-pragmatists speak of truth they seem most often to mean something about the objects."

their data at the moment are actually perceived or only imagined. So the evidence or justification for their claims is not passively received.

This has two important consequences. First, we can now see why Kant describes these disciplines as "in a position to demand and expect none but assured answers to all the questions within [their] domain[s]..., although up to the present [these answers] have perhaps not been found" (A488/B508).

Kant's official explanation for this optimism is that these sciences are not dependent on anything outside the mind itself. Their questions, he says, are "domestic questions," whose "key" *does* lie within us, and whose answer "must issue from the very same sources from which the question proceeds" (A476/B504). But now we can see that he is simply invoking the spontaneity of the exploratory imagination that is employed in these sciences. The mind is free to produce its own data without any need for passive receptivity. To be sure, these are still human sciences; and gathering evidence within these sciences is still governed by our limited spans of attention. Thus for instance our *Figure* 1 analysis with its incomplete conscious episodes still characterizes the perceptual experience of the mathematician as he draws his lines and constructs his triangles. That is why mathematics can still have some unanswered questions at any given moment. But because all that drawing and constructing can be done in the mathematician's imagination, Kant is confident that the science can be systematically unified in a way that guarantees those questions can be answered (see, e.g., A464/B492). So he will not let that temporary ignorance influence the notion of ultimate mathematical truth. The force of the exploratory imagination has cancelled the semantic effect of the anchored projections. Semantically *Figure* 1 is once again a mere flourish, and the mathematician has a clear ticket to the realist semantics. That is the first consequence of abstracting from sensation.

The second consequence is that Kant must now take special pains to assure that mathematical success is really *truth*. Since the exploratory imagination can be used to justify mathematical judgments without producing any actual perception, Kant worries that mathematics will fail to satisfy the basic assertabilist criterion for empirical truth, the criterion that requires reducibility to actual perceptions. He sometimes phrases this semantic worry in terms of "objective validity," the requirement that mathematical concepts (and those of transcendental philosophy) be applicable to actual empirical objects.[20] Though we have seen that mathematics and transcendental philosophy are

---

[20] Objective validity is defined in terms of concepts because it is a formal condition, one which characterizes an entire class of judgments. Truth, by contrast, is a material condition which applies to individual judgments one at a time.

realistic sciences, they are not noumenal. And the way Kant guarantees this is by limiting their imaginative projections to the realm of "possible experience."

for though a pure intuition can indeed precede the object *a priori*, even this intuition can acquire its object, and therefore objective validity, only through the empirical intuition of which it is the mere form. Therefore all concepts, and with them all principles, even such as are possible *a priori*, relate to empirical intuitions, that is, to the data for a possible experience. (A239/B298)

We can now understand this "relation to empirical intuitions" as the requirement that the mathematician and transcendental philosopher must augment the exploratory imaginative experiments which accompany their research by adding the explicit assumption that the projected scenarios are actually (humanly) perceivable. They may not "abstract" from the spatial (and/or temporal) aspects of their paradigm cases.[21] To be sure, it is psychologically impossible to dispense with the sensory content of imagination,[22] but nevertheless the restriction to experienceable objects must be made explicit. For without this added assumption, the concepts of mathematics and transcendental philosophy would "have no objective validity, and in respect of their representations [would be] a mere play of the imagination or of understanding" (A223-24/B271; see also Anth. 7: 168).

IV. Ethical Assertabilism

We can answer the remaining objections — about omniscience, about the self-in-itself, and about the ethical imagination — by simply noting that determining the goodness of a maxim is to ethics what determining the truth of a judgment is to the theoretical sciences. It is the mark of "semantic success." For semantics is not merely the study of "truth conditions" for theoretical judgments. Semantics in its most general sense is the study of those factors which make our judgments successful within the different projects in which those judgments occur. Indeed, we have in ethics a straightforward

---

[21] In transcendental philosophy this distinguishes the thought experiments which accompany concepts having objective validity (the schematized categories, for instance) from those thought experiments which must be employed when we consider the unschematized categories. (See my "Where Have All the Objects Gone?" for more details.)

[22] "So no matter how great an artist and even enchantress imagination may be, it is still not creative, but must get the *material* for its images from the *senses*" (*Anth.* 7: 168).

continuation of Kant's assertabilism. An empirical judgment is semantically successful (i.e., true) if it is justifiable by sensory experience. Similarly, in ethics, a maxim is semantically successful if and only if it is justifiable by way of the universalizability test. This is the observation that will lay to rest the remainder of our open questions.

A. *Omniscience*. Now we can see why Kant includes ethics in that special circle of optimistic sciences. For the methodology of ethics is closer to that of phenomenology and mathematics than it is to that of empirical science.

Our everyday ethical deliberations, our evaluations of our maxims and choices among them, our applications of the universalizability test, all of these invariably consist of the exploratory imagination at work. In these activities we use imagination — just as the mathematician does — to conjure at will any ethical situation we need. I can imagine myself changing places with my destitute colleague. Macbeth imagines a realm of ambitious murderers. And so, Kant will say, just as in mathematics, the "key" to answering ethical questions lies within that very same reason which posed the questions. This inner control is what assures us, however uncertain we may be at the moment about the moral worth of some maxim, that in the long run, this moral question, indeed every ethical issue, will be resolved! That is why Kant holds the doctrine of ethical omniscience.

B. *The Self-In-Itself*. We speak of ethical agents in the context of moral decision making, a context, we have seen, whose questions are decidable, and whose semantics follows *Figure* 3. But *Figure* 3 gives the entire semantic content of the concept of a thing-in-itself. To be a thing-in-itself is to be independent of the conditions of sensibility. Semantically these conditions are those which yield undecidability and *Figure* 1. Thus, a thing-in-itself concept is one which dictates that the judgments in which it appears must be assumed to be decidable and, equivalently, bivalent; just as depicted in *Figure* 3.

That is why in ethics the concepts of an acting self and of its various actions and motives are thing-in-itself concepts. This is a semantic decision (as we now understand semantics) and not an ontological one. There is no other-worldly entity being posited here. Judgments about the ethical self are said to be "unknowable" simply because the deliberation which grounds these judgments explicitly flouts the limitation to possible experience. But when we view these very same concepts not as constituents of maxims, but rather as parts of empirical judgments (when we view the motion of Macbeth's dagger not as an action but as a temporally determined event) then we must rest the assertability of our judgments about that motion on sensory experience. In this case the standards of assertabilist truth will require that we model those judgments in a semantics which respects our imaginative projections and looks like *Figure* 1. And Kant argues in the Second Analogy that this sort of semantics will justify the principle of causal determinism.[23]

C. *Ethical Imagination.* Finally, let's turn to address Kant's reason for banning imagination from ethics. Here we need to contrast ethics with mathematics and transcendental philosophy on the question of objective validity. As we have seen, ethical deliberations must be action guiding and ethical concepts must subsume observable actions. In order to obtain the same sort of applicability in mathematics Kant had to curb mathematical abstraction by adding a special requirement to the projective mental experiments that underlie the necessity of mathematical truth. He added the requirement that each element of the schematic survey must be perceptually realizable. As we saw, without this requirement mathematics would be a mere "play of the imagination."

In the ethical projections, however, we do take this extra abstractive step. Not only can we eliminate the perceivability requirement, we *must* eliminate it. There are two reasons for this:

(1) In ethics, the objectivity of our maxims depends upon their being valid (i.e., it depends upon their stated ends being obligatory) for all "rational beings." But we have seen that the only thing that distinguishes us from other rational beings is our spatio-temporal faculty of intuition. Thus the thought experiments which establish ethical objectivity must explicitly apply to non-spatio-temporal beings.

(2) Were we to restrict these projective thought experiments to humanly perceivable situations (and specifically to situations which are temporally ordered), then we could not avoid the reasoning of the Second Analogy (in particular the argument from temporal fixity). But then we would have to assume that all actions are determined by empirical causes, and that would undermine the possibility of practical freedom.[23]

Kant phrases the lifting of this restriction in terms of his definition of imagination; and this is where we need to correct our provisional understanding of that faculty. Imagination, strictly speaking, is not merely the faculty of projecting non-actual objects and mental situations. It is instead that faculty with the added restriction that the projected situations must be actually perceivable. A faculty which lacks this restriction in fact or which does not

---

[23] See my "Transcendental Idealism and Causality," in W. Harper and R. Meerbote (eds.), *Kant on Causality, Objectivity and Freedom* (University of Minnesota Press, 1984).

make it explicit, cannot be called imagination. That is why the projective faculty at work in ethics cannot be called imagination. And that is why Kant officially bans imagination from ethical deliberation.

This ban is also at the heart of the doctrine of autonomy. The ends that are posited by those maxims which can be fully universalized have passed a test which, as we now see, must be viewed as entirely conceptual. Officially this test uses no imagination and thus takes no account of the special nature of human sensibility. That is the meaning of Kant's claim that these ends are legislated by pure reason alone.

Once again this distinction between conception and imagination cannot be based on introspection. And Kant's decision to ban imagination from ethics must be a semantic and not an introspective decision. For if one looks introspectively at the actual scenarios that the mind calls up in the process of universalizing, then of course all their animate and inanimate elements are perceivable. Kant himself admits this (see KpV 5: 68). Nothing else could be possible. So in actual deliberation we do use imagination in the full Kantian sense. But what is missing here, and what must remain missing, is the *assumption* that the perceivable aspects characterize and limit the survey.[24]

All of this perspectivism — this choice between using our concepts in ethical or empirical judgments — is, I believe, loosely consistent with the currently popular "double aspect" interpretation of Kant's solution to the third antinomy. According to this interpretation, there is a single self which is viewed from two perspectives, the perspective of an empirical appearance, and the perspective of a thing-in-itself. I would simply add that the empirical and ethical perspectives are distinguished by their semantic assumptions, and that this is the best way to understand the difference between viewing the self as an appearance and viewing it through pure reason as a thing-in-itself.

This perspectivism also sounds suspiciously close to a sort of semantic relativism that has been championed by Nelson Goodman.[25] But in this case I want to resist the equation. For one thing, there is an ordering of perspectives in Kant which is not present in Goodman's views. Kant ranks the ethical perspective as primary. But more importantly, in contrast to Goodman, Kant does not have two different theories of truth underlying the ethical and theoretical projects. There is, on my reading, a single, assertabilist theory of semantic success that holds for all our intellectual projects: science, mathematics and ethics alike. To that Kant has added a "critical" recognition that

---

[24] Thus taking natural law as a "type" (KpV 5: 70) simply amounts to considering natural laws under a special set of assumptions.

[25] See, for instance, *Ways of Worldmaking* (Hackett, 1978).

different projects will have different evidential criteria and thus different semantically dominant "faculties." But, I repeat, there is a unified, undivided notion of semantic success underlying the entire critical philosophy.

V. Ethical Omniscience?

It would be nice to stop here. Though there remain many details to be supplied, still the picture I have sketched so far hints at a rather neat package. In one stroke we get a unified critical philosophy, based on a philosophically respectable principle (assertabilism), which combines in turn with understandable epistemic assumptions to answer our various objections. It explains Kant's seemingly mysterious views about things-in-themselves and imagination, and even that initially surprising claim of ethical omniscience. Indeed, though Kant is often attacked for his moral realism (his view that in any moral situation there must be a unique and consistent course of action prescribed by duty),[26] we now see that he espouses this doctrine only because it is a consequence of his much more radical view of ethical omniscience.

But no matter how well we might now understand the systematic reasons for this last doctrine — Kant's ethical optimism — I cannot end without at least noting that Kant's view is still anomalous. The belief that every ethical question can be decided (indeed, decided by pure reasoning) even in the fullness of time, this belief runs against Kant's own awareness of ethical ambiguities and moral dilemmas. And it certainly clashes with the tenor of much modern ethical wisdom. Let me now speak briefly about these clashes.

We are not talking here of a larger-than-life Macbeth or of Kant's infamous pathological liar. But rather most of us are concerned with ordinary people like ourselves, who must choose between the pulls of career and family, or who, like the student in Sartre's famous example, must decide on short notice between apparently conflicting duties. (In Sartre's story the student must choose between his duty to support his mother and his duty to join the resistance thus aiding his country and perhaps all mankind.)[27] Cases like these

---

[26] Kant says: "A conflict of duties ... would be a relation of duties in which one of them would annul the other (wholly or in part). But a *conflict of duties* and obligations is inconceivable ... For the concepts of duty and obligation as such express the objective practical *necessity* of certain actions, and two conflicting rules cannot both be necessary at the same time: if it is our duty to act according to one of these rules, then to act according to the opposite one is not our duty and is even contrary to duty" (MS 6: 223).

[27] Sartre, *L'Existentialisme est un Humanisme* (Les Editions Nagle, 1946).

have indecision or at least uncertainty about moral worth written all over them. And these are problems for Kant, because even the best of wills and the firmest of commitments to act from duty cannot avail if, as many of us suspect, in cases like these duty itself is unknown!

I believe that Kant will explain this suspicion by his distinction between pure and applied moral philosophy.[28] Kant defines *ethics* (sometimes called *pure ethics*) as the discipline concerned with evaluating maxims (determining their "semantic success" in my terminology). But in any actual choice-situation the agent's practical options must be described and the alternative maxims must already be formulated before Kant's ethical test can be applied. Kant makes it quite clear that we should not think of pure ethics as a decision procedure for morally worthy behavior or of these tests as providing algorithms for deciding between opposing possible actions. In particular, evaluation depends upon description of our choices, and ethics alone does not provide a set of basic concepts with which to construct these descriptions. In Kant's own terms, we need a faculty of *wit* or *judgment* in order to determine the ethical options and judge the conflicting motives that might effect an ethical situation (G 4: 389; TL 6: 410). This faculty would not belong to pure reason (practical or theoretical), and so it could well be uncertain and fallible.

Once again, Macbeth can provide a good example. Lady Macbeth attributes his indecision to "the milk of human kindness," a debilitating sentimentality that undermines the "sickness" which should attend ambition (i.5). We have seen that she is wrong. It is as much moral reasoning as it is sentiment which inhibits Macbeth. Macbeth himself recognizes this. He admits that his ambition is inconstant (it "o'erleaps itself" he says, "And falls on the other side" i.7); but, as we have seen, he knows that it is the call of duty and not mere sentiment which opposes it — the duty of a kinsman, a subject and a host, and fully universalized Kantian duty. Yet Shakespeare suggests that Macbeth too is not fully aware of his motives and drives. It is less ambition that leads Macbeth to stab Duncan than it is the desire to seem manly before his wife. (That is the import of Act i, Scene 7, lines 31-82.) The literary point here is that Lady Macbeth does not know her husband well enough — does not have enough information — to assess his deepest motives, and neither does Macbeth himself. The Kantian point is that these ascriptions of motives and ends to others and even to ourselves are matters of observation and empirical inference. And as in empirical observation, we may often lack full and final information.

So the picture we get is that ambiguity and indecision come in at the applied

---

[28] See, for instance, A55/B79 and TL 6: 380, 409.

level of describing the options and formulating the maxims. And, at that level, indecision might even be inevitable. But if we assume (perhaps *per impossibile*) that this descriptive work has been completed, then the remaining pure ethical evaluations, the universalization tests, are totally decidable.

As I said, I believe that this analysis is close to Kant's own. Pure ethical theory, when divorced from the need for native judgment, will be able to attain the systematic structure that Kant linked with decidability (see A54/B78). To be sure, questions in the pure theory might not be answerable on the spot or in any short time. The limits of intellectual attention are no different in ethical deliberation than they are in transcendental philosophy or mathematics. So, as in these theoretical sciences, in ethics too, at any given point there may well be unresolved issues. But, again just like mathematics and transcendental philosophy, pure ethics can be certain that its intellectual methods will eventually solve any problem in its domain.

I must, however, say that — at least for me, and I suspect for others as well — the skepticism still lingers about this doctrine of omniscience, even in *pure* ethics. I believe that there are three reasons for this skepticism.

(1) In this post-Quinean era we are no longer confident that we can so easily separate the pure from the applied, the intellectual from the observational, in the way that is demanded by Kant.

(2) Nor is it clear that, were this separation possible, human action could be systematized in the way that Kant supposes. Kant often equates the completeness (and by this he means decidability) of a science with our ability to organize (his word is "unify") that science under a set of principles. In ethics much of this comes through in his remarks about the bases for harmony in the *kingdom of ends* and his frequent reduction of morality to a single overarching principle. Yet many of us are skeptical today that any such unified theory can be adequate to human ethical experience.

(3) Finally, even if the laws of morality could be so systematized, there remains the modern suspicion that systematic *a priori* sciences are not immune to undecidability, even in the fullness of time. We now believe that, because of its immense complexity, even mathematics will have unsolvable problems. To be sure, we should not fault Kant for failing to anticipate this modern skepticism. He is in the good company of at least Frege and Hilbert. But reflecting on this modern belief leads us to suspect that "pure" ethical theory may well go beyond ordinary deliberative ability, even for what Kant calls an "enlightened moral consciousness."

To persist in the doctrine of ethical decidability while recognizing the grounds for our modern suspicions might lead us to hold that pure ethics requires a special direct intellectual/ethical intuition to resolve moral dilemmas.[29] Or perhaps we might hold that the moral law — like so many other Kantian concepts — serves as a mere regulative ideal, even in practical philosophy. Or perhaps we might resolve — again as so many others have done — that if there is a foundation for our ethical choices, then this foundation must be heteronomous in some way or other.

I will not presume in this brief essay to decide which of these options is least unKantian. I do not think that will be an easy decision.[30]

Duke University

[29] Much as Gödel has posited such an intuition in mathematics.

[30] I would like to thank the National Endowment for the Humanities for support allowing me to attend the Institute on Kantian Ethical Theories at Johns Hopkins University in the summer of 1983. I am grateful to the participants at that institute and especially to its Directors, Professor Jerome Schneewind and David Hoy, for guiding my first steps in studying Kant's ethical writings. Research for this paper was begun in the summer of 1985, when I visited the Bergman Center for Philosophical Studies at the Hebrew University of Jerusalem. That visit was partially supported by an NEH summer stipend. I would also like to thank Professor Yirmiyahu Yovel for arranging that visit and for several stimulating discussions which influenced my thinking on the topics covered in this paper. This paper also benefited greatly from the comments made on an earlier version by the participants in the Carnegie Mellon University philosophy colloquium.

Yirmiyahu Yovel

The Interests of Reason:
From Metaphysics to Moral History

When studying the relation of Kant's practical philosophy to the theoretical, one tends to stress either a set of *structural* analogies and similarities or the *material* way in which Kant supposes the two domains to complement one another. My own approach in this paper will be to link them programmatically, from the standpoint of Kant's *philosophical program* and the "interests of reason" which are said to underlie it. This, for Kant, is the standpoint of the "architectonic of reason," the meta-philosophical theory which refers to reason as a system of ends or rational interests, and explicates the way in which these ends are to co-exist and be harmonized in the pure system of reason — that is, in the thought and action of rationally-enlightened humans. As a by-product it also explains the conflicting and impure modes in which these rational interests are manifest historically in the course of reason's self-evolution and before its pure system has been fully and coherently brought to light.[1]

By Kant's "philosophical program" I do not mean a subjective interest of Kant as author but what he takes to be an objective interest of reason itself. This interest is defined by the "essential ends" of reason (Kant's term, A839/B867) and their state of explication in a given philosophical culture. In this respect Kant views himself as responding to a "need of reason" (again his term, Prol. 4: 367/116) which is both structural and historical. Kant's philosophical program is designed to satisfy this need in two stages, first in the theoretical and then in the practical branch of his system. Thereby it links them from the viewpoint which provides "architectonic" unity to the system as a whole. The same architectonic viewpoint also makes it possible to understand Kant in the way he understood himself, that is, by reading his actual work in light of his meta-philosophy.

---

[1] For a more complete discussion of the architectonic of reason and its historization, see my *Kant and the Philosophy of History* (Princeton University Press, 1980, 1989), especially the Introduction and Chapter 6.

Y. Yovel (ed.), Kant's Practical Philosophy Reconsidered, 135-148.

Reason as Interest

Philosophy, to Kant, is a goal-directed activity. It expresses "essential ends of human reason" as they stand in relation to one another within the pure system of philosophy, or (before the latter is fully uncovered) within a certain philosophical culture. To understand a philosophical system in a rational way, we have to understand it in view of the "unifying goal" that runs through all the parts and gives them architectonic, that is, rationally-teleological unity. Moreover, the unifying goal must not be borrowed from some external interest — political, theological, aesthetic, technological, etc. The goal must be set by reason itself and should express its nature as the pursuit of ends which are inherently rational, rather than as a mere instrument for promoting goals that are set beforehand by other interests. Human rationality is not merely a means and an auxiliary to something else but an end in itself. Its instrumental capacity — the power to calculate, to infer, to foresee, to design a strategy and adjust means to an end — should be used above all in the service of its own interests, the inherent ends which human rationality sets to itself by its own nature. These Kant calls the "essential ends of human reason"; they specify the principle that rationality should be pursued as an end in itself in all domains of knowledge and action.

Rationality as Goal-Oriented Autonomy

Rationality as end in itself is also, to Kant, the only coherent conception that maintains the autonomy or freedom of reason. Human reason, though limited, is nevertheless autonomous, not only because it prescribes to itself the norms it must obey, but also because it sets to itself the goals for which it mobilizes its instrumental capacity. *Both* these modes of self-determination are necessary conditions of autonomy — and rationality. Obeying a precept that the agent cannot recognize as derived (at least in principle) from the legislation of her own free reason is neither moral, nor rational, nor an act of autonomy. Similarly, using one's intellectual powers to further a goal prescribed by pleasure — or by political interest, economic advantage or technological efficiency and the like — does not testify to reason's autonomy but rather to its subordination, and therefore cannot count as genuinely rational. This alienated use of reason was expressed in medieval theology by the dictum that "philosophy is the handmaiden of Revelation." The analogous phenomenon in politics is often called "ideology" (following Marx and contemporary *ideologiekritik* in Germany). In modern economics, utility analysis, decision theory and game-theoretical models, rationality is reduced to a strategic skill — the capacity to maximize certain values which are externally given, to optimally adjust means to ends and offer the most efficient solutions to problems whose aims are presupposed. This, Kant would hold, is not "reason" (*Vernunft*) proper but its reduction to "understanding" (*Verstand*) or to mere intelligence, which is a subordinate skill and, severed from its inherent ends, heteronomous and not truly rational.

The view that rationality is an interested, goal-oriented activity also follows from two other major ideas of Kant. First, rational norms are not there, ready-made, existing *an sich* in some Platonic universe, but are *constituted* by the rational subject. The dynamic element of being-constituted is part of the meaning of the rational norm and a condition for its power to obligate. Being rational involves in Kant the dynamic move whereby the ego reconstitutes the rational norm to which it subordinates itself. Rationality thus involves sub-mission to self-imposed limitations, which reflect the immanent ends of the ego itself. Becoming rational is thus realizing rationality for its own sake within the subject's sphere of cognition and action — and thereby realizing one's own innermost structure. That this is equally the descripton of freedom, or autonomy, according to Kant's explication of this concept, is of course no accident.

Secondly, since human rational powers are finite, no one can be always rational. Every person must relate to rationality as a goal and hence also, to a certain extent, as a lack. At the outset, because of his or her limitation, the human person is not characterized as *being* rational but as *having to become* rational. The essential ends of reason are not clearly and necessarily realized in him — but must become so. Human rationality, as inherently limited, is thus the *pursuit* of its own realization. Hence the crucial concept of an "interest of reason" that pervades Kant's works, expressing itself in a ple-thora of dynamic metaphors like the "need" or "aspiration" of reason. Since human rationality is finite, there is an inevitable gap, at least at the outset, between the structural "end of reason" and the actual state of the subject (or of a given society or culture).

Philosophy and the Interests of Reason in Historical Contexts

Philosophy thus has a teleological nature: it is the realization of the funda-mental ends of rationality. Indeed, Kant defines philosophy as "the science of the relation of all knowledge to the essential ends of human reason," calling it also *teleologia rationis humanae* (a teleology of human reason, A839/B867). However, because of the finitude of human reason, the concept of an end-of-reason has not only a structural sense but also a developmental one. By its ideal structure, human reason is a coherent system of ends. It balances within itself both "regional" interests, like theory or practice, and "horizontal" interests which cut through the specific regions, such as the critical or the metaphysical interests of reason. Furthermore, the horizontal interests are harmonized, among other things, by a special hierarchical balancing of the regional interests (e.g., the Primacy of Pure Practical Reason).

Yet this harmony characterizes reason only in its latent or ideal model. So long as human reason has not become fully aware of itself and shaped through consciousness in accordance with its essential form, so long as it remains in relative obscurity and lacks complete explication, its essential ends (or some of them) are likely to fall into opposition and create an antinomy in its midst. Consequently, reason has another interest which, architectonically, is the most comprehensive and vital of all — the interest to overcome its inner antinomies and partial states of explication, and constitute itself as a harmony of interests. In other words, the historical (evolutionary) end of reason is the actualization of its inherent structural ends.

Moreover, the historical end of reason assumes each time a specific form, determined by the particular way in which its structural ends relate to each other *at a given stage of their evolution.* It is not sufficient, therefore, that a philosophical system (1) has coalesced through a "unity of purpose," which (2) expresses the fundamental ends of reason. The purpose which unites the philosophical system must also (3) be identical with the *specific* form which the historical end has assumed at a given stage, as a result of an incongruity between the fundamental ends of reason. If now we agree to call this latter, specific end the "need of reason" (a metaphor common in Kant), then we may say more briefly: a philosophical system is one whose unifying end corresponds to the "need of reason" at a given stage of reason's evolution.

How Does this Model Apply to Kant's Own System?

This model of philosophy in general, presented towards the end of the first *Critique*, seems to be actually satisfied by Kant's account of the "unifying purpose" of his own system, as given in the Prefaces to the first *Critique* and other programmatic texts. This purpose is the *critical renewal of metaphysics.* It corresponds to a need of reason, born of the antinomy which has arisen between two fundamental interests of reason at a given stage of its development: the metaphysical interest on the one hand, the critical interest and the spirit of the Enlightenment on the other.

The metaphysical interest inheres in reason throughout its whole evolution, gradually assuming higher degrees of rational explication — from magic and primitive religion to higher theology, dogmatic rationalism and, finally, to critical rationalism. The critical interest is equally a fundamental end of reason, of which, however, the mind becomes aware only after it has undergone considerable elucidation and rational development. The antinomy produced in reason between its metaphysical and critical interests has, therefore, a historical and essentially *modern* character; the antinomy occurs because reason has already matured and become critical and reflective, and yet has not attained complete elucidation and self-consciousness. Hence the link between the need to resolve this antinomy and the need to bring reason's self-explication to its *final* stage (which concludes the history of philosophy) — both overlapping in the "unifying goal" of Kant's *Critique*.

This goal is to be realized through a "revolution in the mode of thinking," the pattern of all significant intellectual advances according to Kant — in the sciences, in religion, and also in philosophy. The revolution caused by the *Critique* will conclude the tortuous historical journey of philosophical reason and lead it to complete self-explication. It will, thereby, both actualize and expound the true nature of reason as a harmonized system of interests. The ensuing philosophy will not only contribute to the sum of human *knowledge* but will redeem a distortion in culture and bring about a sort of mental emancipation. This may be understood in two ways.

First, the *Critique* is not a mode of philosophical self-consciousness only but also of self-*limitation*, whereby reason restrains itself in accordance with the laws of its own structure. The latter, however, is the Kantian definition of autonomy, or positive freedom, in general; hence *the Critique involves an act of autonomy already in the cognitive domain*, and is comparable, from this standpoint, to the autonomous act of morality (for which it serves as a latent paradigm) and also to the civilizing self-limitation involved in the transition from the "state of nature" to the civil state.

Secondly, by resolving the opposition that manifests itself in reason, the *Critique* is to enable the enlightened individual to express his rational powers and interests in a balanced, undistorted manner, without having to repress or discard one essential interest because of the other. In this respect the *Critique* does not only resolve a logical antinomy but redeems an alienated state of mind: it concerns the philosopher's individual existence as a rationally-interested being and the tensions within the culture in which he or she lives — a fact that Kant's dry scholastic idiom and lofty use of the term "reason" sometimes makes his readers overlook.

Kant's Unifying Goal as Realized in the System

Having identified Kant's "unifying goal" as the creation of a *critical metaphysics*, let me briefly sketch how this program is supposed to join the various parts of Kant's system together and be realized in them.

In general terms, the metaphysical interest is reconciled to the critical interest first by establishing a limited "metaphysics-as-science" in the cognitive field, and then by diverting the extra-scientific surplus of metaphysics to channels of moral and historical action (praxis). Moreover, frustrating the metaphysical interest in its higher, speculative quest is a necessary precondition for satisfying this interest by way of a *metaphysics of practive.*

I shall survey this move according to its main stages. They parallel, more or less, the Analytic and the Dialectic of the Critiques of speculative and practical reason.

1. *The Critical Metaphysics-as-Science*

In the first stage a new metaphysics, transcendental but not transcendent, is to be created. The new metaphysics no longer opposes the critical principle but incorporates it within itself. Metaphysics in general is, for Kant, an a priori science dealing with supersensible issues and linked to the problem of existence; and the major demand of critical reason is to avoid all existence-claims wherever no relevant empirical observation can be adduced. The new transcendental metaphysics satisfies this demand, because it claims to know and determine of itself no actual entity whatsoever — neither within nature nor beyond it. Transcendent metaphysics, the traditional kind that Kant calls "dogmatic," pretends to know supersensible *entities* existing beyond nature. By contrast, the new metaphysics only claims to know the existence-*conditions* of the natural existents themselves, that is, it claims to determine a priori the synthetic-logical structure of nature in general as a unified system — a structure which all its existents share and embody and by virtue of which they count as — and are — empirically objective. This metaphysics, therefore, is immanent and not transcendent, critical and not dogmatic. It remains an a priori science dealing with supersensibles, although the latter are no longer separate entities, but the metaphysical constituents of natural objects and the ontological conditions of their objective existence or actuality (*Wirklichkeit*). Critical metaphysics thus maintains its special link to the problem of existence, not by actually ascribing existence to supersensible entities, but by expounding the super-empirical conditions for determining objective existence in general and thereby offering a systematic explication of its meaning.

Through this shift, transcendental metaphysics not only satisfies the critical principle but makes it part of its own system. One of the a priori conditions for objective existence requires that candidates for such existence be observable in space and/or time and be the product of empirical syntheses. In this manner, the critical principle that empiricist philosophy has professed onesidedly and as mere dogma, now finds its proper place and rational "deduction" — that is, derivation and justification — within the new critical metaphysics, where it functions as one of the *non*-empirical conditions for the existence of empirical objects. Since Kant believes he has found the complete list of these conditions and given them systematic unity, he feels entitled to declare that, thus far, his program "succeeds as well as could be desired, and promises to metaphysics, in its *first* part [i.e., the Analytic of the first *Critique*]... the secure path of a science" (Bxviii).

To understand Kant's claim of success we should emphasize that the science he offers in the Transcendental Analytic is not a theory of knowledge merely but, with regard to nature, also a theory of being, an ontology. This is due to the Copernican revolution, which states that the epistemological conditions for knowing real entities in nature are the same as the ontological conditions for these entities to actually be what they are. Hence, in uncovering the necessary structure of knowing the world, we have ipso facto uncovered the fundamental structure of the world itself. In other words, we possess the system of primary forms and principles which, by structuring the objects in nature, constitute their objectivity and thereby their actual existence. Thus, without actually determining the existence of any particular object, transcendental science describes the logical-metaphysical substrate of nature in general (*natura formaliter spectata*) and of everything that can validly claim objective existence.

According to the Copernican revolution, the conditions for correctly describing objective entities and states of affairs are equally the conditions for these entities and states of affairs to *be* what they are and what the description claims them to be. From the Copernican perspective, therefore, all analysis of the structure of knowledge is equally an analysis of the structure of the known reality. Moreover, the ontological significance of the Transcendental Analytic is also what accounts for its epistemological force. Knowing a priori the conditions of the possibility of real objects in nature, we rightly claim to know something about the real world even before we turn to observe it. This a priori knowledge, to be sure, is as yet "empty" or only conditional; as long as it has not been linked to observation and measurement, and thereby realized in an empirical synthesis, this metaphysics of knowledge lacks interpretation and cannot determine the existence of a single object. Yet it already tells us, conditionally, something significant about the real world: we know that if nature exists at all, then, necessarily,[2] all its objects are effects of causes, all are observable and mathematically quantifiable, all exist in time and stand in some reciprocal relation, etc. It is by virtue of its ontological significance that transcendental science allows us to know the supreme laws and essential structures of any possible world, even before we can assert its existence, and without knowing the material aspect of its objects or the *particular* formulas that govern its laws. The Analytic is thus supposed to figure as critical metaphysics, which yields the a priori or "supersensible" foundation of the natural world and its objects; and without making particular existence-claims, it provides a systematic explication of the meaning and conditions of empirical existence as such.

2. Metaphysics as Speculation: The Ultimate Objects

Cognitively, however, the "metaphysics-as-science" has succeeded only within a restricted domain. Its range is confined to existents that are *conditioned* in a dual sense: (1) each is conditioned by others in a causal chain, and (2) all are conditioned by the structure of the knowing mind; that is, they are "phenomenal" and not "things-in-themselves." Consequently, the "first part" of the system has failed to attain that which, in the final analysis, is the highest objective of metaphysics: the absolute (or unconditioned) and the total. This form of the metaphysical interest is incompatible with the critical interest and must, in its cognitive mode, be thwarted by it. This too is done in two stages, one in the domain of knowledge, the other leading beyond it.

First, the transcendent-directed drive of the metaphysical interest is re-oriented into immanent use, producing (in the "regulative idea") a *heuristic methodology of the natural sciences* that replaces dogmatic metaphysics.

---

[2] The kind of necessity involved here is characteristic of Kant's view of metaphysics. It is neither logical nor empirical necessity, for it is not derived from the analysis of the meaning of terms or from observable fact. The necessity here is of a synthetic kind we may call meta-empirical, or metaphysical in Kant's sense; it does not obtain from the standpoint of formal logic, but from that of Kant's new transcendental logic, which endows empirical states of affairs with necessary links even though their negations are not self-contradictory. At the same time, this metaphysics — unlike Spinoza's, or other rationalists' — is unable to explain why nature exists at all and why its particular contents are what they are: these facts remain rationally inexplicable and irremediably contingent.

Instead of leading to spurious speculations about God, the soul, and the cosmos as a whole, the same metaphysical interest that usually leads reason astray is here deflected into immanent use, and serves as a methodological guideline and spur for expanding our valid empirical knowledge, both in gaining greater information about natural phenomena and in providing a more profound and continuous systematization of what we already know.

Yet this is only part of the shift. The ultimate form of the metaphysical interest is not abolished, but rather re-channelled from its devious cognitive mode into the field of moral and historical praxis. The second part of the shift consists, then, in transferring the ultimate metaphysical concerns from one regional interest of reason to the other, thus creating a *metaphysics of ethical practice* (*Metaphysik der Sitten*). If reason, in its cognitive interest, cannot know the absolute and the total, then in its practical use it can *engender* and *shape* them. This allows them, too, to figure within the legitimate range of critical reason, the objects not of human knowledge but of human creation. Moreover, thwarting the cognitive pretense of reason to attain the absolute is itself a precondition for satisfying it in the practical domain, since free morality must not presuppose a divine lawgiver. To be autonomous, morality must be grounded in the rational will of man, not of God, so that denying reason's ability to determine God's existence is also a critical prerequisite of morality, politics, and historical action — all being based on human reason and legislation rather than on God's transcendent guidance. Thus a further systematic link is secured between the first and the second *Critiques*, derived from the same "unifying goal."

3. *The Metaphysics of Ethical Practice*

Transforming the metaphysical interest into a metaphysics of ethical practice is the *Critique*'s major enterprise after it had established a restricted metaphysics-as-science in the field of knowledge. The metaphysics of ethical practice is also divided into two stages roughly corresponding to an Analytic and a Dialectic, but now a major difference should be noted. In the field of knowledge, totality and unconditionality referred to the same objects (God, or the universe as a whole) and formed a systematic pair within the Dialectic. Indeed, the concept of totality provided the logical interpretation of the concept of the absolute, its translation from the vague language of aspiration to that of distinct logical structures. In the field of praxis, in contrast, the two concepts are relegated to different domains: the (moral) absolute discussed in the Analytic takes the form of the categorical imperative and is attained already on the level of individual acts; whereas the (moral) totality is expressed in the ideal of the Highest Good put forward by the Dialectic, and is to be attained, or rather promoted, by the combined historical effort of the human race.[3]

4. *The Absolute: The Moral Law*

The theory of the categorical imperative explicates the role of reason in producing morality. Every moral act has an absolute value and, moreover, it creates this value of itself. Since moral acts derive exclusively from reason (which manifests itself in them as "practical"), they offer a legitimate channel in which reason's search for the absolute can be validly satisfied. The critical transformation of reason's ultimate quest into this practical channel is, in Kant's view, a realization of its fundamental structure: it re-directs reason from a devious *cul de sac* (the spurious attempt to *know* the absolute) into its genuine task (the duty to *create* it as moral value). This has also a semi-religious effect, since the moral law legislated by human reason inherits the elevated and awe-inspiring qualities that religion ascribes to divine decrees. Moreover, the moral act is supposed to evoke in the agent a mental repercussion potentially as powerful as the experience of the sublime. Hence, in transforming the ultimate metaphysical concerns of the human mind with their halo of sublimity and infinity, the critique does not merely put forward an abstract philosophical principle but, thereby, performs an act of profound cultural and existential implications.

5. *The Totality: The Historical End*

The theory of the categorical imperative relates to individual and disconnected acts. Every act recreates the absolute value in itself, independently of other acts by the same agent or by other persons, and regardless of the kind of *world* they help to produce. The flaw in this picture is that another basic interest of reason — totalization — is still missing. This flaw is however

---

[3] I use 'Analytic' and 'Dialectic' in a broad systematic sense rather than as part-titles in the second *Critique*. In the sense I use, the Dialectic includes such issues as the kingdom of ends, the religious and political doctrines, or the moral physico-theology at the end of the third *Critique* (and many others), even though they appear in other Kantian texts. Thus, the major bulk of the *Groundwork* falls within the Analytic.

corrected in Kant's Dialectic and its predominant idea of the "Highest Good." The Highest Good is a synthesis of the ethical idea with empirical reality, which ought to be realized by human action in history; it is the *name* of an ideal world to come ("the best of worlds") that the human race should establish on the basis of the existing natural world by reshaping its orders and endowing them with a new, human meaning and moral reorganization.

In its fully developed sense, the Highest Good functions as the regulative idea of history; in its light, all the disparate actions of men and women and all the domains of their collective endeavor (politics, law, education, etc.) should unite in leading to one comprehensive end. The historical end does not detract from the absolute character of the moral action but supplements it with the element of totalization. The imperative "act to promote the Highest Good in the world" (which we may call *the historical imperative*) requires that every moral action should have absolute value in itself (i.e., be performed from the categorical imperative) and at the same time contribute to promote the historical goal.

This picture has yet to be completed by observing the position of religion, aesthetics, and the theory of the practical postulates.

6. *The Religion of Reason*

Kant's theory of religion expresses the same transformation we have been discussing. It transfers to the ethics of human reason all the divine attributes and exalted emotions that were traditionally associated with the historical religions and with the will of God expressed in their commands. What is now considered divine is the autonomous law of human reason and no longer the decree of a transcendent will. Furthermore, it is *human* action that is now required to bring about "the kingdom of God upon earth," that is, to create a moral world in the midst of the natural world and using its materials. The religion of reason thus negates the historical religions in their origin while preserving and transforming their essential message, which is declared to be exclusively moral and anchored in the authority of the rational *human* will. God is neither presupposed by this religion as lawgiver, nor admitted even as an actual being. The religion of reason, true to the critical move and expanding it, disclaims any cognitive import. It teaches no truth — either metaphysical, historical, or para-scientific. Its primary role is to reshape the metaphysical interest into a moral-historical ideal, i.e., the Highest Good represented in the metaphor of the "kingdom of God on earth"; and in addition, organized as a "church," it is meant to provide the institutional means for the propagation of that ideal through moral education. Consequently, the supreme status and elevated mental states that used to be associated with revealed religion are now transferred to the domain of moral history, in which the ultimate drives of the metaphysical interest have been invested.

7. *The Quasi-Speculative Appendix: The Postulates*

This transference has also a quasi-speculative appendix, the theory of the practical postulates. In essence, this theory authorizes a rational agent (engaged in performing a moral action) to believe that the minimal conditions required to make his action metaphysically possible are satisfied even if this belief can neither be proved nor disproved by ordinary cognitive methods. Thus, in the context of moral action and in this context alone, the agent has *rational* grounds for believing that he or she possesses metaphysical freedom, both in the sense of free choice and indetermination by natural processes, and the power to intentionally intervene in these processes; the agent is also rationally entitled to believe that the world is so made that it can respond to moral action and be reshaped by it into a good world (as if the world had been created by "a moral world-creator" who had impressed this potentiality upon it). These are cognitive propositions that no other cognitive propositions can prove or refute; yet in the context of moral action, reason allows them to be accepted as assuredly as religious believers would accept them on *non*-rational grounds. In this way, the ultimate objects are readmitted into the critical theory as objects not of knowledge but of a morally justified "rational faith."

Elsewhere[4] I have questioned the validity of this method of postulation and the principle of the "primacy of pure practical reason" upon which it is based. Among other flaws, it warrants a procedure whereby, under certain conditions, one learns something about the real world from moral considerations of duty and Ought. Moreover, rather than offering a rational argument, this method seems to involve "reason" in an act of dogmatic authorization, as if it were a pontifical power; which may lead an unsympathetic critic to claim that the whole theory of the postulates is based on a logic of self-deception.

And yet, it is crucial to realize that the theory of the postulates occupies a subordinate and secondary position in Kant's system. The existence of God, freedom and immortality is postulated as *auxiliary* to the Highest Good and

---

[4] See the Epilogue of my *Kant and the Philosophy of History.*

its prospect of realization; nor is it into these postulates that the *Critique* re-directs the metaphysical interest, but rather into the idea of moral history which alone gives meaning and validity to the postulates themselves. In retrospect, when the program of the *Critique* has been carried out, the highest end-concept which unifies the system thus produced turns out to be the Highest Good, as the supreme moral-historical ideal under which all the interests of reason (both "regional" and "horizontal") are to be systematized.

Conclusion

Looking at Kant's system programmatically from the standpoint of the "unity of purpose" which unites its various parts and the interests of reason which it proposes to satisfy, we found that, on their deep, architectonic level, Kant's practical and theoretical doctrines are linked by the underlying pro-gram to create a critical metaphysics. In yielding a "metaphysics of ethical practice," morality, politics, religion, and their encompassing domain of moral history, are to provide human reason with a legitimate field in which to satisfy the metaphysical interest in its ultimate and totalizing thrust. What the critique of knowledge had to frustrate, the philosophy of ethical action can and ought to make possible. Although we may not affirm any absolute *entities* to exist, human action ought to create the absolute as *norm and value* and imprint it upon nature. Moreover, discrete moral actions will not do; the overall face of the world must be reformed in a totalizing effort, in which further sectors of human life and experience are reshaped in light of the moral idea and brought under its dominion.

This involves a re-channelling of reason's transcendent metaphysical drive back into the immanent domain, and its transformation from a futile effort to *know* the world as one totality into the task of reshaping it as a *moral* totality. The metaphysical query, "what is the ultimate purpose of being," is trans-formed and given its answer by moral history: the world exists for the sake of the *moral* world it can and should eventually become through human action in history. In consequence, the ultimate objective of metaphysics is no longer Truth or Being as such but the Good, more precisely, the Highest Good, taken as a historical ideal.

Critical metaphysics thus begins as theory and ends as praxis; it starts by explicating the a priori structure of nature and ends by projecting a semi-messianic ideal, for which it also provides the drive to act and the grounds for hoping it can be achieved. Unwittingly (and even without directly relying on Kant), this transformation was reproduced in many nineteenth century ideologies, which sought to transfer the power of religious commitments and beliefs to channels of social and political reform.

However, Kant's move is, I think, untenable in terms of the same concepts he uses at the basis, those of the "interests of reason." A case can be made for accepting the metaphysical interest of reason as a *sui generis* interest, unassimilable to those of action and morality. A harsher critic will even see this move as irrational, a form of self-deception in which a genuine interest of reason is repressed, masked under the guise of another interest and silenced by the humdrum of daily social action and endeavor.

This is another, perhaps deeper significance of the primacy of the practical interest in Kant, which cannot be admitted either in itself or in Kant's own terms, because it does infringe upon the autonomy of a genuine rational interest and subordinates it to another. The cognitive metaphysical interest cannot be obliterated without distorting human rationality: if the ultimate questions of this interest are found to have no critical answer, so be it; this philosophical discovery has a salutary value in itself, and points to the genuine rational stand; the proper response to this discovery is neither to dismiss the metaphysical queries as meaningless, nor to pretend answering them: both alternatives are equally irrational. There must necessarily remain a gap, a tension, between the queries and their impossible answer, and this gap is the *genuine* and authentic feature of the human situation.

I take this to be Kant's own position, the pure and strict (and also radical) meaning of his critical move. But if so, then Kant should have refrained from the alleged "sublimation" of the ultimate cognitive queries by transporting them into another domain, a move that distorts a genuine metaphysical interest and must end up in its repression and illusory satisfaction.[5]

The Hebrew University of Jerusalem

---

[5] For a precise and more detailed critique of this issue, see the Epilogue of my *Kant and the Philosophy of History*, esp. pp. 287-306. I should add that historically, too, the messianic movements that submerged metaphysical energies in absolute social and political schemes have, by this unwarranted shift, produced not only intellectual distortion but enormous suffering and evil.

Otfried Höffe

Kant's Principle of Justice as Categorical Imperative of Law

Since Kant published the *Groundwork* more than two hundred years ago, the concept of the categorical imperative has been under such scrutiny that one might be tempted to consider the subject exhausted. Using the categorical imperative of Law as a catchword I would like to counter this temptation by drawing attention to an as yet little-noticed aspect of the concept.

We are familiar with two distinctions from the traditional discussion of the categorical imperative: the difference between the basic form ("universal law," G 421/88) and the three subordinate forms (universal law of nature, G 421/88; "humanity...always at the same time as an end," G 429/96; "the kingdom of ends as a kingdom of nature," G 436/104); and that between the highest moral principle and substantive moral rules. If there is a categorical imperative of Law, these distinctions do not suffice, and we must differentiate between two conceptual levels within the moral principle, in that way obtaining three levels of the categorical imperative: a general categorical imperative indifferent to any distinction between Law and virtue; the application of this general concept of the categorical imperative to the two basic realms of human praxis, Law and virtue, leading respectively to the categorical imperative of Law and the categorical imperative of virtue; and the substantive legal and ethical principles of categorical obligations within these basic realms.

My main concern is with a somewhat neglected area of Kant's moral philosophy, viz., his moral theory of Law. In Rawls's *Theory of Justice* and the Kantian interpretation of "Justice as Fairness" (Rawls, par. 40) Kant's moral philosophy acquires new systematic importance. Rawls and other "neo-Kantians" among contemporary philosophers, such as Apel and Habermas, refer almost exclusively to the *Groundwork* and the second *Critique*. However, the appropriate texts are, in fact, Kant's works in legal philosophy, especially the *Elements of Justice*.[1] My paper will be primarily concerned with an

---

[1] Kant's theory of Law was initially received very favourably by philosophers and

Y. Yovel (ed.), Kant's Practical Philosophy Reconsidered, 149-167.

analysis of these works, secondarily with a renewed legal and political ethic, based upon a specially legal categorical imperative.

1. *Is There a Categorical Imperative of Law?*

There are many arguments for the second level, and thus for a categorical imperative of Law. The principal argument is this: the *Groundwork* outlines a metaphysics of morals in general, a program which Kant later carried out with his philosophy of Law as its first part. Since the categorical imperative constitutes the moral criterion developed in the *Groundwork*, it will also be valid for the philosophy of Law.

The second example with which Kant illustrates the application of the categorical imperative in the *Groundwork* is taken from the legal domain. Prohibition of false promises falls under the principle *pacta sunt servanda*, whose "legislation is contained in *Jus* and not in Ethics" (RL 220/20).[2] The law of contract, to which the (contractual) promise belongs, even acquires a specific significance in the *Elements of Justice*; here Kant speaks of a "trans-cendental deduction" (RL 272). If Kant is generally sparing in his use of the concept of the transcendental in his practical philosophy, he is even more miserly in his use of the notion of transcendental deduction.

The fact that the categorical imperative emerges, though only incidentally, under the common "rudimentary-concepts" of the *Metaphysics of Morals*, also speaks in favour of a categorical imperative of Law (RL 221/22; 222f/23f). Moreover, Kant calls the *Elements of Justice* "metaphysical," by which he means knowledge, the validity of which is prior to all experience (RL 205f/3f); consequently, the title clearly shows that Kant is seeking an *a priori* principle of Law. Finally, the Preface calls the concept of Law (Justice) a pure, hence pre-empirical, concept (RL 205/3).

It might be argued that since the *Groundwork* provides the foundation for both parts of the *Metaphysics of Morals*, that is, for the *Elements of Justice* as well as for the *Doctrine of Virtue*, its categorical imperative should be the general imperative, indifferent to the distinction between Law and virtue. Yet there are reasons for denying that this is the case. Law and virtue differ in the

---

jurists, but later fell into disregard due to the influence of Hegel's *Philosophy of Right* (1821) and the historical school of justice (v. Savigny), only to acquire renewed significance in neo-Kantianism, e.g. with Cohen, Stammler (cf. Ebbinghaus 1973), though at the cost of a mistaken interpretation (see below section 3).
[2] Cf. the famous example of the deposit in KpV 27.

kinds of obligation they impose. Thus, Law is defined by the competence (authority) to impose obligations on persons whereas Ethics pertains to self-obligation. Law and Ethics relate to each other as external to internal coercion respectively. Where one accomplishes moral duties out of a free and personal conviction Kant speaks of morality, and where such free self-obligation is absent, Kant speaks of (mere) legality. Now the fact that Kant sets personal motivation at the core of the *Groundwork* speaks against the claim that the categorical imperative in the *Groundwork* is a general categorical imperative indifferent to the Law/Ethics distinction. Insofar as it is concerned with "acting from duty," that is, with morality and not legality, the categorical imperative developed in the *Groundwork* cannot be a general imperative but is, rather, an imperative specific to Ethics or Virtue.

The evidence for the specific ethical significance of the categorical imperative in the *Groundwork* is so abundant that a few examples will suffice. Already in the Preface to the *Groundwork* (390/58) the as yet undeveloped metaphysics of morals is subordinated to the investigation of the "idea and principles of a possible pure will." But, according to Kant, "pure will" acts "from duty" (398/66) and out of "reverence for the law" (400/68); hence it is defined in relation to morality, not legality. Finally, regarding the object of morality, the moral good, the Preface says that it is not sufficient that it should *conform* to the moral law, it must also be done *"for the sake of the moral law"* (390/58).

In the *Groundwork* this programme is carried out in the famous introductory sentence, according to which "it is impossible to conceive anything at all in the world as good without qualification, except a good will." Here, again, the good will stands for morality and not legality.

Even in the examples in the *Groundwork*, through which Kant tests the applicability of the categorical imperative, what is at stake is the fundamental motivation. Kant clearly sees no need to determine in what the morally required or prohibited consists; he takes this as self-evident. What he wants to show is what it means to satisfy the moral duty in those not infrequent cases in which duty does not coincide with, but rather contradicts, self-interest. For that reason Kant constructs his examples in such a way as to show that the morally correct action is endangered by a conflicting self-interest. Whoever abides by it even in this situation can be said to act out of duty, that is, not just legally, but morally as well.

Morality is not, of course, contained in the criterion of universalizability to which the categorical imperative is sometimes conveniently reduced. Two further elements are required. In the first place, the categorical imperative begins with the exhortation, "Act...!" To that extent it is not primarily a *principium diiudicationis*, but a *principium executionis*, not an evaluative but a motivational principle. In the second place, the object on which universalizability bears does not consist, as in the traditional reading of the categorical imperative, in any particular set of action rules: universalizability is required by maxims. And according to the *Doctrine of Virtue*, it is precisely here that the distinction between virtue, or ethics, and law lies. In chapter six, Kant says that Ethics gives laws "only for the *maxims* of actions" whereas the Law (*Jus*) gives such laws directly for actions.

As distinct from the usual rules of action, maxims have to do with determinations of the will, which are not objective schematisms but principles imposed by the actor himself, subjectively, on his own deeds and forbearances. Furthermore, maxims represent rules of the second order. They are principles which give rules of action of the first order their normative orientation. Maxims determine the manner in which a person leads his life as a whole. For example, one is following a maxim in living according to the resolution to be considerate or inconsiderate, to respond to results vindictively or magnanimously, to be helpful or indifferent in critical situations. Maxims, according to their verbal meaning of (*sententiae*) maximae, are the *ultimate* self-imposed (legislated) principles of the will.

Were the third element of the definition omitted, so that maxims were understood as any principles of the will whatever, the categorical imperative would remain indifferent as regards the ultimate motivation. This still leaves open the issue, whether the morally correct, universalizable principles are heeded for their own sake or out of self-interest, for example, in order to avoid legal sanctions. In this way a categorical imperative which is indifferent to the distinction between law and morality could be acquired. However, prescinding from the fact that this might mean giving up the potent concept of the higher-order principles of the will, one is still deviating from the arguments of the *Groundwork* for the explication of a pure or good will. In any event, though, what this shows is that the distinction between the general and the ethically specific categorical imperative is very tenuous, and that perhaps Kant did not always respect the distinction in the *Groundwork*.

If one follows the specific ethical interpretation of the *Groundwork*, however, including the resulting interpretation of the categorical imperative, the following consequence is inevitable: contrary to what the title seems to suggest, and contrary to the views of interpreters like G. Scholz (151ff.), the *Groundwork* does not lay the basis of the whole metaphysics of morals, but only a part thereof, viz., ethics. Of course, the *Groundwork* nowhere denies a categorical imperative of Law. But neither does it develop its necessary basis, that is, the general moral imperative. Up to this point, it could be inferred from the negative result of the inquiry into a categorical imperative of Law, that Kant either does not take it as an object of moral investigation or else has not clearly distinguished between Law and Ethics (or virtue). However, since Kant concerned himself with moral legal philosophy, with natural law, well before his critical period and never gave up this interest (cf. Ritter, 168ff),[3] we can reject this second supposition as well.

Because Kant, like so many thinkers of the past, but unlike almost all significant philosophers of our century, took a strong interest in Law and was aware of its specificity, many of his interpreters have tried to understand the problematic unity of the *Groundwork* (and the *Critique of Practical Reason*) with the *Elements of Justice* in light of the theory of virtue, that is, Ethics, ascribing to it, for instance, the function of protecting moral freedom. According to this ethically relative interpretation of Law, the specifically ethical interpretation of the *Groundwork* is confirmed, but not recognized as a limitation; since Ethics precedes Law, the investigation of a categorical imperative of Law seems superfluous.

This "moral ennoblement" of Law (Kersting, 46) in fact constitutes its "ethification" and is erroneous; it is justified neither by the essence of the subject matter, nor by Kant. To be sure, Law should protect freedom; it is, however, directed not to moral ("inner") freedom, but to freedom of action ("external freedom").

The desired "harmonization of Law and Ethics" (Kühl, 57) is therefore conceivable neither through the subordination of Law to Ethics nor through their separation, but only from a juxtaposition of Law and Ethics and their common subordination to the moral point of view, that is, the general categorical imperative.

It may be that Kant occasionally expressed himself inaccurately. He speaks, for example, of a "universal law of freedom" (RL 230/34) which leads one to confuse the law of freedom with the principle of moral subjectivity, the transcendental freedom. But on the whole his affirmations are clear and distinct. Law has the competence (authority) to impose obligations on others; Ethics and Law relate to each other as self-coercion to external coercion. But because self-coercion by definition cannot be governed by external force,[4] moral freedom cannot be protected by the Law in any case. Though an

---

[3] For the question whether Kant's philosophy of Law is uncritical, see also Busch, Ilting, Sänger.

[4] "Another can indeed *compel* me to do something that is not my end (but only a means to his end), but he cannot compel me *to make it my end*" (TL 381/39. I used M.J. Gregor's translation in the *Doctrine of Virtue*).

"ethification of Law" presumes encroachments which are morally illegitimate, it cannot guarantee moral freedom.[5]

Nevertheless, the claim that the categorical imperative of the *Groundwork* is
valid only for Ethics comes up against opposition, and critics can appeal to
one of the arguments I have adduced in favour of the categorical imperative of
Law, viz., the example of the false promise which involves legal duty. It
therefore seems most plausible to follow Dreier (291ff) and accord to the
categorical imperative of the *Groundwork* the status of a criterion for moral
behaviour in general, hence for legality rather than morality. According to
Dreier we can introduce a distinction between a juridical notion and a moral
one. In the case of a juridical notion, we do not require moral purity of
motivation, while in that of moral action, moral purity of motivation is
required.

This interpretation, insofar as it maintains that the *Groundwork* is concerned with legal questions as well as moral ones, and that the categorical
imperative can be taken in a juridical and a moral sense, is undoubtedly
correct. But the conclusion that the *Groundwork* and its categorical imperative refer to both the moral and the legal spheres is somewhat paradoxical.[6]

This paradoxical outcome results from the frequently overlooked twofold
definition of Ethics. In a formal sense, ethical virtue consists of "self-
coercion" of the "inner freedom" (TL Introd., sec. I, X). Here ethical virtue
and Law stand in opposition to one another, and the *Groundwork*, which
thematizes morality, is valid with respect to ethical virtue only, and not with
respect to Law, which is restricted to legality. Seen from the perspective of
their contents, however, legal duties are on the one hand to be distinguished
from ethical duties, while on the other, according to Kant, it belongs to the
nature of ethical virtue to satisfy duties, which, for this reason, he also calls
"indirect ethical duties" (RL 221/21). The *Groundwork*, therefore, is the
theory of Ethics in the widest sense of the term, viz., a groundwork of morality
which stipulates ethical virtue in a purely formal sense only, not Law, but
which refers materially to ethical virtue in the widest sense of the term

---

[5] Ladd (xi) says quite correctly: "It is no business of the state or... of other individuals
to try to make men moral."

[6] See Höffe 1979. In opposition to the opinion of many interpreters, that Kant's moral
principle is first of all a principle of Law/ Justice (e.g. Ritter, 340, also Dreier, 292),
closer examination reveals that rather the exact contrary turns out to be true. Kant's
first moral-critical writings, the *Groundwork* and the *Critique of Practical Reason*,
define that "first principle of morality" which embraces Law via the disposition to
Law and indirect ethical duties, but does not thematize it as Law, i.e., as the aggregate
of externally coerced claims.

(including legal duties). Materially, therefore, the *Groundwork* furnishes the basis for the entire *Metaphysics of Morals*; formally, however, it does so only for the second part, the Ethics.

In the domain of duty, too, the *Groundwork* brings morality into relief, extolling a "juridical morality" or a "disposition to trust the Law," whose "reverence for Law" (TL, Introd., sec. VII) extends beyond what is enforceable, what is due, to what is meritorious (ibid.) and seeks to satisfy what is legally prescribed, not out of fear of punishment, but freely, and also does so in all those peripheral zones which remain hidden from the "arm of the law," like a deposit without witnesses. Kant's philosophy of Law therefore contains a conceptual *instrumentarium* wherein the relationship between Law and morals can be understood as more finely differentiated than that usually advanced — separation or unity.

Law and Morality

materialiter

Legislation by pure practical reason

juridical   ethical

	juridical	ethical
Morality / *formaliter* \ Legality	juridical morality	ethical morality
	juridical legality/ legal duties[a]: give to each his due	ethical legality/ virtuous duties[b]: self-perfection happiness of others

a. indirect ethical duties   b. direct ethical duties

The categorical imperative of Kant's first moral critical writings is indeed more general than the ethically specific one understood from a material point of view; it consists in the ethical command: "do your duty from the motive of duty" (TL, Introd., sec. VII) referring to both legal duties and the duties of virtue. In order to acquire the general categorical imperative, the formal aspect of morality ("from duty") has to be abstracted (see Gregor, 18); the required imperative is "do your duty," to which it may be added "for whatever motives."

Because the aspect of motive, of morality, is embedded in the concept of a maxim, according to the basic formula of the *Groundwork*, the general categorical imperative is acquired as soon as the expression "maxim" is replaced by that of "principle," which is neutral as far as morality is concerned and signifies an arbitrary, not necessarily self-decreed principle. The required imperative therefore reads: "act only according to principles which can be conceived and willed as a universal law."

First, we can formulate a categorical imperative confined to virtue in a formal sense, i.e., a categorical imperative specific to morality, but materially including Ethics as well as Law. It reads: "act only according to maxims which can be conceived and willed as a universal law." Or, simply: "act internally only according to universalizable principles!"

As distinguished from the categorical imperative specific to morality, there is the categorical imperative specific to legality. It reads: "act externally only in agreement with principles which can be conceived and willed as a universal law!" But we cannot identify the categorical imperative specific to legality with that categorical imperative which is the moral criterion for Law and State. For in addition to the formal difference between morality and legality, *materialiter*, a further distinction between juridical legislation and ethical-moral legislation is still to be drawn. The categorical imperative of legality limits legality to the sphere of juridical legislation of pure practical reason. In juridical as opposed to ethical legislation, the categorical imperative of Law undergoes a thematic change; through the element of legality, as distinguished from morality, it incurs a motivational shift.

Without discussing the details, two limiting conditions can be formulated here. *First* the categorical imperative of Law refers only to duties to others and not to duties to oneself. According to Kant, even if one's own perfection can be morally required, and actions like suicide can be morally proscribed, men cannot demand these obligations of one another; they are under no obligation to one another to perform them. In short, duties to oneself are not a legitimate part of an authorized legal order of coercion. Kant therefore generally adheres to this restriction in his philosophy of Law. For at the very beginning he is concerned with the coexistence of freedom of action in the relation of individuals to each other and not that of an individual to himself. An exception, however, is matrimonial law which Kant infers from a "duty of man to himself" (RL 280).

In the domain of duties to others, the *second* limiting condition, duties which are done out of one's virtue or integrity have to be distinguished from duties owed to someone. As long as behaviours and attitudes like benevolence and sympathy, love of one's neighbour or, in a secularized form, solidarity, are moral obligations in the sense of meritorious duties, their accomplishment is not due to others; they do not constitute enforceable legal duties.

In addition to its thematic determination, the categorical imperative of Law has this motivational peculiarity, that what is morally demanded need not be performed as a result of personal conviction: mere compliance with the law suffices. Thus the categorical imperative of Law does not pertain to personal convictions concerning one's duty (convictions concerning lawfulness); self-interest is sufficient for the adherence to this imperative. This "sufficiency" has the crucial consequence that the enforcement of Law, that is, what is morally right, or justice, must coincide with self-interest. Therefore, it must lie in the very self-interest of people to pay their debts, and that must be beneficial to everyone. Further, self-interest must result in the fulfilment of what is in one's own interest. The first aspect is discussed by Kant under the title of "Private Law"; in order to prevent misunderstanding, it would be better to speak of a natural justice, that is, men's duties to one another unenforced by any positive legal or political system. Kant labels the second aspect "Public Law"; I speak of political justice whose actualization is guaranteed by political power.

Within the domain of external actions Kant distinguishes a pre-public Private Law, which is valid independently of the State, i.e., from the Public Law (RL 242/48). In this way we have — while still in the realm of principles — a third level at which a categorical imperative of Private Law and one of Public Law can be derived. And for the sake of completeness let it be remarked that both domains of Law are each in its own way subdivided, viz., Public Law is subdivided, for example, into State Law, Law of Nations and International Law. Within State Law, Criminal Law acquires a special significance; its categorical imperative would be a moral principle of the fifth level.

Levels of the Categorical Imperative (CI)

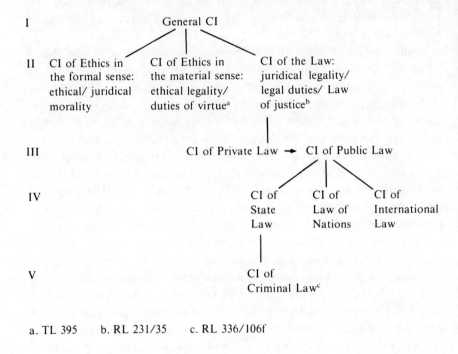

I
General CI

II   CI of Ethics in   CI of Ethics in   CI of the Law:
      the formal sense: the material sense: juridical legality/
      ethical/ juridical   ethical legality/   legal duties/ Law
      morality   duties of virtue[a]   of justice[b]

III   CI of Private Law → CI of Public Law

IV   CI of   CI of   CI of
                                               State   Law of   International
                                               Law   Nations   Law

V   CI of
                                               Criminal Law[c]

a. TL 395   b. RL 231/35   c. RL 336/106f

2. *The Categorical Imperative of Law in Kant's Elements of Justice*

Whereas in the *Groundwork* the purpose is to develop a general categorical imperative, the task of the *Metaphysics of Morals* is to specify the domains wherein this general concept applies. Therefore a categorical imperative of Law has to be present already in its first part, the *Elements of Justice*. As a moral concept and criterion of Law in general, the categorical imperative of Law would have its place in a general philosophy of Law which Kant places before the two main parts in the Introduction to the *Elements of Justice*: Private Law and Public Law. But whereas the Introduction to the *Doctrine of Virtue* (395) stipulates the categorical imperative as its first principle, the *Elements of Justice* is disappointing in this respect. The word appears neither in the title of a paragraph nor in the text nor does Kant introduce any modified expression, such as "categorical practical proposition." Nevertheless, it would be rash to regard this as a disconfirmation. For apart from the *modus imperandi*, the categorical imperative is equivalent to the moral law, respecting the fundamental law of pure practical reason (cf. KpV, §7). In §C of the Introduction to the *Elements of Justice* Kant formulates a "universal principle of Law/Justice" which in accordance with the moral point of view of the *Elements of Justice* is the "universal moral principle of Law" or the "moral principle of Law as a whole."

The universal principle of Law comprises, *first*, the conceptual elements of the general categorical imperative: (1.1) the requirement that there be an action which (1.2) is unconditionally binding and (1.3) which contains the standard of categorical obligation, universal lawfulness. *Secondly*, these conceptual elements are specified in such detail as is appropriate to the particular circumstances of Law, namely (2.1) legality ("act externally"), not morality (inner motivation), and (2.2) within legality appropriate to its juridical aspect, i.e., the compatibility of free will ("that the free use of your free will is compatible with the freedom of everyone"); ethical legality (duties to oneself and those out of respect and esteem to others) however remains excluded. *Finally* (2.3), being universal, the principle of Law enters neither into the object of Private Law (the external mine and yours), nor into that of Public Law (the public assurance of the external mine and yours), but is valid for the overall domain of the Law. In this way there is not merely a structural analogy between the universal principle of Law and a categorical imperative of Law. Rather, Kant's universal principle of Law *is* the principle of pure legal-practical reason in the *modus imperandi*, viz., the stipulated categorical imperative of Law.

There is a passage in one of Kant's works on legal and political philosophy, published after 1781, in which he speaks of a categorical imperative of Law. It occurs in *Zum ewigen Frieden* (*Perpetual Peace*) that appeared prior to the *Metaphysical Elements of Justice*. Why Kant drops the expression and does not use it in the *Metaphysical Elements of Justice*, is not made clear in the course of his development. A closer look at his *Reflexions*, however, could eventually provide an answer to this question.

It is possible to speak of a moral principle of Law in two senses: either as a principle that grounds the obligatory nature of the rules of Law or as a standard to which legal principles ought to conform. For it is morally required that either legal relations in general obtain between men or that those legal relations be determined by certain principles. For Kant's categorical imperative of Law, it is essential that both requirements be related to each other. To be sure, the imperative mentioned in §C does not yet require that a public juridical state of affairs be established.[7] The obligation *exendum e statu*

---

[7] For this reason the categorical imperative of Law is not, as Brandt supposes (238), included in the "law of permissiveness" of Private Law (§ 2), but in the more general

naturali comes much later, not in the Introduction to the *Elements of Justice* but in the transition from Private Law to Public Law; to put it in Kant's terms, it concerns the "transition from the mine and the yours in the natural state to the mine and the yours in juridical states in general" (RL §§ 41-43).

But apart from this, the imperative of Law lays down, first, the reciprocal restriction on the freedom of external action, whereby a mere or purely natural relation will be negated and a (doubtless, pre-public, i.e., natural) legal relation will be grounded; and second, it requires that the legal relations be formed according to a universal law whereby they become an inner-legal principle. The legal-moral *ought* comprises both the legitimation and the limitation of coercion in the relations between men.

3. *Is the Categorical Imperative of Law a Concept a priori?*

According to Kant, moral law and all moral concepts "have their seat and origin in reason completely a priori" (G 411/79). This contention applies also to the categorical imperative of Law. However, it involves a presupposition that even an orthodox Kantian would not like to regard as a priori: the coexistence of responsible agents. It is a contingent and historically recent fact that there are responsible agents who live in the same world and mutually influence one another through their actions. For that reason the legal task cannot be necessarily a priori as such, but at most in relation to this experiential fact. Despite what Kant believed (RL 205f, 3f), already the main "text," and not only the "annotations" of the *Elements of Justice* contains an empirical element.

To be sure, the empirical fact is not the justification of the (categorical) obligation; it concerns only the circumstances of its application. Further, it is an element which is unproblematical. Kant's presupposition is restricted to a plurality of persons who act voluntarily in the same world. Hence, however critical one might be of legal obligations or sceptical of their philosophical grounds, one should not take umbrage at this presupposition: for (1) whether it be a matter of inner ("virtue") or else external restrictions on freedom ("Law"), a discussion of the legitimacy or else illegitimacy of the restriction of freedom has sense only if there is freedom at all. Thus, freedom (of action) is necessarily the common presupposition of virtue and Law. However (2) the specific legal problem — the external, social restriction of freedom — is a

---

"law of permissiveness" of practical reason in the Introduction to the *Elements of Justice* (§ C).

reasonable subject for discussion only where there is another freedom which could restrict the first one. In that sense, the presupposition of a plurality of free agents is unavoidable. It should be noted that the radical counterproposal to legal relations does not consist in a world without responsible beings but in a society without Law. Consequently, there is an a priori, but a relative one, relative to the presupposition of coexistence — and that relative a priori is sufficient.

In his famous Inaugural Address, *Two Concepts of Liberty*, Isaiah Berlin suggests that in his political philosophy Kant, due to his concept of reason, is hostile to the negative concept of freedom, namely, the freedom to do and to forbear doing whatever one wants (37ff). Inasmuch as Berlin refers to the *Groundwork* for the view that Kant would condemn all that is "non-rational" in the name of "reason" he is correct in his claim but unjustified in reproaching Kant on this basis. For in the *Groundwork* the goal of the political community is not in issue at all; even if the *Groundwork* includes the Law in content, this is achieved formally with only respect to that side of morality which, though requiring the self-restriction of the will (*Willkür*), is not characteristic of Law and its political administration, but only of virtue. The negative freedom which Berlin demands for politics and finds lacking in Kant is treated in its proper place, in the *Elements of Justice*; and in the second chapter of the *Common Saying* Kant says with unmistakeable clarity that the Law must not turn men into autonomous, constantly self-determining individuals: "each may seek his happiness in whatever way he sees fit, so long as he does not infringe upon the freedom of others" (TP 290/74). Berlin cites Kant directly: "nobody may compel me to be happy in his own way,... a Paternal government ...is the greatest despotism imaginable" (22). Nevertheless it does not suffice to leave men their freedom to act. A legal order has to account for the conditions under which the coexistence of free agents is in general possible: "each may seek his happiness in whatever way he sees fit, so long as he does not infringe upon the freedom of others to pursue a similar end which can be reconciled with the freedom of everyone" (TP 290/74).

Because Kant presupposes freedom of action as given, a "speculative" interpretation like Shell's is disputable: "Through man's concept of right he first opposes nature and begins to discover his own freedom" (109). That man needs to discover his freedom is not a legal question for Kant, and in any case it is rather a Hegelian than a Kantian thesis.

Inasmuch as Kant succeeds in deriving the tasks set before the Law exclusively from the presupposition of the coexistence of persons, he gets by without specifying any merely empirical particularities of man, such as his society, his history and the nature in which he lives. The legal task is valid in "all possible worlds" in which responsible agents live. Kant himself did not demonstrate in the *Elements of Justice* that this in fact validly holds. But one can reason it out by way of a thought experiment, the basic elements of which can be gleaned from the Kantian definition of the task set before the Law.

The thought experiment is known as the "state of nature." In agreement with the most radical critics of Law, it posits a coexistence altogether free of Law. For that reason this "primary" state is distinguished not only from the state of nature as a historical assumption, but also from that "secondary" state of nature of Locke (*Second Treatise*, 4.6) and of Nozick (10f) in which men already possess inalienable rights. *Prima facie* their argument may appear more realistic, hence more reasonable in comparison with those of philosophers like Hobbes. However, they do not in fact think radically enough. For in a well-founded philosophy of Law, inalienable rights are not presuppositions but, on the contrary, demand proof; the thought experiment has therefore to start with a coexistence without those rights.

The thought experiment is the assumption of a socially unrestricted freedom of action which belongs to the primary state of nature. As no preceding obligations need be acknowledged, in this social perspective subjects are wholly free to posit and pursue "their" goals; in relation to other subjects they have a "right to everything."

The unrestricted freedom of action may be taken as a historical premise which holds good only for the "detached subject of the modern era," or more specifically still, for the early capitalist burgeoisie (cf. Macpherson). This opinion, however, fails to recognize the methodological significance of the state of nature theorem, namely, that in order to deal with the legitimation of the restriction of freedom, the opposite position is tentatively adopted — that there are no social restrictions — only in order to find that this assumption leads to contradiction, and hence, is not conceivable. The thought experiment of the primary state of nature thus constitutes a type of reflexion which begins with the conception of an unrestricted freedom and leads to the introduction of the social perspective.

It would likewise be wrong to interpret the unrestricted freedom of action as a "psychical indeterminism," whereby human desires are not subject to instincts, needs, interests and passions. For apart from the question whether they depend secondarily on socio-cultural conditions, instincts, etc. come "from within," and for that reason are premises of the state of nature theorem, and are left to the (subjective) will (*Willkür*).

Finally, it would be mistaken to conceive of the unrestricted freedom of action as man's omnipotence over nature. For in the thought experiment of the state of nature only the social aspect, that is, the interaction between free human beings, is in question: the external but non-social limits of freedom are not discussed, and are thematized no more than the inner limits. In strict adherence to the issue in point, i.e., the necessity or dispensability of moral restrictions on freedom, the primary state of nature is defined as the absence of Law, absence being construed in a radical sense: there are no legal obligations, and any other such absences remain beyond consideration.

The "right to everything" that holds in the state of nature signifies that property, labour power, even the life and limb of one person are not protected from interference by other persons. Thus, from a social perspective, the assumption of unrestricted freedom entails a problem, for a subject's decision to act in a certain way can conflict with that of another. To be sure, the conflict arises already at the moment in which the decision to act of one person conflicts with the decision of the other person. It is thus of secondary importance whether the conflict results in a struggle to the death, or whether one party deems the risk of death not worth taking, or the cause not worth fighting for. To this extent the thought experiment I am proposing is not tied to Hobbes's *bellum omnium contra omnes*, nor to the anthropological assumption that man's leading goal is self-preservation and happiness, nor to the claim that the leading goal together with the assumption of equality ("each can kill and be killed") and the mediating concept of the endless struggle for power lead necessarily to a state of war. The inevitable problem of the idea of the primary state of nature is likewise not a result — as it is in Rawls (§ 22) — of the distribution of the advantages and disadvantages of cooperation.[8] It derives more formally, hence more convincingly, from the freedom of action in its social perspective. On this assumption mutual restriction takes place independently of all changing empirical conditions, that is, independently of whether the parties are mutually dependent or unrelated, aggressive or peaceable, as well as independently of how powerful and threatening they are.

On closer observation, whoever adopts the position of the radical critics of Law and assumes a coexistence wholly devoid of restrictions set upon freedom, runs into a sort of contradiction. Unrestricted freedom, the "right to everything," turns out to be a "right to nothing" from a social perspective. Since in principle my freedom of action is unrestricted, nothing, in principle, is forbidden to other persons — neither taking my life nor my possessions — nothing limits the freedom of one's peers.

Consequently, the limits imposed upon human freedom do not arise solely from the external or inner nature of men. They are found neither exclusively in the "vicissitudes of instinct" (*Triebschicksale*) nor alone in the scarcity of

---

[8] For the relation of Rawls to Kant see Höffe 1984.

goods, the limits to growth, the perhaps economically conditioned debasement of the human character, nor in the obstinacy of external nature, nor in any combination of these factors. They are grounded in the freedom of action, viz., in an unrestricted discretion to act, which confronts an equally unrestricted freedom. Putting the same point in an anthropological way: inasmuch as man is a free and at the same time a social being, he not only aids and abets but also restricts his peers as well. Therefore in addition to the possibility of cooperation there is also the possibility of conflict.

These fundamental considerations hold up even if we refrain from examining the empirical questions, such as how do actual conflicts arise and how does one react to them — with a struggle, with resignation or by attempting negotiation. For in each case the conflicting parties renounce their "right to everything." In negotiations this happens freely and reciprocally; in resignation freely but unilaterally; while in struggle under compulsion and unilaterally on the part of the loser. Thus, the thought experiment that started from an unrestricted freedom of action comes up against a state of necessary restriction as soon as the social perspective is introduced. The result is not that there must be a restriction, still less that there must be law. These would be normative statements, perhaps moral statements which have no place in the pre-moral duty of obeying the law. The result is, rather simply, restriction obtains (exists). In whatever way the restriction of freedom occurs, it is unavoidable from the social perspective.[9]

Given this result, the pre-moral task to be solved by Law must be regarded as a relatively necessary one. Assuming the coexistence of free human beings as the object of Law, reciprocal restriction of freedom of action is inevitable. Nevertheless, it is not unavoidable at the point where one person's freedom confronts the mere need or desire of another. For an unfulfilled wish or an unsatisfied need may well be quite painful to those concerned, and even lead to agression. But taken as they are in themselves these are first of all interior factors; since they do not come into contact in the same external world, they can coexist. In other words, one can worry about the state of one's own desires, prohibit the intervention of others and in turn remain indifferent to the wishes and needs of others. For that reason there is a moral problem here — Kant is by no means an exponent of hard-heartedness — but it is a question of interior not exterior legislation, that is, of virtue, not Law. Restriction of freedom of action is necessarily present only where the limited freedom of one person comes into conflict with that of another. This is precisely the task of Law which Kant mentioned in § B of the Introduction to the *Elements of*

[9] For a systematic and more detailed discussion see Höffe 1987.

Justice, the question, namely, how in abstraction from all intentions one person's freedom (will) can be reconciled with another person's freedom (will).

The thought experiment of a primary state of nature vindicates Kant's claim and proves — on the assumption of the coexistence of free human beings — the legal problem of the reciprocal restriction of freedom of action to be an a priori valid, and to this extent, a purely rational problem. In the course of the *Elements of Justice* further legal tasks emerge which arise from "basic facts" of human existence, and extend well beyond the fact of a plurality of responsible beings; so, for instance, there are the differentiation of the sexes in Marital Law, the procreation of children in Parental Law (RL §§ 24-29). As against an ever richer empirical anthropology, the task set for the Law remains a *relative a priori*.

Now, legal obligations are the outcome of two factors, the normative principle of evaluation (the general categorical imperative) and the pre-moral tasks to be solved by Law. Since the latter always involve an empirical aspect, the fundamental legal obligations are not discovered in a purely rational way. In Kant's insufficiently clear language: "a metaphysics of morals cannot be founded on anthropology, although it can be applied to it" (RL 217/16).

Not until the standard of morality is applied to the unavoidable social problem — the reciprocal restriction of freedom — is the moral concept of the Law acquired. For that reason, after the ethical-functional interpretation, the view that Law for Kant is nothing but the condition of the possibility of the coexistence of free agents (Geismann, 56) should be criticized. Geismann is quite correct in excluding morality (autonomy, virtue) from the foundations of Law. But however evidently Kant separates Law from Ethics, he does not separate it from the moral point of view.

On the other hand, as the categorical imperative of Law does not succeed without the pre-moral definition of the task set before Law, we can agree with Williams, for whom the (general) categorical imperative is not "the only court of appeal for the rules of justice" (60). However, that does not mean, as Williams suggests, that the rules (more precisely, the principles) of justice "also have to pass the positive test of whether in fact they allow individuals to live in harmony with each other in society." In particular, it is not here a matter of an "empirical question" (ibid.). For in universally compatible freedom of action, a principle of justice was discovered which is categorically valid a priori as far as coexistence of freedom of action is concerned. Of course, in order to specify this principle, empirical considerations are necessary. To be sure, Kant argues pre-empirically and tries to establish legal institutions such as property, contract, marriage, the relation between parent and child, public legal states and criminal law, as categorically binding. In order to prove this, there are other basic givens of the *conditio humana*, such as corporeality and sexuality which must be taken into account. But for Kant these factors are not the ground for obligation, but rather the circumstances of its application. So the following result remains: the categorical imperative of Law has an a prioristic nature in its moral interpretation and an empirical nature in its circumstances of application whereby the empirical nature involves first general knowledge and then more specific knowledge.

University of Freiburg
Switzerland

Bibliography

Berlin, I. *Two Concepts of Liberty.* Oxford: Clarendon Press, 1958.
Brandt, R. "Das Erlebnisgesetz oder: Vernunft und Geschichte in Kant's Rechtslehre," in Brandt (ed.), *Rechtsphilosophie der Aufklärung.* Berlin/New York: de Gruyter, 1982, 232-285.
Brown, S.M. "Has Kant a Philosophy of Law?" *Philosophical Review* 71 (1962): 33-48.
Busch, W. *Die Entstehung der kritischen Rechtsphilosophie Kants.* Berlin/ New York: de Gruyter, 1979.
Cohen, H. *Kants Begründung der Ethik nebst ihren Anwendungen auf Recht, Religion und Geschichte* (1877). Berlin, 1910.
Dreier, R. *Recht-Moral-Ideologie: Studien zur Rechtstheorie.* Frankfurt a.M.: Suhrkamp, 1981.
Ebbinghaus, J. *Gesammelte Aufsätze, Vorträge und Reden.* Hildesheim: Georg Olms, 1968.
Ebbinghaus, J. "Kants Rechtslehre und die Rechtsphilosophie des Neukantianismus," in G. Prauss (ed.), *Kant. Zur Deutung seiner Theorie von Erkennen und Handeln.* Köln: Kiepenheuer & Witsch, 1973, 322-336.
Freud, S. "Das Unbehagen in der Kultur," in *Gesammelte Werke,* XIV. 6th ed. Frankfurt a.M., 1976.
Geismann, G. "Kant als Vollender von Hobbes und Rousseau," *Der Staat* 21 (1982): 161-189.
Gregor, M.J. *Laws of Freedom.* Oxford: Blackwell, 1963.
Hassner, P. "Immanuel Kant," in L. Strauss & J. Cropsey (eds.), *History of Political Philosophy*, 2nd ed. Chicago: Rand McNally, 1972, 554-593.
Höffe, O. "Recht und Moral: Ein kantischer Problemaufriss," in *Neue Hefte für Philosopie,* Heft 17. Göttingen: Vandenhoeck & Ruprecht, 1979, 1-36.
Höffe, O. "Is Rawls' Theory of Justice Really Kantian?" *Ratio* 26 (1984): 103-124.
Höffe, O. *Politische Gerechtigkeit. Grundlegung einer kritischen Philosophie von Recht und Staat.* Frankfurt a.M.: Suhrkamp, 1987.

Ilting, K.-H. "Gibt es eine kritische Ethik und Rechtsphilosophie Kants?" Hans Wagner zum 65. Geburtstag. *Archiv für Geschichte und Philosophie* 63 (1981): 325-345.

Kersting, W. *Wohlgeordnete Freiheit. Immanuel Kants Rechts- und Staatsphilosophie.* Berlin/ New York: de Gruyter, 1984.

Kühl, K. *Eigentumsordnung als Freiheitsordnung. Zur Aktualität der kantischen Rechts-und Eigentumslehre.* Freiburg/ München: Alber, 1984.

Ladd, J. Translator's Introduction, in *I. Kant. The Metaphysical Elements of Justice.* Indianapolis: Bobbs Merrill, 1965, ix-xxxi.

Macpherson, C.B. *The Political Theory of Possessive Individualism: From Hobbes to Locke.* Oxford: Clarendon, 1962.

Nozick, R. *Anarchy, State and Utopia.* Oxford: Blackwell, 1974.

Rawls, J. *A Theory of Justice.* Oxford University Press, 1973.

Reich, K. *Rousseau und Kant.* Tübingen: Mohr, 1936.

Riley, P. "On Kant as the Most Adequate of the Social Contract Theorists," *Political Theory* 1 (1973): 450-471.

Ritter, C. *Der Rechtsgedanke Kants nach den frühen Quellen.* Frankfurt a.M.: Klostermann, 1971.

Sänger, M. *Die kategoriale Systematik in den "Metaphysischen Anfangsgründen der Rechtslehre." Ein Beitrag zur Methodenlehre Kants.* Berlin/ New York: de Gruyter, 1982.

Scholz, G. *Das Problem des Rechts in Kants Moralphilosophie.* Köln, 1972 (Dissertation).

Shell, S.M. *The Rights of Reason: A Study of Kant's Philosophy and Politics.* University of Toronto Press, 1980.

Williams, H.L. *Kant's Political Philosophy.* Oxford: Blackwell, 1983.

Alexis Philonenko

Histoire et Guerre chez Kant

On ne saurait dire que Kant ait été un philosophe passionné par la guerre comme le fut Tolstoï; sa signification concrète ne l'a peut-être même pas intéressé. En ce sens ce n'est pas un philosophe susceptible d'être comparé à Gibbon, Voltaire, Montesquieu. Nulle part dans ses œuvres officielles, je veux dire celles publiées de son vivant et avec son consentement, nous ne trouvons d'allusion ou mieux une remarque très détaillée au sujet d'un conflit européen de grande envergure. Appuyé sur l'*Esthétique transcendantale* Schopenhauer en fera son profit en proclamant que la devise de l'histoire est *Eadem sed aliter*. En revanche Kant est un géographe averti. De nos jours les géographes n'hésitent pas à lui rendre hommage. Et après Avenarius on reconnait volontiers en Kant un des pères de la géographie moderne. Si nous consultons en outre le Bd. 15 des œuvres de l'Académie royale prussienne des sciences, nous découvrons, surtout pour la période de l'*Anthropologie des années 80*, un ensemble de matériaux très riches. Il est clair pour l'historien de Kant que s'il vise la notion de guerre en se limitant à la seule notion de conflit il ira à l'échec: Kant, même si sa philosophie l'a inspiré, n'a pas écrit *Guerre et paix*. En revanche une stratégie indirecte combinant la théorie transcendantale et l'anthropologie pourrait, à notre sens, ouvrir une perspective.

1. La notion de finalité est au cœur du problème. S'il n'y a aucune finalité historique concevable en un sens transcendantal rigoureux, il sera extrêmement clair que la notion de guerre se dissoudra en nos mains et deviendra d'une fluidité proche du néant. On s'accorde à reconnaître deux sens à la notion de finalité chez Kant. Le premier, bien connu, est celui de *finalité transcendante* dont le schéma (trop souvent attribué à Bernardin de Saint-Pierre) sous sa forme simpliste est le suivant: l'herbe est *faite pour* l'herbivore et celui-ci *pour* le carnassier. Tous les grands commentateurs de Kant[1] s'en sont tenus là. Le positivisme allemand ou français fait de même. Quelques-

---

[1] J'ai cité les principaux dans mon *Oeuvre de Kant* (Vrin, 1972), T. II.

Y. Yovel (ed.), Kant's Practical Philosophy Reconsidered, 168-182.

uns ont même cru que Kant ne faisait qu'entériner une sentence issue d'un consensus dont Voltaire, par exemple, était l'interprète éloquent. Même le meilleur "critique" de Kant, je veux dire Bergson, se range à ce point de vue. Critiquant Kant dans l'*Evolution créatrice*, il affirme que celui-ci a pris conscience de la fragilité de la finalité externe dogmatique et que pour la sauver il l'a ramenée à l'individu. Mais, précise Bergson, réduisant ainsi le concept au seul individu, loin de le sauver Kant l'exposait davantage aux coups et c'est pourquoi Bergson affirme: "la finalité est externe ou elle n'est pas."[2] Si cette critique était fondée il conviendrait d'attribuer à Kant une conception abdéritiste de l'histoire qu'il évoque pour la repousser.[3] Sans dessein, aveugle, confondant sans cesse l'essentiel et l'inessentiel, notre espèce s'acharnerait à détruire ce que par ailleurs elle a obtenu au prix de travaux aussi pénibles qu'obscurs. On sait que tel n'est pas le point de vue de Kant. Seule par conséquent une analyse approfondie du concept de finalité dans le criticisme peut procurer une issue plus heureuse.

2. Les thèses fondamentales sur la finalité sont contenues dans la IIe partie de la *Critique de la faculté de juger*. Le §63 est l'exposition polémique et métaphysique du concept, le §64 est sa déduction transcendantale subjective, le §65 est la déduction transcendantale pure du concept, le §67 enfin en esquisse les modalités d'application. Nous lirons avec beaucoup d'attention l'exposition polémique. Son but avoué est de détruire le concept de finalité externe dogmatique où la finalité est conçue comme un ensemble de solutions toujours déjà préparées pour l'homme et ces solutions, comme on le voit chez Mendelssohn et tant d'autres, sont posées par des jugements thétiques. L'angle sous lequel Kant développe sa critique dans le §63 est remarquable: c'est celui déterminé par la *géographie humaine*, science des relations de l'homme avec son environnement. L'exemple central est celui de la symbiose du renne et de l'homme.[4] Toutes les relations observées dans le Grand-Nord — par exemple le bois de flottage — sont interprétées par la philosophie dogmatique comme des *principes de solutions* et celui qui du point de vue kantien a été le plus loin est Mendelssohn dans sa *Lettre aux amis de Lessing*. On connaît l'essentiel du thème: un missionnaire se promène avec un Groenlandais sur la banquise, et celui-ci, devant les feux roses de l'aurore se réfléchissant dans les glaces éblouissantes de la banquise s'écrie: "Ah! Puisque ceci est beau, combien plus beau doit être celui qui l'a fait". La finalité-solution, la finalité

---

[2] Bergson, *L'Evolution créatrice* (PUF, 1983), p. 41.
[3] AK. VIII, 18.
[4] A. Leroi-Gourhan, *La civilisation du renne* (Paris, 1936).

externe absolue (*darum-weil*), qui permet le raisonnement analogique du Groenlandais (troisième preuve de l'existence de Dieu, "la plus ancienne et la plus respectable") est utilisée au maximum, puisqu'elle porte sur la question la plus fondamentale et la plus angoissante pour l'homme: "Dieu existe-t-il?" Et supposé que cette connaissance soit donnée comme une solution toute faite (le spectacle irréfutable de la banquise), alors on peut avec Mendelssohn déterminer des séries de solutions finales.

Si l'on admet le principe mendelssohnien il n'y a pas à proprement parler d'histoire et de progrès: il existe seulement des ensembles de complexes de solutions finales que l'homme méconnaît tragiquement. Il va de soi que l'exemple du Groenlandais n'est pas du tout innocent: au 18e siècle, c'est l'*Unter-Mensch* par excellence et les jugements de Buffon sont éloquents.[5] Et le sens du propos de Mendelssohn s'éclaire: si l'*Unter-Mensch* s'élève si facilement du spectacle de la banquise à l'Etre suprême, combien, avec nos lumières, ne devrions-nous pas nous élever plus aisément à la solution de la question suprême! Dès lors on aperçoit que toute une *Weltanschauung*[6] s'édifie dans la finalité externe dogmatique.

La réponse de Kant à Mendelssohn est double. D'une part il repousse sans réserves le principe de jugements de finalité externe comme "*absolus*", sans noter toutefois qu'utilisés *hypothétiquement* de tels jugements peuvent posséder une valeur indicative. Et c'est pourquoi dans le *Projet de paix perpétuelle* tous les exemples repoussés dans le §63 sont récupérés d'un point de vue, non dogmatique, mais hypothétique, c'est-à-dire régulatif. Ceci est extrêmement important. Il y a pour Kant un usage scientifique des jugements téléologiques. On considérera ce point comme le moment systématique formel transcendantal. Mais d'autre part, c'est en posant la question de savoir pourquoi le Groenlandais a dû se réfugier dans des terres aussi inhospitalières que Kant réfute Mendelssohn d'un point de vue transcendantal matériel. Le Groenlan-Nord, vers le froid, qui est *privatio entis et bonis*,[7] est par excellence l'homme envers l'homme qui engendre la *guerre*. L'*Untermensch* chassé vers le Grand-Nord, vers le froid, qui est *privatio entis et bonis*[7] est par excellence l'homme qui ne sait pas *s'adapter* à l'homme. *Il n'y a pas de finalité-solution, il y a une finalité-adaptation.* La dynamique de la résolution des problèmes constitue l'histoire. L'*Untermensch* définitivement vaincu est l'illustration de la déchéance dans l'horizon de la nature depuis le sommet de l'histoire. On ne

---

[5] A. Philonenko, *La théorie kantienne de l'histoire* (Vrin, 1986), p. 34 et suiv.

[6] Ib., pp. 57-62.

[7] Sur le sens métaphysique du froid, cf. A. Pézard, *Dante sous la pluie de feu* (Vrin, 1950).

peut expliciter encore ici tout le sens de la pensée kantienne — contentons-nous de dire qu'il entrelace dans une relation soutenue par la notion d'adaptation guerre et histoire, et l'*Anthropologie des années 80* reliera la guerre à la morale par la théorie des passions, reprise dans les écrits de 1784 à 1795. Tout est selon Kant (en ceci héritier de Rousseau)[8] *problème*. La loi téléologique de l'histoire est le principe d'adaptation suivant lequel l'homme évolue ou n'évolue pas. En ce point reliant le moment systématique formel avec l'élément matériel du concept de finalité externe, nous ne dépassons pas au point de vue *métaphysique* la présentation *a priori* du concept de finalité externe (adaptation). Il faut s'élever à sa *déduction transcendantale subjective.* Le §63 rédigé dans une perspective polémique ne pouvait donner plus qu'une exposition métaphysique *a priori.* Le §64 nous donnera dans des relations concrètes (subjectives) la déduction subjective qui suffira à notre propos.

3. Le §64 n'a pas été mieux compris que le précédent. La guerre, problème que l'homme en général et aussi comme individu pose à l'homme, est une relation de finalité externe (les adversaires sont op-posés), dynamique (la guerre est mouvement), interne (les op-posés forment une totalité), enfin ouverte (la guerre est l'exigence d'une adaptation). Or nous pouvons concevoir une telle totalité dynamique ouverte externe-interne d'après l'analogie avec la déduction transcendantale subjective de la finalité dite interne qui n'est aucunement comme le croit Bergson la simple harmonie d'un individu *vivant.*

Dans le §64 l'exemple choisi est celui de l'arbre. Il est bien vrai que c'est seulement par le schématisme de l'analogie que Kant pourra transposer au niveau de l'homme (au-delà de l'articulation)[9] les résultats obtenus. La déduction subjective (parce qu'elle fait intervenir un concept comme exemple saisi *in concreto* dans l'intuition) a pour fin essentielle la fondation du principe de *système*, nécessaire pour justifier formellement Linné et matériellement Blumenbach.[10] Puisqu'il n'est pas dans notre dessein d'entrer dans la problématique de la synthèse et du système,[11] relevons seulement les moments fondamentaux. En premier lieu *un* arbre (*une* guerre) est une totalité *fluide*, qui se définit en trois moments: les parties qui sont en interaction (relation

[8] A. Philonenko, *J.J. Rousseau et la pensée du malheur* (Vrin, 1984), vol. I.
[9] Fichte, *GA*, I, 382-383.
[10] Blumenbach, *Handbuch der Natur-Geschichte*, § 19.
[11] H. Cohen, *Kants Begründung der Ethik*, 2e ed. (Berlin, 1910). Je renvoie aussi à mon *Oeuvre de Kant*, T. II, à mes *Etudes kantiennes* (Vrin, 1982) et à ma *Théorie kantienne de l'histoire*. On peut consulter aussi mon introduction à ma traduction de la *Kritik der Urteilskraft*.

dynamique où, par exemple, les feuilles protègent le tronc qui les nourrit);
l'auto-production de l'arbre (de la guerre comme limitée — il y a des guerres et
pas seulement la guerre) comme *individu*; enfin *l'espèce* (*Gattung*) ou l'arbre
envisagé du point de vue de la génération (de la guerre comme principe, par
exemple, de peuplement de la terre). En second lieu donc cette totalité fluide,
où les parties déterminent l'individu qui détermine l'espèce et réciproque-
ment, est un triple nexus: nexus des parties entre elles, nexus des parties avec
l'individu, et enfin de l'individu avec l'espèce. Dans la mesure où la causalité
est ici une relation susceptible d'être lue dans les deux sens, elle est à la fois
réelle et idéelle.

En ce point de la déduction subjective (*in concreto*) du triple nexus finalis
doit apparaître la détermination de la finalité au sens transcendantal: elle est
l'organisation ou encore la totalité *fluide* des déterminations. Pragmatique-
ment cela revient à définir la finalité comme possibilité et réalisation de la
greffe. Levons donc ici une source de malentendus: l'organisation n'est pas le
vivant.[12] Dans un arbre, précisément au niveau de la détermination du rapport
comme triple nexus finalis, chaque feuille peut être considérée comme un
arbre existant pour soi. Un arbre est donc un rapport entre *des individus*
(finalité externe-interne) et pas du tout, comme le veut Bergson, un individu.
La finalité est un rapport qui doit être considéré comme détermination d'une
collectivité et c'est en effet le statut de l'arbre en lequel Kant affirme que
chaque feuille peut être considérée comme un arbre existant pour soi, se
nourrissant de l'autre comme un parasite,[13] ou encore comme greffé. Je ne puis
ici entrer dans la théorie de la notion de greffe au 18e siècle, mais il est clair
qu'une greffe suppose deux moments en relation réciproque d'adaptation,
soit de finalité interne-externe dynamique ouverte. La limite théorique de la
finalité, donc ce qui suppose l'intervention d'autres concepts régulateurs, est
l'impossibilité de la greffe et les penseurs du 18e siècle (surtout Fichte) font
intervenir *l'articulation*. Dans le règne de l'organisation (dont s'occupe seulement la seconde partie de la *Critique de la faculté de juger*) la greffe n'a pas de
limites; mais l'individu pur qui forme un pour-soi et non une collectivité

---

[12] KU, §65.

[13] Image essentielle chez Kant. J'évoque ici cette image pour établir que chez Kant la
greffe n'est pas nécessairement, pour ainsi dire, pacifique. Entre le greffon et le greffé
des problèmes peuvent survenir. Rares au niveau de l'organisation dans le monde
animal, les structures parasitaires sont, en fait, des greffes conflictuelles. Au point de
vue politique la substitution dans l'esprit du Souverain d'un point de vue opposé à la
pensée de la volonté générale est un principe de dissociation du corps de l'Etat. Cf. A.
Philonenko, *Théorie et praxis dans la pensée morale et politique de Kant et de Fichte en
1793* (Vrin, 1976).

suppose pour être conçu comme *pour-soi* un autre concept que celui qui illustre la finalité dynamique externe-interne.

Dès lors qu'on distingue ces rapports on peut concevoir comment la finalité comme organisation permet de concevoir l'histoire et la guerre. En premier lieu, bien qu'élevé au-dessus de la simple finalité l'être humain (l'homme, être articulé), peut être regardé analogiquement à un double point de vue. D'une part comme collectivité, il constitue une *organisation* dont le schème est semblable à celui de l'être-organisé (la plante). On m'épargnera un commentaire de la célèbre note du §65.[14] D'autre part la métaphore végétale illustre ce qu'il y a de plus profond en l'homme; par exemple "le mal radical" est un mal qui a des racines, qui ont plongé jusque dans le cœur de l'homme, et il faut les *extirper*.[15] Que si l'on relie ces deux moments, collectivité et mal radical (mais non *définitif* puisqu'il peut être extirpé en théorie), on obtiendra d'abord la guerre interne qui elle-même se lit sous deux déterminations, l'une sociale, l'autre domestique. Guerre sociale: dans l'Etat, bien qu'il se trouve en eux une disposition sur laquelle rien de mauvais ne puisse être greffé, la disposition au bien,[16] les individus sont greffés les uns sur les autres par la médiation du conflit suscité par leurs passions fondamentales: l'avarice, la soif d'honneurs, la soif de domination. C'est une grande question que de savoir jusqu'où cette guerre peut être féconde. On voit ici combien une juste appréciation de la finalité externe-interne dynamique ouverte est nécessaire pour entendre Kant. La guerre sociale marque les époques dans l'histoire et par exemple la *politesse* (avec le faux jour que lui a si justement prêté Rousseau) est une *époque* de l'histoire.[17] C'est un rapport d'adaptation finale qu'il ne faut pas négliger (quelle erreur ce serait!), une greffe dont la valeur éthique doit être soigneusement mesurée. Que si l'on passe à la guerre domestique (*Mann und Männin*), qui oppose l'homme et la femme et que décrit l'*Anthropologie des années 80*, nous trouvons une détermination fondamentale évoquée un peu brièvement dans les *Conjectures sur les débuts de l'humanité*. Dans les débuts de l'histoire humaine à l'intérieur de la greffe que forme le couple le mâle domine. Il marche devant et la femme suit chargée comme un animal. L'homme est en effet d'une beauté absolue, tandis que la beauté de la femme est imparfaite, relative.[18] Pour compenser sa faiblesse la femme va jouer sur la greffe, refuser

---

[14] AK. V, 375.
[15] A ce sujet voir mes notes dans la traduction que j'ai donnée de *La Religion dans les limites de la simple raison* (in *Oeuvres philosophiques de Kant*, T. III, ed. F. Alquié, Gallimard, 1980).
[16] Ibid.
[17] AK. VIII, 113.
[18] AK. XV, Refl. 1301.

l'acte sexuel. Certes de ce refus naît d'abord au point de vue théorique une plus grande compréhension de la *durée*, non du temps. Mais surtout en se refusant la femme se pose comme conscience indépendante, libre, capable d'opposition. Dès lors intervient la *dialectique de la séduction*. Deux points sont importants en ceci. Il n'y a séduction que si l'on admet la liberté de l'autre en tant qu'autre et que si le but qu'on se propose n'est pas de se l'approprier — relation *d'avoir* — mais de réaliser l'union (greffe) qui est une relation *d'être*. Dans l'*Anthropologie des années 80*, Kant est très clair sur ce point. Le second moment à relever est la quasi-infinité de la dialectique de la séduction placée sous le signe de l'exigence. La séduction va alors contraindre dans la guerre domestique l'homme à *travailler*, exactement comme le serviteur chez Hegel. Il ornera sa maison, puis sa demeure, il cherchera à trouver dans la nature les belles parures (fourrures) susceptibles de compenser la beauté relative de la femme, et creusant au fond de la terre il trouvera les pierres précieuses. En séduisant la femme par son travail, l'homme non seulement se transforme lui-même, devenant plus raffiné, mais encore domine la nature. Je laisse ici à la réflexion de chacun la richesse de cette dialectique: elle comprend tous les acquis de la célèbre dialectique hégélienne de la domination et de la servitude et même plus puisqu'elle conduit au système de la civilisation comme "accord pathologiquement extorqué".[19] Mais aussi bien faut-il relever que les deux moments déduits tombent l'un à l'intérieur de l'autre puisque guerre sociale et guerre domestique tombent l'une en l'autre et que le diamant qui étincelle au doigt de la femme résume cet univers de la politesse. *Mutatis mutandis*, il y a corrélation entre le diamant, travaillé, sorti de sa gangue brute, puis taillé, et la femme plus raffinée, plus distinguée (mais non pas nécessairement plus morale).

4. On s'aperçoit donc comment à partir d'une analogie avec la finalité dynamique, ouverte externe-interne, qui ne se limite pas comme le croyait Bergson, à un individu, on peut penser la guerre en son principe et en ses formes. En son principe dans la mesure où la norme primaire est toujours et partout l'exigence d'adaptation et en ses formes, par exemple, la guerre sociale et la guerre domestique. Il me paraît inutile ici en analysant le §65 de confirmer ces vues par l'exposé de la déduction objective réfléchissante du concept de finalité-adaptation. Il convient, dès lors que le fondement est assuré, que la guerre est liée à l'histoire, de prendre la mesure de cette dernière pour prendre la mesure externe de la guerre.

La question qui se pose (et qui peut-être éclaire le caractère schématique et

---

[19] AK. VIII, 21; cf. *La théorie kantienne de l'histoire*, p. 96 et suiv.

abstrait de la pensée kantienne, par opposition à celles de Voltaire et de Hume) est de savoir en quel point se situe l'humanité dans son mouvement que Kant veut regarder comme un progrès. Il ne s'agit pas de se reposer comme on le fait toujours sur le seul concept de politesse; capitale, cette notion n'est pas suffisante. Nous trouvons dans l'*Anthropologie des années 80* une réflexion extrêmement précieuse. Je cite l'essentiel de la Refl. 1453: "Il y a seulement deux siècles que nous sommes entrés en relations avec d'autres parties du monde par delà les mers. Amérique, Japon, les Iles des Mers du Sud — une grande partie du monde est à moitié animale et mal peuplée. Nous ne possédons que depuis un siècle l'idée du système de la constitution civile d'un grand Etat en Angleterre. Au point de vue du droit international nous sommes encore des barbares. Nous ne possédons pas de système susceptible d'unifier les religions. Nous n'avons pas encore à proprement parler de système d'éducation."[20] Il y a ici des rapports complexes à élucider. Le premier, celui qui saute aux yeux, est que pour Kant l'humanité est tout à fait *adolescente*: elle ne possède que depuis un siècle le modèle concret d'une constitution politique cohérente. Rome, Byzance, le Saint-Empire germanique, les royautés de structures non constitutionnelles (la France jusqu'en 1789), voilà autant de modèles périmés, anciens, archaïques. Les désordres de l'Empire romain et même de la République romaine prouvent la *puérilité* (mot grave chez Kant) de ces systèmes. Le droit international se réduit à une chimère puisque nous sommes des barbares et *cette chimère est littéralement enceinte de guerres*. Notre système d'éducation est imparfait — dans les *Réflexions sur l'éducation*, Kant minore sévèrement la découverte de Gutenberg. Comme le montre l'exemple de l'enseignement primaire même en Prusse on fabrique plutôt des analphabètes — tout prêts à céder au discours machiavélique — que des hommes abrités par les faibles leçons du passé. Et si l'on veut mieux mesurer le lieu où se trouve l'humanité, qu'on réfléchisse sur l'Afrique, "une grande partie du monde à moitié animale et mal peuplée"; il faudra coloniser, effectuer un travail de romain et puis aussi évangéliser avec pour seul *Leitfaden* l'Evangile, puisque nous ne possédons pas de *System* susceptible d'unifier les religions. Comme Fichte,[21] Kant croit l'humanité très jeune. La possibilité de la voir succomber dans la barbarie en raison des guerres énormes que tous ces problèmes vont susciter n'est nullement exclue, car on l'a vue pour le Groenlandais, la possibilité du *déclin*, de la glissade vers

---

[20] AK. XV, 634. Voir aussi ma présentation des *Réflexions sur l'éducation de Kant* (Vrin, 1974), et la description dans mon *Introduction* de la scolarité en Prusse.
[21] A. Philonenko, *Théorie et praxis dans la pensée morale et politique de Kant et de Fichte en 1793* (Vrin, 1976), IIe partie, introduction.

l'*Unter-Mensch*, n'est pas une simple idée, mais un fait. L'humanité est, en dépit de son ascension au système de la politesse en Europe, extraordinairement jeune, fragile et dans la balance de l'histoire ses forces ne pèsent pas lourd face aux gigantesques difficultés.

Kant se veut néanmoins optimiste en garantissant la fondation de la guerre et de l'histoire dans la structure d'adaptation par analogie avec le concept réfléchissant de finalité externe-interne, dynamique, ouverte par l'Idée d'un dessein caché de la Providence ou de Dieu ou de la Nature (termes donnés pour équivalents dès la *Critique de la raison pure*). Le fait, si fortement développé dans l'*Idée pour une histoire universelle au point de vue cosmopolitique*, que l'humanité ne comprend pas son labeur,[22] atteste à la fois le fait que l'humanité est une adolescente à peine murie et la possibilité immanente au système kantien, comme Théorie des Idées, de récupérer la téléologie à l'intérieur des limites de la Raison pure. Il nous est impossible de décrire ici tous les liens de cette dialectique et nous avons même négligé de le faire dans notre *Théorie kantienne de l'histoire*, car cela suppose l'élaboration d'une *Théorie kantienne de la religion*. Notons seulement que d'une part la doctrine kantienne est infiniment plus appuyée sur la conception de la finalité transcendante (Nature, Providence, Dieu, trois termes dont la synthèse forme un *monogramme* qu'il convient de déployer dans le schématisme systématique de la Religion) que ne l'a pensé l'Ecole positiviste de Marbourg et que d'autre part la lucidité kantienne n'est pas le fait d'un cerveau philosophique dressant des plans sans regarder le monde concret.

On s'est trop souvent abusé en s'appuyant sur la garantie du "dessein caché de la nature". On a cru à un progrès mécanique se trouvant mesuré d'une part par le développement du peuplement de la planète et d'autre part par la substitution graduelle de la guerre commerciale à la guerre criminelle. C'est sans doute la leçon du *Projet de paix perpétuelle* et c'est aussi la lecture de Proudhon dans *Guerre et Paix*.[23] Mais il faut demeurer ouvert sur les dérapages possibles et pouvant conduire à la nuit barbare. D'après *La Religion dans les limites de la simple raison*, les Empires suivent un cycle clair. Dans un premier temps ils fédèrent des provinces, puis vient l'unité systématique globale et peu après l'Empire se décompose dans un sens ou dans l'autre, suivant une ligne, non pas droite, mais empruntant dans son tracé tous les cas possibles.[24] Dans ce chemin et souvent *media dell camino* un Empire pour garantir son unité systématique devient un Royaume barbare. Kant — dans la

---

[22] AK. VIII, 19.

[23] A. Philonenko, *Essais sur la philosophie de la guerre* (Vrin, 1976).

[24] Herder a la même conception de la nature de la courbe du progrès de l'humanité.

mesure même où il dit que le modèle politique ne date que d'un siècle, ce qui signifie qu'on ne l'utilisera peut-être pas toujours — redoute d'immenses dérapages et notre histoire ne lui a pas donné tort. Ce que je voudrais dire seulement à propos du commerce, forme de conflit pacifique à en croire Proudhon, moins avisé que Kant, c'est que dans le meilleur des cas, dans celui où il se substitue aux conflits sanglants, on peut le considérer du point de vue de la finalité-adaptation comme la substitution d'une forme de greffe à une autre. Mais le commerce n'est que le commerce; il n'exclut pas, loin de là, la malhonnêteté, la duperie. Kant n'a aucune complaisance pour les commerçants. Même s'ils sont loyaux ils ne sont pas pour autant moraux. Et puis le commerce par principe et par définition n'est pas loyal: c'est quand même une forme de guerre — peu glorieuse,[25] car on n'y risque pas sa vie — avec ses structures: l'argent, les changes (trompeurs: du verre contre de l'or), l'embargo, etc. On en vient à se demander en quoi le commerce comme guerre non sanglante est un progrès par rapport à la guerre militaire. En ceci sans doute: le commerce ne peut se développer sans abaisser les barrières linguistiques. Certes il ne fonde pas un Etat de paix, mais un langage commun.

C'est ici le lieu — puisque nous venons d'examiner le bilan de l'humanité adolescente et de ce fait incapable d'éviter des guerres sanglantes — de développer le concept de la guerre militaire, aspect le plus criard dans l'Idée générale de la guerre, dont les autres formes (guerre sociale, guerre domestique, guerre commerciale, guerre religieuse, etc.) sont sans doute plus riches. Kant ne possède aucune notion de stratégie, de structure opérationnelle. Il n'a pas étudié les guerres et en tous les cas s'il sait quelque chose, il le cache fort bien. Il a deux idées. D'une part il reprend, après Fichte, la parole du Grec: "Que la guerre crée plus d'hommes méchants qu'elle n'en conduit au tombeau". Ne négligeons pas l'héroïsme où comme les sauvages[26] l'homme atteint au sublime en se comportant négativement par rapport à sa propre vie. Mais n'exagérons rien: les sauvages font peut-être mieux que l'homme moderne. Donc nul pathos de l'héroïsme — c'est une naïveté qu'on peut laisser à Hegel. En gros les héros sont la minorité et les assassins la majorité (ce qui en somme est normal). D'autre part Kant trouve que la guerre coûte

---

[25] Dans la *Religion dans les limites de la simple raison*, Kant souligne qu'en leur guerre perpétuelle les Indiens sauvages atteignent en un sens au sublime, car ils dépassent le lien qui les attache à la vie. De même Rousseau dans le *Premier Discours* évoque cette vertu militaire chez les Anciens (les Scythes) et se moque du guerrier moderne. Cf. A. Philonenko, *Rousseau et la pensée du malheur*, vol. I.
[26] Voir la note précédente. Là où on rencontre l'héroïsme dans la guerre moderne on ne dépasse pas le niveau du sauvage. Hegel aurait dû y penser.

trop cher: le bénéfice d'une guerre n'est jamais à la hauteur des investisse-
ments (supposant de lourds impôts). On est toujours perdant et tant que
l'humanité fera la guerre elle sera perdante, glissant vers la dés-adaptation.
Kant imagine bien qu'excédés les peuples se révolteront contre leurs princes
barbares, car verser ses économies pour en fin de compte donner naissance à
des assassins, c'est tout de même la pire affaire qui soit. Mais si l'on trouve
quelques allusions très claires en ce sens dans le *Nachlass*, la philosophie
politique de Kant qui condamne absolument "le droit de résistance"
(*Widerstand-Recht*)[27] interdit aux peuples un tel mouvement. Il n'y a qu'à
espérer en une Sainte-Alliance, en un Projet de paix perpétuelle, qui fonde
réellement une Société des Nations. Quand la guerre militaire cessera-t-elle?
Quand le commerce deviendra-t-il vraiment loyal, quand la guerre sociale
(*Herrsucht, Ehrsucht, Absucht*) s'évanouira-t-elle? Quand les femmes
s'occuperont-elles de leur cuisine, de leurs enfants, de l'Eglise et de rien
d'autre? etc. L'ensemble de ces questions définit le niveau qui est le nôtre dans
l'histoire. Car ce sont les questions qu'on peut poser qui définissent dans leur
entrecroisement une *époque* de l'histoire. Il me semble que ce faisceau de
questions définit assez bien notre situation dans l'histoire. L'homme est un
adolescent qui selon l'analogie de la finalité externe-interne dynamique
ouverte doit s'adapter à des problèmes complexes dont l'entrecroisement est
délicat.[28] La seule question qui demeure consiste à savoir si en droit, et non
seulement en fait comme nous l'avons fait dans ce paragraphe, la guerre sous
toutes ses formes peut être dépassée dans une histoire où par exemple la
philosophie transcendantale comme *science*[29] serait reconnue en son plein
droit, où la guerre des philosophies s'effacerait devant les progrès de ce qui ne
serait plus *philosophie*, mais *science transcendantale*. En fait cette question est
celle du mal radical dont la notion ne peut se séparer de l'Idée de l'espérance,
comme troisième question fondamentale du système kantien.

Avant d'aborder cette difficile question, je voudrais souligner un point.
Kant ne peut évidemment être présenté comme un philosophe de la technique.
Au demeurant cela n'aurait point été sage de sa part. Il n'allait pas reprendre à
lui tout seul l'entreprise réussie de Diderot et de d'Alembert. De même plus
tard Fichte ne se préoccupera pas de reprendre de manière systématique la

---

[27] On connait à ce sujet la belle dissertation de W. Haensel. J'y renvoie souvent dans
mon travail *Théorie et Praxis dans la pensée morale et politique de Kant et de Fichte en
1793*.
[28] Kant sait fort bien que des guerres militaires ont été entreprises pour imposer le
commerce.
[29] *La théorie kantienne de l'histoire*, Ch. 8, p. 211 et suiv.

théorie de la physique qu'il jugeait parfaitement menée à son terme dans la *Critique de la raison pure.*[30] Et les exemples de techniques sont rares dans les œuvres officielles de Kant (la chaussure de Camper; l'aérostat dans le texte de 1793 dirigé contre Mendelssohn). En revanche les brèves notations sur l'histoire des techniques et de leur découverte dans l'*Anthropologie des années 80* permettent d'assurer que Kant avait conscience de la possibilité de *retombées technologiques.* Que pour ce qui est de la guerre il les ait vues est excessivement problématique. Il me semble qu'en dehors d'une amélioration de la *discipline*, il n'a rien perçu avec une grande clarté. Toutefois la philosophie qui demeure ouverte et ne s'arrête pas, pour ainsi dire, en 1807 — Hegel voyant passer l'Esprit du monde — on peut intégrer une théorie de la "retombée technique" dans le système transcendantal.

5. Nous voici enfin conduits à la notion de mal radical, principe transcendantal de la limitation de l'histoire et de la greffe considérée en général. Le mal radical est le monogramme des passions qui s'unissent dans le Moi comme *ego.* A partir du mal radical s'explicitent bien des vices, mais surtout la soif de domination, celle d'honneurs et enfin celle de possession. Qu'on n'attende pas ici une exposition de la doctrine des passions chez Kant: ces grands éléments nous suffisent et sont bien connus. Aussi longtemps qu'ils règnent, même dans le domaine de la *politesse*, il va de soi qu'on ne peut s'élever de l'insociable sociabilité, ou encore de l'histoire dialectique (celle de la guerre dans toutes ses formes) à l'histoire non dialectique (sous toutes ses formes, par exemple disparition de la dialectique de la séduction).

Pour définir l'égoïsme, ou encore le mal radical, Kant use d'une image très importante: la courbure, le bois courbe.[31] Il en use dans la VIe proposition de l'*Idée pour une histoire universelle au point de vue cosmopolitique*, dans la *Religion dans les limites de la simple raison* et dans la *Doctrine du droit.*[32] E. Troelsch a manqué la portée de cette détermination en se contentant de dire qu'il s'agissait peut-être d'une métaphore affectionnée par Kant.[33] En réalité

---

[30] A. Philonenko, *La liberté humaine dans la philosophie de Fichte* (Vrin, 1966); cf. R. Lauth, *Die transzendentale Naturlehre Fichtes nach den Prinzipien der Wissenschaftslehre* (Meiner, 1984).

[31] *La théorie kantienne de l'histoire*, p. 100 et suiv.

[32] AK. VIII, 23; VI, 100; VI, 233.

[33] E. Troeltsch, *Das Historische in Kants Religionsphilosophie* (*Kantstudien*, 1904). Troeltsch ne donne aucun commentaire sur le mot 'Krum'. Il se contente d'écrire: "*Offenbar ein lieblings Wort*". Voir mes commentaires dans mes notes à ma traduction de *La religion dans les limites de la simple raison*, in Kant, *Oeuvres philosophiques*, T. III, p. 1327 et suiv.

elle est capitale et intervient à des moments stratégiques. Le bois courbe est une métaphore qui remonte à Augustin — par là Augustin désigne le pécheur qui au lieu de s'élever vers Dieu et Dieu seul, se courbe vers les prétendus biens finis de la terre. Mais la courbure n'est pas, apparemment, absolument déterminante chez Augustin, car bien que condamnant l'égoïsme, évidemment impliqué dans la recherche des bien finis, elle n'entraîne pas une condamnation sans appel: en effet cela rendrait incompréhensible le second commandement qui nous ordonne d'aimer notre prochain comme nous nous aimons nous-mêmes. Il y a donc chez Augustin une limitation de la courbure. Avec Luther la courbure devient absolument déterminante: Luther ne fait pas, comme Augustin, la moindre place à un amour raisonnable de soi (un amour raisonnable supposerait quelque sainteté, ce dont nous sommes bien loin!) et il interprète le second commandement tout autrement. S'aimer soi-même est prendre conscience de la courbure et la détester, se détester donc: "aimer signifie se haïr soi-même":[34] "*Igitur, credo,* écrit Luther, *quod isto precepto* 'sicut te ipsum' *non precipiatur homo diligere se, sed ostendatur vitiosus amor, quo diligit se de facto, q.d. curvus es totus in te et versus in tui amorem, a quo non rectificaberis, nisi penitus cesses te diligere et oblitus tui solum proximum diligas*".[35] Nygren établit ainsi les équivalences luthériennes: *curvus = curvus in se (incurvatus in se) = versus in sui amorem.* L'homme fait d'un bois si courbe (*aus so krummem Holz*) ressemble à un bois qui se réfléchit en lui-même et par là non seulement on obtient une image précise de l'égoïsme, mais aussi une image plastique du passage d'une histoire dialectique à une histoire non-dialectique: il faudrait charpenter (comme dit Kant) quelque chose de droit à partir d'un bois tellement courbe. Mathématiquement c'est la quadrature du cercle.

Cette quadrature, Kant l'explique dans la VIe proposition de l'*Idée pour une histoire universelle au point de vue cosmopolitique* en insistant sur l'idée qu'"animal qui a besoin d'un maître" (ce que conteste Herder),[36] l'homme ne peut le trouver que parmi ses semblables — ce qui revient à nous faire tourner dans un cercle vicieux. Il s'agit bien de la quadrature du cercle: il n'y a pas de passage du courbe au droit. Et pourtant! L'homme a eu un maître: *le Saint de l'Evangile*, comme dit Kant dans les *Fondements de la Métaphysique des Mœurs*, et il l'a tué. Pour approfondir ce point il nous faudrait ici passer à la

---

[34] "*Est enim diligere se ipsum advisse*". Cf. ref. et commentaire in A. Nygren, *Erôs et Agapè* (Paris, 1952), T. III, p. 283, note 706.
[35] Com. *Römerbriefvorlesung* (*Epitre aux Romains*), Weimar 56, 518; cf. Pascal, *Pensées*, Ed. paléographique Zacharie Tourneur (Vrin, 1942), p. 294.
[36] Herder, *Ideen zur einer Philosophie der Geschichte*, VIIIe Buch.

théorie kantienne de la religion. Mais cela nous entraînerait trop loin. L'homme a tué, conduit à une "mort ignominieuse", le seul Maître qui pouvait par son exemple et son enseignement ("mes commandements ne sont pas difficiles") le redresser. Toutes les autres instances (Gouvernement d'un bon prince, d'une Assemblée, d'une démocratie) sont des approximations très insuffisantes par rapport au Christ. Voici donc la limite de notre histoire: incapables de briser notre courbure, nous demeurons enchaînés à l'histoire dialectique sous toutes ses formes et naturellement à la guerre.

D'un point de vue non pas pratique mais théorique, la triple unité synthétique de l'histoire, suivant la corrélation déterminée par H. Cohen[37] comme *Selbstzweck-Endzweck*, est susceptible d'être conçue. Première synthèse (IIIe proposition de l'*Idée pour une histoire universelle au point de vue cosmopolitique*) l'homme qui ne possède ni instinct, ni armes naturelles (soit pour se défendre, soit pour se nourrir) doit aller *du rien au tout*. Un moment important de cette synthèse est la population s'étendant sur le globe par la médiation de la guerre. La seconde synthèse est celle du courbe au droit. Dans la Ve proposition de ce texte Kant évoque une forêt où, luttant les uns contre les autres pour aspirer à la lumière, les arbres se redressent et poussent "beaux et droits". C'est l'image non pas du bien moral, mais de la politesse. Enfin les guerres doivent cesser: troisième synthèse — c'est celle qui conduit du clos à l'ouvert. Les nations s'élèvent de la guerre militaire à la guerre commerciale. Au point de vue théorique, la triple synthèse de l'histoire est concevable: du rien au tout, du courbe au droit, du clos à l'ouvert. L'unité de cette synthèse est la corrélation précitée.

Mais il est clair que la détermination *éthique* de la conception de l'histoire (l'impossibilité de réduire la courbure) contredit la détermination conceptuelle issue de la considération de la synthèse au point de vue de l'entendement. C'est pourquoi, en dépit de ses considérations sur les sciences, et même sur la philosophie comme science, Kant s'est toujours senti incapable de rejoindre la conception eudémoniste, non seulement de Herder, mais aussi d'un Condorcet et de tous les tableaux simplement empiriques des progrès de l'esprit humain qui fleurissaient alors. Il n'y a qu'une issue. Mais l'homme n'en détient pas la clef. Ce serait la révolution (je dis bien: la *révolution*) qu'opérerait Dieu lui-même dans la grâce d'un pardon effectif extirpant le mal radical définitivement. Alors bien sûr le pas métaphysique de l'histoire dialectique à l'histoire non dialectique serait franchi; la guerre sombrerait dans l'oubli. Dans cette pensée l'homme trouve enfin la vérité de l'histoire et de la

---

[37] *Kants Begründung der Ethik* (Berlin, 1910), p. 504 et suiv.

guerre, et c'est recueilli dans "l'esprit de la prière", comme dit Kant, qu'il doit à travers les mots de la prière tendre vers cette Idée. Ainsi nous voici encore une fois renvoyés à la théorie kantienne de la religion qui donne tout son sens à l'espérance. On ne le dit pas assez: *La Religion dans les limites de la simple raison* est une théorie d'abord synthétique, puis systématique de l'espérance. Que m'est-il permis d'espérer? La grâce divine instaurant l'histoire non dialectique comme communion des Saints et à l'intérieur de cette communion la disparition de ma courbure. Espérance difficile, espérance qui demande effort et rigueur. Kant n'oublie pas ces mots de Luther: "Omnia incurvata, je cherche en Dieu..."[38]

Université de Haute Normandie

---

[38] Luther, *Edit. de Weimar*, T. XL, 2, p. 325, 7 et suiv.

Megumi Sakabe

Freedom as a Regulative Principle: On Some Aspects of the Kant–Herder Controversy on the Philosophy of History

1. Although much work has been done on Kant's philosophy of history, it seems to me that there remain many points to be reconsidered regarding its relation to his whole system of critical philosophy, especially to his practical philosophy. The problem is all the more complicated, because in Kant's philosophical thought the philosophy of history is not fully integrated into the system of his critical philosophy. I will discuss the following points, mainly from the perspective of the interpretation of some aspects of the Kant–Herder controversy on the philosophy of history.

(1) Kant uses the distinction between regulative and constitutive principles and that between imagination and reason to highlight the confusion between them in Herder's thought. Keeping his methodological advantage over Herder, he makes it clear that the philosophy of history is an intermediate domain between theory and praxis or, from another point of view, between imagination and reason.

(2) In "Conjectural Beginning of Human History," published immediately after his criticism of Herder, Kant presents his own views as to the beginning of the history of mankind, using the concept of freedom as a regulative principle for "understanding" the conduct of others by "mimesis" or simulation by his own consciousness of freedom.

(3) In "Conjectural Beginning" Kant determines "quasi-performative" as well as "regulative" qualification of teleological principles. This step plays a considerable role in the advancement of Kant's philosophical thought towards his third *Critique*.

(4) In his controversy with Herder as to the problem of Averroism, Kant explicitly qualifies his vision of human history as a regulative principle (in contrast, perhaps, to the postulate of the immortality of the soul as a quasi-constitutive principle).

183

Y. Yovel (ed.), Kant's Practical Philosophy Reconsidered, 183-195.
© *1989 Kluwer Academic Publishers.*

2. In his "Review of Herder's Ideas for a Philosophy of the History of Mankind, Part Two," Kant writes on "poetical" features of Herder's description of races as follows:

It is not our intention here to pick out or analyze any of the bountiful number of beautiful passages rich in poetic eloquence which will recommend themselves to every reader of feeling. But just briefly we want to question whether the poetic spirit that enlivens the expression does not sometimes also intrude into the author's philosophy; whether synonyms are not valued as definitions here and there and allegories as truths; whether instead of occasional neighborly excursions out of the area of the philosophic into the sphere of poetic language the limits and domains of both are not completely disarranged; whether frequently the tissue of daring metaphors, poetic images, and mythological allusions does not serve to conceal the corpus of thought as under a farthingale instead of letting it glimmer forth agreeably as under a translucent veil. (Rez. 8: 60/45)

Clearly, though his language is euphemistic, Kant is very critical of Herder's confusion between poetical and philosophical languages: confusion between synonyms and definitions, between allegories and truths, and so on. On the other hand, however, it is undeniable that Kant admits the effectiveness of poetical expressions properly employed: the thin stuff of metaphors, poetic images and mythological allusions can "let the corpus of thought glimmer forth agreeably under a translucent veil"!

In other words, what Kant criticizes here is not the metaphorical or "tropical" transposition of language in general, but confusion between that sort of transposition and the philosophical use of language. Metaphorical or tropical transposition of language can well be put to use by the creative imagination. I contend that what Kant criticizes here is confusion between the level at which the imagination operates and that at which reason operates.

In any case, it seems very striking that both the distinction between the two uses of language (i.e., the poetical and philosophical) and criticism of their confusion are closely related to the well-known distinction between the constitutive and the regulative use of principles and criticism of the conflation of these two uses. Though Kant does not employ explicitly the terms "constitutive" and "regulative" in his "Reviews," in fact, as we shall see, the main point of his argument can be reduced to criticism of the lack of this sort of distinction in Herder's philosophy of history.

In the Supplement to his "Review of Herder's Ideas, Part One," Kant sums up the motivation of Herder's philosophy of history as follows:

The idea and final purpose of Part One (I say One as there is the likelihood of several subsequent volumes of the work) consist in the following. The spiritual nature of the human soul, its permanence and progress toward perfection, is to be proved by analogy with the natural formings of matter, particularly in their organic structure, with no recourse to metaphysics. (Rez. 8: 52/36)

However, in Kant's opinion, this ultimate aim cannot be achieved because of an essential defect in Herder's method. There may well be an organic force (organische Kraft) which, operating either as "animal soul" or as "spiritual force," etc., generates a series of organic systems culminating in man, a series which will continue to evolve and will reach a higher, more refined stage of life. But, admitting the continual gradation of natural kinds beyond man, it is not possible to have insight into this inferred invisible realm of creatures. For, it is *different* beings who occupy the successively more perfect stages of natural organization. Man can certainly infer by such an analogy that somewhere beyond earth, say, on another planet, there may be creatures embodying a level of organization above human beings. But this does not mean that a particular individual reaches that stage. That is, there is simply no connection between the expectation that in the future "moral" or even "metaphysical" causes will generate a more perfect man and the postulation of a hierarchy of levels in the realm of nature. To explain the phenomena of human mind as a result of the invisible organizing force of nature is clearly a case of explaining what one does not grasp by what one grasps even less.

But this is still metaphysics, and what is more, very dogmatic metaphysics, even though our author renounces it, as fashion demands." (Rez. 8: 54/38)

Admitting (not without irony) the courage with which the author dares to challenge excessive timidity as to the limits of reason, Kant nevertheless expresses the following hope regarding the further development of Herder's work:

It is to be hoped that philosophy, whose concern consists more in the pruning than the sprouting of superfluous growth, may guide him [the author] to the consummation of his enterprise, not with hints, but precise concepts, not through conjectured, but through observed laws, not through the intervention of winged imagination, whether metaphysical or sentimental, but rather through a reason, bold in the project but careful in the execution. (Rez. 8: 55/39)

What Kant rejects here, is the short circuit, so to speak, between "imagination" and "reason," which, due to the lack of sufficient methodological reflections, inevitably tends to "dogmatic metaphysics," or to confusion between "hints" (Winke) and "precise concepts" (bestimmte Begriffe), between "conjectured" and "observed laws," or between "winged imagination" (beflügelte Einbildungskraft) and "careful reason" (behutsame Vernunft).

The main points of Kant's criticism of Herder's philosophy of history can be summarized as follows:

(1) The basic defect in Herder's thinking resides, ultimately, in the short circuit between imagination and reason. Or, employing terminology often used in Kant's other writings, in the confusion of (levels of) "regulative" and "constitutive" principles. The same criticism applies to the confusion of "poetical" and "philosophical" languages or, on a larger scale, to the confusion of principles of thinking.

(2) Closely related to point (1) is the criticism that in Herder's thinking there exists no clear distinction between the realms of theory and praxis, physical determination and practical freedom, the world of natural history and that of morally responsible individuals, or, in a word, phenomenal and noumenal worlds.

(3) In reference to Herder's (methodological) monism and his theory of continuity (chiefly inherited from Hamann and Leibniz: there is even continuity between "verbum" and "ratio" as is clear from Hamann's famous phrase, "Poesy is the mother tongue of mankind"), Kant sets forth a set of clear, methodologically well-regulated distinctions between nature and morality, theory and praxis, regulative and constitutive principles, and finally, imagination and reason.

As we saw above, Kant speaks favourably of "a reason, bold in the project but careful in the execution" (eine im Entwurfe ausgebreitete, aber in der Ausübung behutsame Vernunft). At the same time, he disapproves of "conjectured (not observed) laws." But does this necessarily mean that he cannot admit any leap of "winged imagination" or its "conjectures"? (In fact, in some contexts, Kant greatly admired Herder's competence as a "poet," as we can see, for example, in the lines quoted above: "the bountiful number of beautiful passages rich in poetic eloquence.") Or, to the contrary, do we not inevitably need some bold leap of creative imagination, or even "poetical" imagination in the original sense of the word, to "expand [ausbreiten] the reason in the project," assuming, of course, that it is well-regulated methodically? In other words, do we not also need bold poetical "conjectures" as regulative principles to orient our thinking? Or, historically speaking, can we not discover under the surface structure of Kant's philosophy of reason a lower stratum issuing from "heuresis" or "inventio" as a branch of the tradition of European rhetoric?[1]

---

[1] Here one should also recall the historical development of the notions of "critica" and "iudicium" since Roman and Renaissance philosophies.

3. In his "Reviews," as we saw above, Kant criticized confusion between "conjecture" and "observation," "winged imagination" and "careful reason" as well as between poetical and philosophical languages. But, this does not mean that Kant will not, in any context, admit the bold leap of "winged imagination." If it is methodically well-regulated by reason, Kant is even willing to give himself voluntarily over to the exercise of the creative or "poetical" imagination. In the "Reviews," Kant spoke of a "reason, bold in the project but careful in the execution." But does not the bold expansion of reason inevitably require the aid of imagination?

In any case, in the "Conjectural Beginning of Human History," published a year after the "Reviews," Kant, borrowing a framework from mythical descriptions of Genesis, allows himself a bold leap of imagination, one which seems, in a sense, even more bold and "poetical" than Herder's, because it is regulated in advance by strict methodological reflections.

At the outset of this article Kant writes:

It is surely permissible to insert here and there conjectures into the progression of an historical account, in order to fill gaps in the record. For what precedes the gaps (the remote cause) and what follows them (the effect) give a fairly reliable clue to the discovery of the intermediate causes, which are to make the transition intelligible. (Mut. 8: 109/53)

Lacking sufficient historical knowledge, we are permitted to fill gaps of intermediate causes by extrapolation through "conjectures" of our imagination (which might sometimes even be poetical). In particular, when we do not examine the successive process of the history of human actions but its first beginning, our advantage is methodically greatest. For in this case, one need not imagine (erdichten) himself the first beginning, but one can simply speculate as to the original natural conditions of human beings by the "analogy of nature," that is, by analogy with its actual natural conditions.

Hence a historical account of the first development of freedom from its original predisposition in human nature is something altogether different from an account of the progression of freedom. For the latter can be based on records alone. (Mut. 8: 109/53)

Nevertheless, this sort of historical description, based largely on conjecture, cannot claim the same status as positivistic historical description whose grounds are not "mere natural philosophy." "Conjectures" must declare themselves "at best only as permissible exercise of the imagination guided by reason, undertaken for the sake of relaxation and mental health."

But precisely because of this difference, and because I here venture on a mere pleasure trip, I may hope to be favored with the permission to use, as a map for my trip, a sacred document; and also to fancy that my trip — undertaken *on the wings of the imagination, albeit not without a clue rationally derived from experience* — may take the very route sketched out in that document. (Mut. 8: 109-110/53-54, my emphasis)[2]

Just as the "Reviews of Herder's Ideas," after presenting a mythical model of Genesis, brought examples of historical "conjectures" by means of imagination, here Kant indicates his own views as to the way to reconcile such conjectures of winged and in some sense poetical imagination with claims of reason.

To describe concretely "a historical account of the first development of freedom from its original predisposition in human nature," Kant starts from what cannot be deduced by human reason from preceding natural causes, that is, the existence of man: specifically, the existence of fully-grown man living as a single pair (to avoid the immediate occurrence of war or struggle) in a fertile and peaceful garden. Moreover, this first man is supposed to have had, from the start, the ability to walk in an erect posture, to talk and to speak, that is, speak using coherent concepts, namely to think.

Thus, avoiding over-indulgence in unnecessary conjectures regarding the development of man from his natural primitive state, Kant starts with man with sufficient inherited "skills." "For my sole purpose is to consider the development of manners and morals [des Sittlichen] in his way of life, and these already presuppose the skills referred to" (Mut. 8: 111/55).

As opposed to Herder, who insists on the continuity between man and other animals and tries to trace the numerous successive steps from the one to the other, Kant needs only apply the "analogy of nature" to conceive of man with fully developed skills and consider only the development of the moral factors in his actions. Note that it is just the distinction between natural causality and the causality from freedom established in the *Critique of Pure Reason* that made possible application of this procedure in the philosophy of history.

Beginning with the suppositions mentioned above, Kant sketches the stages of the development of human reason or his consciousness of freedom:

(1) The man who has hitherto followed only the guide of instinct as if it were the voice of God, choosing his food through his senses of smell and taste, now, with the awakening of reason, becomes aware of visual features of food

---

[2] It is noteworthy that in addition to its relation to Herder's "Ideas," "Conjectural Beginning" can also be regarded as Kant's (perhaps indirect) response to Herder's remarkably bold leap of imagination in his "Oldest Sources of the Human Race" (1776). For a classical description of this point, see R. Haym, *Herder nach seinem Leben und seinen Werken* (Berlin, 1800-85), I: 564-67, 612-13; II: 247-60.

previously unnoticed, thus extending his cognition of food beyond the limits of mere instinct. This extension of his sensual abilities through reason, however, once accompanied by imagination, tends to operate even *counter* to his natural impulses and becomes "concupiscence" and "luxuriousness." In a famous passage of the Old Testament, the awakening of reason is related to a myth of the apple of wisdom and seduction by the snake. What is decisive here is that "He discovered in himself a power of choosing for himself a way of life, of not being bound without alternative to a single way, like the animals." By revealing to man the infinity of his desire and choice, newly-awakened reason, inevitably evoking man's uneasiness and timidity, leads him to the "brink of an abyss." But, once conscious of his freedom, like it or not, man can never again return to the state of servitude "under the rule of instinct."

(2) After the instinct of nourishment, comes that of sexuality. Here, too, certain changes took place under the influence of the newly-awakening reason. The attraction of sex, while in other animals mostly temporary and seasonal, becomes constant and augmented through imagination. The fig leaf symbolizes a more advanced stage of the exercise of reason. For, as a symbol of abstinence from direct animal impulse, it implies consciousness of some predominance of reason over sensual impulses. Desires are internalized and prolonged. Attractions which previously were only a matter of feeling now become idealized. Animal impulses gradually change into love. The feeling of the merely agreeable turns into that of the beautiful. Concealment of what might inspire contempt, together with good manners as a desire to inspire feelings of respect in others, mark a step towards the moralization of mankind.

(3) The third step in the development of human reason was the awakening of deliberate expectation of the future. This faculty can be regarded as the most definite indication of human supremacy, because it proves man's ability to prepare for remote purposes destined by his vocation. At the same time, because of the uncertainties of the future, it is the least conquerable origin of worry or anxiety. Perhaps, the hope vested in succeeding generations only constitutes consolation for that sort of fear of the future.

(4) Fourth and last came the definitive step of reason exalting man above the level of the life of mere animality: consciousness (however obscure) that man is ultimately the end of nature. Man becomes aware that other animals are not his comerades, equal to himself, but are means granted him for the attainment of his purposes. This idea entails (perhaps somewhat obscurely) its counterpart: one should not have this instrumental attitude to his fellow men, but must regard every other man as having equal right to utilize the gifts of nature.

Thus man had entered into a relation of equality with all rational beings, whatever their rank, with respect to the claim of being an end in himself, respected as such by every one, a being which no one might treat as a mere means to ulterior ends. (Mut. 8: 114/59)

Now, driven out of the cradle of nature, in spite of the hope expressed in the myth of the paradise, man has no way to return to his primitive state. Rather, in the midst of all the pains and distresses of this world, reason encourages man to further develop the faculties given him by nature.

Thus, in these descriptions of the conjectured beginning of the history of humankind, after making certain suppositions regarding the natural "skills" of man, Kant imagines boldly, in a framework borrowed from Genesis, the successive stages of the awakening of human reason or consciousness of freedom in the primitive state of nature. What undeniably governs this rational reconstruction or extrapolation of the intermediate stages of the development of the consciousness of freedom from its original natural state is the departure from our own consciousness of freedom. Kant, of course, could not foresee the epistemological discussion about "understanding" and "explanation" in the wake of Droysen and Dilthey. But, in fact, I believe precisely because he did anticipate that sort of distinction (which is closely related to his distinction between "regulative" and "constitutive"), he exceeded Herder methodologically in the philosophy of history. Moreover, Kant clearly grasped that this extrapolation in the domain of human history is carried out not by the process of "explanation" but by that of "understanding," which is a sort of simulation (mimesis) by our own consciousness of freedom.[3]

The following passage concerning interpretation of the myth of original sin can be regarded as yet another typical example of the application of the method of "understanding" by Kant:

Such an exposition teaches man that, *under like circumstances, he would act exactly like his first parents, that is, abuse reason in the very first use of reason, the advice of nature to the contrary notwithstanding.* Hence he must recognize what they have done as his own act, and thus blame only himself for the evils which spring from the abuse of reason. (Mut. 8: 123/68, my emphasis)[4]

In this procedure of "understanding" the origin of vice by means of the

---

[3] Cf. G. H. von Wright, *Explanation and Understanding* (Cornell University Press, 1971).

[4] Comparing these lines of "Conjectural Beginning" with Aristotle's famous description of "mimesis" in tragedy (*Poetics*, 1451b), one is struck by the close resemblance between them.

simulation (mimesis) of our own consciousness of freedom, evidently freedom is not used as a constitutive principle for our own conduct but as a regulative principle for the "understanding" of the conduct of others.

Is it not precisely in this (provisional) detachment from the actual situation of one's own conduct that one can obtain the free space for the bold leap of winged imagination? And is it not also in this free space of the imagination that historical discourse or narrative presents poetical or fictional features in a process of "idealization"?[5]

4. It is true that the main concern of understanding in the philosophy of history is the past conduct of humankind. But this does not mean that past historical facts can be understood quite independently of our vision of the future. As in our conduct or action there must be some comprehension of or projection into the future, so too in the understanding of past conduct of others one cannot but have some conception in mind of our own future. In a word, the "understanding" of he past cannot be separated and isolated from our "hope" concerning the future.

Hence, in his "Conjecture," Kant would seem to emphasize the interrelation between understanding the past and our vision of or hope for the future in the "teleological" space of our own historical consciousness:

It is true that Providence has assigned to us a toilsome road on earth. But it is of the utmost importance that we should nevertheless be content, partly in order that we may gather courage even in the midst of toils, partly in order that we should not lose sight of our own failings. These are perhaps the sole cause of all the evils which befall us, and we might seek help against them by improving ourselves. But this we should fail to do if we blamed all these evils on fate. (Mut. 8: 121/66)

In the concluding paragraph of the article, which immediately follows his interpretation of original sin, Kant writes as follows:

This, then, is the lesson taught by a philosophical attempt to write the most ancient part of human history: contentment with Providence, and with the course of human affairs, considered as a whole. For this course is not a decline from good to evil, but rather a gradual development from the worse to the better; and nature itself has given the vocation to everyone to contribute as much to this progress as may be within his power. (Mut. 8: 123/68)

In this teleological space of "understanding" and "hope" which is situated

[5] Among the many recent discussions about the nature of historical narrative, see especially, P. Ricœur, *Temps et récit III, Le temps raconté* (Paris: Seuil, 1985), pp. 203-75.

between "knowledge" and "action" (or rather "detached" from them) Kant freely exercises his productive and at times even poetical imagination which, in my opinion, may be even described as "mytho-poetical" or, if you like, "fonction fabulatrice." Having established the distinction between "regulative" and "constitutive" (which basically, as we saw, corresponds to that between "understanding" and "explanation"), Kant finds the way to assign imagination a positive role and situate it among other faculties of the human mind. (In "Conjectural Beginning of Human History," Kant in fact presented a method of positively assessing poetical language or fictional discourse as a sort of "mimesis" in line with the "as-if" qualification of regulative principles in general. For example, recall the passage quoted above: "that my trip — undertaken on the wings of the imagination, albeit not without a clue rationally derived from experience — may take the very route sketched out in that document.")

As we saw, Kant in fact exercises his imagination even more boldly than Herder in the philosophy of history because of his methodological superiority over Herder. For Kant is not simply opposing Herder's view, but rather, is actively responding to the boldest leap of Herder's imagination since his "Oldest Sources of the Human Race." Kant situates himself in a kind of "dialectical" relationship with Herder, and in this fruitful dialogue, he goes even further than Herder in the exercise of his poetical and mythical imagination. Thus, one could say that Kant can be more "poetical" or "mytho-poetical" than Herder in his bold leap of the imagination.

In passing, I think that Kant's views of natural teleology were considerably influenced by his determination, in the domain of the philosophy of history, of the status of the teleological principle as regulative for "understanding." And this determination of the teleological principle in the domain of natural history or natural science in general, must have been decisively influenced by Kant's previous investigation into the origins and application of that principle in the domain of human history.

Contrary to the generally accepted view as to the development of Kant's philosophical reflections on the teleological principle, I strongly emphasize the important, indeed definitive role played by his deliberations on the status of this principle in "Conjectural Beginning of Human History": the status of this principle as a regulative principle has its origin in the "mimesis" occurring in our own consciousness of freedom.

We find an unmistakable echo of these considerations in the following passage from an article published two years after the "Conjectural Beginning," namely, "On the Use of Teleological Principles in Philosophy," in which Kant argues as regards the definition of an organism:

So the concept of a faculty of a being which is of itself *purposive*, yet has *no purpose* or aim to accomplish either in itself or in its cause — as some special basic force [*Grundkraft*] of which no example is given in experience — is completely made up and empty, i.e., without the slightest guaranty that any object whatsoever could correspond to it. So whether the cause of organized beings is to be found *in* the world or *outside* it, we must either renounce any determination of their cause, or think of an *intelligent being* as the cause. (UG 8: 181-182)[6]

It would be very interesting to trace the development of Kant's views on the teleological principle from here to the *Critique of Judgement* and reexamine its status together with that of aesthetic judgement. For, generally speaking, the problem of "reflective judgement," issuing from the long tradition of "iudicium" and characterized by Kant as a medium between the domains of theory and praxis, has naturally much to do with the philosophy of history as well as with practical philosophy. But we cannot enter into further consideration of this problem here. For the present, I confine myself to some remarks characterizing Kant's philosophy of history.

In his philosophy of history, Kant utilizes freedom as a regulative principle for the "understanding" of the past conduct of others. At the same time, this process of understanding through simulation or mimesis necessarily involves projecting into the future. It is because of this fact that, however positivistic it may be, historical discourse inevitably includes moments of fiction (poiesis) or even of myth.

It would seem that imagination (or reflective judgement), which occupies an intermediate position between knowledge and action (or theory and praxis), is essentially ambiguous. To some degree, due to the detachment of imagination from actual situations, its determinations are formed outside the dichotomy of theory–praxis, or even independently of those of explanation–understanding, constitutive–regulative. Does not this ambiguous character mean precisely that the so-called descriptive historical discourse has a "quasi-performative" nature?

As we have seen, Kant says:

This, then, is the lesson taught by a philosophical attempt to write the most ancient part of human history: contentment with Providence, and with the course of human affairs, considered as a whole. For this course is not a decline from good to evil, but rather a gradual development from the worse to the better; and *nature itself has given the vocation to everyone to contribute as much to this progress as may be within his power.* (Mut. 8: 123/68, my emphasis)

[6] See also Sakabe, "Kant on Anthropology and Natural History," *Acta Institutionis philosophiae et aestheticae* (Tokyo: Centre international pour étude comparée de philosophie et d'esthétique, 1984), 2: 105-113.

Does not the historical discourse naturally partake of this vocation of nature (Rufen der Natur) in its "quasi-performative" character?

Kant also talks of a "pleasure trip" led by the map of "a sacred document." This detour — the "pleasure trip" on the wing of imagination — is detached from reality and played through the "mimesis" or simulation of the consciousness of freedom. Was it not a kind of "catharsis" which was realized so as to make one hear and follow more attentively that "vocation of nature"?

5. At the end of his "Reviews of Herder's Ideas," Kant tries to rebut Herder's two critical arguments against his "Idea for a Universal History from a Cosmopolitan Point of View" (1784). One concerns the problem that if man is an animal he necessarily requires a master, and the other concerns the presence of some traits of Averroism in Kant's philosophy of history. Herder's argument regarding the second point, that is, against Kant's Averroism, is as follows:

If someone said that not the individual man but the species could be educated, he would be speaking unintelligibly for me since race and species are only general concepts, except to the extent that they exist in individual beings.... As if I could speak of animality, minerality or metality in general and adorned them with the grandest attributes which, however, contradict one another in single individuals!... Our philosophy of history should not follow this way of Averroistic philosophy." (Rez. 8: 65/51).

Kant rebuts Herder's argument by saying that if kind means nothing but the feature shared by all members of a group, Herder is right:

But if by human species we understand the totality of series of generations proceeding into infinity (the indeterminable) — and this meaning, after all, is quite common; and if it is admitted that this line of descent ceaselessly approaches its concurrent destination, then it is no contradiction to say that this line is asymptotic in all its parts to this line of destiny, and on the whole, coincides with it. In other words, no single member in all of these generations of the human race, but only the species, fully achieves its destination. (Rez. 8: 65/51)

The progress of the human race towards the ultimate goal of its history is here considered using the metaphor of the infinitely "asymptotic" line, which might very well symbolize the "regulative" character of Kant's vision of the history of humankind.

The mathematician can offer explanations on this matter. The philosopher would say that the destination of the human race in general is perpetual progress, and its perfection is a simple, but in all respects very useful, Idea of the goal to which, conforming to the purpose of providence, we have to direct our efforts. (Rez. 8: 65/51)

Let me repeat the following lines: the "perfection [of the destination of the human race in general] is a simple, but in all respects very useful, Idea of the goal to which, conforming to the purpose of providence, we have to direct our efforts." Is it not self-evident that in these lines Kant qualifies "the destination of the human race in general" as "a simple, but in all respects very useful, Idea of the goal," that is, a genuinely "regulative" principle for the orientation of our conduct?

Kant concludes his "Reviews" by alluding to the fact that it is in Herder's philosophy rather than in his own that the inclination to Averroism is most pronounced.

Still, this misunderstanding in the polemical passage cited above is only a trifle. More important is its conclusion: "Our philosophy of history should not follow this way of Averroistic philosophy." From this it may be concluded that our author, so often offended by everything hitherto passed off for philosophy, will now, once and for all in this exhaustive work, give the world a model of the true art of philosophizing, not in fruitless verbalisms but in deed and example. (Rez. 8: 65-66/51-52)

Here too we notice extremely interesting methodological controversy between Kant and Herder. Once again, on the basis of the distinction between regulative and constitutive principles, Kant gains a methodological advantage over Herder and performs a bolder methodological leap than Herder.

Having established the "as-if" character and "quasi-performative" nature of his own discourse, Kant goes beyond the incompatibility between the individual and the whole, and takes the swift metaphorical leap from his own consciousness to that of others, from the domain of the individual soul (firmly rooted in the domain of immortality to be postulated in the second *Critique*) to that of the general history of humankind.

In this bold but at the same time methodologically well-regulated leap of the winged imagination, we can see Kant's response to Herder's exercise of poetical or mytho-poetical imagination in his "Oldest Sources" and "Ideas" and, possibly, also find some way of reassessing Herder's philosophy of history in the light of Kant's arguments in his historical and practical philosophy.[7]

University of Tokyo

---

[7] In order to reevaluate the Kant–Herder controversy on the philosophy of history, it would be helpful to extend our study to the full relations between them. It would be especially helpful to examine a work of Herder's later years, *Kalligone*. See Sakabe, "Historia et Ethica chez le jeune Kant et Herder," *Aesthetics* (Journal of the Faculty of letters, the University of Tokyo), 5 (1981): 85-91.

David Heyd

How Kantian Is Rawls's "Kantian Constructivism"?

Introduction

The following is yet another contribution to the vast corpus of Rawlsiana which has grown during the past two decades to reach a size rapidly approaching that of the literature on Kant. But at the same time, it is an attempt to critically examine Rawls's reading of Kant and to come to some conclusions about Kant's ethical theory.

Beginning with *A Theory of Justice*, Rawls persistently presents his theory, especially in its methodological aspects, as Kantian in nature. In his John Dewey Lectures of 1980 he uses the term "Kantian Constructivism" as the title of his three papers and as the concept constituting his principal thesis. Later, in "Justice as Fairness: Political Not Metaphysical" (1985), Rawls further refines his constructivist argument, still insisting on its Kantian origins. In a more recent paper, "The Idea of an Overlapping Consensus" (1987), Rawls elaborates the idea of justice as fairness as a political conception.

Rawls, like many great philosophers, tends to disclaim originality by couching his own theory in a well-established tradition. The method of arriving at the principles of justice is said to be a version of the social contract and the Kantian idea of free and equal persons exercising their autonomous will. This disavowal of theoretical innovation should not be taken either as false modesty or as an attempt to mobilize great names in support of one's cause. It is rather a philosophical statement simultaneously identifying Rawls's own ethical and political views and interpreting the essence of earlier formulations of similar views.

I am grateful to Onora O'Neill who read the draft of this paper very carefully and made numerous incisive comments saving me the embarrassment of some serious blunders. I also learnt much from Otfried Höffe's criticism. I am however aware that both would have liked to see the article even more radically revised than it has actually been.

Y. Yovel (ed.), *Kant's Practical Philosophy Reconsidered, 196-212.*
© *1989 Kluwer Academic Publishers.*

It would therefore be a mistake to take Rawls's reading of Kant as a commentary or a textual analysis that can be subjected to standards of textual interpretation. Rawls's reading is indeed biased. He says himself: "I do not wish to argue here for this interpretation on the basis of Kant's text. Certainly some will want to read him differently" (TJ 252; see also JF 223-24, and KC 552, 559). It is, accordingly, interesting to examine the sense of Rawls's own reading of Kant as well as its limitations and the sense of these very crossroads where a different reading yields interesting implications regarding some unresolved problems in the Rawlsian constructivist program.

My paper, therefore, could be called either To what extent is Rawls's "Kantian constructivism" indeed Kantian? or, How constructive, i.e. Rawlsian, is Kant's ethics? The clarification of these questions may prove illuminating — first in the interpretation of Kant, secondly in the discussion of Kant's impact on modern political philosophy, and thirdly in drawing the dividing lines in the debate between naturalism and constructivism as two major alternative bases for morality and political organization.

Constructivism

What is constructivism? Kant refers to construction in ethics in the context of the discussion of rights as authorizations of coercion:

The law of a reciprocal use of coercion that is necessarily consistent with everyone's freedom under the principle of universal freedom may in certain respects be regarded as the *construction* of his concept [of justice]; that is, it exhibits this conception in a pure a priori intuition... Just as in pure mathematics we cannot immediately deduce the properties of the object from a concept, but can only discover them by means of the construction of the concept, likewise the exhibition and description of the concept of justice is not made possible so much by the concept itself as by the general reciprocal and equal use of coercion that comes under a universal law and is consistent with it. (RL 6: 232-33/37)

This constructivist method suggested by Kant is surprisingly ignored by Rawls. It could have served his Kantian connection much better than other texts, which do not mention construction. Yet, it is important to note that this constructive strategy is offered by Kant for the concept of justice (or "legality"), and not for the specifically "moral" dimension of his ethical theory. This could have been Rawls's reason for disregarding the above quoted passage. Still, O. Höffe is certainly right in criticizing Rawls for confusing the internal (virtue, ethical) with the external (right, legal) levels of the Kantian exposition and for using Kant's analysis of the "moral" for his theory of political justice.[1] Rawls, on his part, says only little by way of a systematic exposition of the concept, although it serves him as the defining characteristic in his Kantian self-image. Rawls formulates the idea of constructivism in a nutshell as follows: "The leading idea is to establish a suitable connection between a particular conception of the person and first principles of justice, by means of a procedure of construction" (KC 516). This succinct description implies some basic propositions about justification in moral and political theory, many of which are certainly of a Kantian nature. The priority of *procedure* over antecedently given ends highlights the role of (possible) *agreement* as the basis for the justification of moral and political principles. Agreement is essentially a result of the exercise of the *will*, which is given priority over the discovery of truth. Any moral construction is grounded on rational *choice* (i.e. choice under certain constraints which will be specified later) rather than on intellectual insight or knowledge. Accordingly, the object of construction is usually a decision on *principles* of action rather than the specification of values or moral facts. Thus, the chief predicate characterizing the product of construction are 'right' and 'just' rather than 'good' or 'true'.

An essential assumption underlying any constructivist view is therefore a *subjectivist* theory of value, implying heterogeneity of legitimate individual objectives and life-plans. Unlike utilitarianism, perfectionism, and intuitionism, constructivism is not committed to any a priori conception of justice (or indeed to any other moral value). It does not strive to implement any independently defined ideal or desirable social structure. Thus, *toleration* is called for on two levels: first, as respect for other people's values and preferences (moral toleration); secondly, as neutrality between competing views concerning the correct method of justifying such values and preferences (philosophical toleration). Toleration on both levels is a condition for the free bargaining which characterizes the Rawlsian version of construction.

Constructivism is obviously an *anti-naturalistic* theory of ethics. As we shall see later in some detail, it shuns most traditional assumptions about human nature — its essential features or metaphysically based evaluations of its different powers. It avoids all moral reasoning which refers to the natural order of things in the world — human or non-human, individual or social, physical or metaphysical (KC 559). The constructivist sees the goal of his enterprise as *practical* rather than epistemological. In contradistinction to the subordination of human cognition to truth, moral agents are described as the

[1] O. Höffe, "Is Rawls' Theory of Justice Really Kantian?" *Ratio* 26 (1984): 105.

autonomous source of the very standards of behaviour by which they choose to abide.

Circularity

But now the philosophical question arises: how can the very idea of construction be made to do any work? For, if indeed no view of human nature is allowed in the theory, *who* are the agents of such a construction? The prospects of solving this problem chiefly lie in the subtle distinction between what Rawls calls "a conception of a person" and what we referred to as "a theory of human nature." The success of the constructivist program is conditioned by the viability of a non-naturalistic, metaphysically neutral, concept of a person. Such a concept must be an abstraction, a non-realistic isolation of certain features thought to be relevant to the very project of construction. Thus, Rawls persistently reminds us that his concept of a person is itself *moral* or *political*. It is a concept of a person *as a citizen*. The only characterization of a person allowed by this model is through the two moral powers: "the capacity for a sense of justice and the capacity for a conception of the good" (JF 233).

This concept of a person, albeit stripped of all psychological features, is dependent upon the idea of social cooperation, which is both a presupposition and the goal of construction. In other words, the point of the specific abstraction of the concept of the person as a contractor in the original position is its deployment in the enterprise of construction, leading to the establishment of a just and well-ordered society. We are thus entangled in a typically circular argument, which Rawls calls "The Three Model Conception":

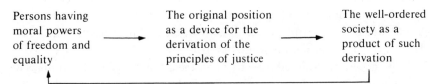

Persons having moral powers of freedom and equality → The original position as a device for the derivation of the principles of justice → The well-ordered society as a product of such derivation

The notion of a well-ordered society is itself the basis for the concept of the person as a citizen, and social cooperation the assumption validating the rationality and reasonableness of these persons in their dealings with others under the veil of ignorance of the original position.

By consciously "closing" the argument in a circle Rawls hopes to achieve his methodological goal of absolute neutrality regarding the nature of human beings, the world and the good. He is guaranteed a self-sufficient line of argument requiring no realistic assumptions. The constraints on the behaviour of the contractors in the original position are all *internal*, that is to say derived from the very idea of what these persons are supposed to do in the negotiation of principles of justice. In Kantian language, they are autonomous, free from any psychological or pathological (natural) conditioning in their pursuit of a moral order.

The Limits of Kant's Constructivism

The question which will be addressed in the rest of this paper is twofold: Is such a constructivist circular model indeed Kantian in nature? and What is its plausibility? My thesis may sound paradoxical: the more constructivist Rawls's argument becomes the less Kantian it is. The evaluation of his theory may give us some clue in support of this claim. Rawls of *A Theory of Justice* could be understood as implying that the original position should express what we *really* are, i.e., free and equal persons. Later on, in both "Kantian Constructivism" and "Justice as Fairness: Political Not Metaphysical," freedom and equality are treated merely as features relevant (or necessary) for the construction of a model. Furthermore, whereas the earlier work draws the lines of a partially comprehensive *moral* theory, the later ones explicitly offer only the basis for a *political* agreement. In these two aspects of constructivism — namely the dissociation from both metaphysical and moral assumptions — Rawls parts company with Kant.

It is of course true that Kant held some basic views which naturally lend themselves to a constructivist interpretation. His moral theory is based on the idea of a person as a rational being, having the power to choose his principles of action autonomously, rather than on a scheme of given values and ends which dictate his behaviour. The power of rational intuition can be ascribed only to God and accordingly the moral law cannot be founded on the knowledge of moral truth couched in the order of things, be it natural (as in Hume) or super-natural (as in Leibniz).

More generally, Kant adheres to a constructivist model in the primacy he attaches to will and choice over cognition, the right (i.e., the way the will is determined) over the good (of the will's objects). The formulation of the Categorical Imperative in terms of universalizability offers an ultimate moral test or decision procedure which is absolutely neutral between antecedent claims for certain values. The formulation of the Imperative in terms of respect for persons as ends also fits the constructivist model in the priority it attaches to the value of the moral agent over that of desirable states of affairs in the world.

Yet, having said all this, one should not ignore the essentialist assumptions in Kant's ethics. Kant could not share the Three Model Conception, for he does not distinguish between procedure and its outcome. Unlike Rawls, he does not have two meanings for freedom and equality — one in the procedural stage of the original position, the other in the social state which is the end-result (although he holds another different distinction between two concepts of freedom). Furthermore, Kant's starting point for his theory is not an abstracted notion of a person having only the features relevant to the project of fair social cooperation. In a way, Kant's concept of the *knowing subject* is closer to the notion of a Rawlsian construction, for it is characterized only by those features that make experience possible. Everything which can be said of the cognitive self is transcendental, that is to say, that which makes the function of this self (cognition) possible. This introduces an analogous form of circularity into the relationship between the knowing subject and the object of knowledge. But in the case of the *moral agent*, Kant insists on a fully independent, real, noumenal self, who is essentially free.

Kant, of course, is conscious of the problem of circularity (G 4: 453/113) and offers a solution to it elsewhere (KpV 5: 5/4n) in terms of the distinction between freedom as the *ratio essendi* of the moral law and the moral law as the *ratio cognoscendi* of freedom. He also speaks of the moral law as "a fact of reason" (KpV 5: 31/31) thus resting the whole construction on a non-natural yet real *fact*.

Kant's avoidance of constructivist circularity is thus based on the traditional metaphysical view of persons. Unlike Rawls, Kant does not raise the banner of philosophical toleration in the above-mentioned Rawlsian sense. For him, the distinction between the noumenal reality of the moral self and the phenomenal self-consciousness of the knowing subject is itself metaphysically real.

Furthermore, an important part of Kant's philosophical motivation in the *Critique of Practical Reason* is to prove the metaphysical reality of freedom and the noumenal self, that is to say, the moral theory is partly instrumental in deciding a profound philosophical issue. The very distinction, so central to Kant's ethics, between the natural world of inclinations and passions and the noumenal world of free will is indeed "problematic" from the point of view of speculative reason, but becomes real from the perspective of practical reason. So, whereas Rawls tries to establish objectivity in moral theory on the basis of philosophical toleration, Kant tries to gain access to metaphysical reality through moral theory, and by that achieve the architectonic goal of the unity of reason. On the one hand, we have moral objectivity founded on neutral grounds; on the other, we have moral theory both pointing to a metaphysical truth and in turn supported by it. Kant refuses to found his moral theory on philosophical toleration because he wants to use moral theory as the ultimate evidence for the redundancy of such toleration!

The Concept of a Person

Unlike the Rational Intuitionist, who believes in the existence of moral *truth* independently of a conception of the nature of human beings, both Kant and Rawls share the view that in moral theory the starting point should be the characterization of the moral *agent*. Both philosophers oppose Hume's empirical or naturalistic conception of the moral agent which includes the basic human psychological motives and drives. The construction of a moral theory must, in their eyes, be founded on some sort of a nucleus in the human subject, isolated from empirical contingencies. Such subjects must be rational, free, and equal, and treat others as also having those features. They should be autonomous, i.e., have a power to decide for themselves the principles of right action. They must be assumed to have some sort of moral sense (conscience, sense of justice, reverence for the moral law, sensitivity to fairness, etc.), although this is not used in the construction itself. But the common constructivist ground ends here, as Kant and Rawls part ways in the characterization of that nucleus.

To play on words, my argument concerning the difference between the two may be put thus: while Kant is concerned with a concept of *a moral person*, Rawls is concerned with *a moral concept* of a person. In other words, Kant offers a theory of human *nature*, although only in its isolated practical dimension, i.e., of moral agency. Rawls, on his part, anxious to avoid any philosophical commitment to a theory of human nature, focuses on the *concept* of a person, which is merely a theoretical construct, an intellectual artifice.

This basic difference implies different approaches to the process of isolating the desired nucleus. Kant, in the tradition of most of his predecessors in moral philosophy since Plato, tries to elicit or extract the essence of human nature (although only on the *practical* level), which in accordance with that same tradition is rationality. Rawls, on the other hand, is typically and consciously engaged in the *abstraction* of those characteristics of human beings that would make them possible representatives in the original position, which is treated as "a device of representation." Accordingly, Rawls insists that the contractors should be viewed as players in a game like Monopoly, who artificially abstract their roles as landlords and entrepreneurs from their real features just for the sake of playing the game (JF 238-39).

What are the constraints on this procedure of isolating the nucleus? In Rawls's constructivism they have to do with the ends of the game, namely the agreement on principles of justice for a well-ordered society. In Kant's theory, the constraints are dictated by human nature. More metaphorically, it is as if a person entering the game of the original position is asked to be what the *game* instructs him to be, while a person entering Kant's moral game is asked to be *himself*, his real self. Rawls's constraints are methodological and the instrument of their implementation is the veil of ignorance. Kant's constraints are substantive and their validity is derived from an a priori deduction from the very concept of reason.

Rawls can therefore exclude all psychological assumptions about human motivation from the original position (JF 239n) and admit that the contractors are just "artificial agents who inhabit a construction" (KC 532). Kant, on the other hand, must prove that even without removing the psychological motives (inclinations), rational will can indeed move real human beings to action; that is to say, human agents can act freely and morally not because we artificially abstract all non-moral idiosyncratic motives, but because we can *choose* to act for moral reasons rather than be driven to act on inclinations.

So for Kant the human agent is always conceived as having natural desires beside reason. Desires are the basic motives of action and the moral law is only the ultimate constraint on their realization. Rawls, on the other hand, by introducing an artificial model of construction allows his contractors to act with complete freedom from the psychological idiosyncrasies of the individual.

In this context it is intriguing to find Rawls speaking of the sense of justice as "a highest order desire" (KC 533), thus introducing into his system a regimentation or value-order in the realm of human motivation. In this, Rawls reminds us of Kant's distinction between higher and lower faculties of desire (KpV 5: 24/23), again as part of a theory of human nature. If indeed Rawls wishes to stick to the constructivist conception of a person, he must explain the term "higher faculty" also in purely constructivist terms, namely, from the point of view of what he calls "fully autonomous citizens of a well-ordered society." From a metaphysically neutral point of view, there can be nothing intrinsically or naturally "higher" in the desire for justice.

Thus, Rawls's claim that the desire for justice is autonomous and "not a desire on the same footing with natural inclinations" (which are heteronomous) can be justified only in constructivist terms, i.e., the desire to be that kind of person as specified by the idea of a citizen in a well-ordered society. But Kant could object to this interpretation of autonomy, since for him the idea of a well-ordered society is "external" to the will itself and thus a heteronomous determinant of that will. Autonomy is defined solely in terms of self-legislation.

One well-known problem of any constructivist program is the extent of empirical information which can be left outside what we called "the nucleus." Rawls believes morality should serve human beings, and thus takes their *general* aims and goals into account. He accordingly outlines a "thin theory of the good," that general scheme of values which, though not logically necessary, characterize all human beings as we know them. Morality is subject to those general empirical constraints because otherwise it would become vacuous. For example, no moral theory can ignore the general human interest in wealth or the bases of self-respect, universally held to be good. Rawls advises us to read Kant as accepting some sort of general empirical constraints (TJ 257), but it seems that the addition of such constraints would run contrary to the spirit of Kant's a priori based ethics.

However, I would not like to take issue with Rawls on the interpretation of Kant on this point (especially as Rawls himself suggests it only tentatively); yet, it cannot be denied that Kant systematically insists on an ideal conception of morality, applying to all rational creatures including those not sharing the specifically human character, needs, or goals (such as wealth or self-respect). Kant is reluctant to make any concessions to the *condition humaine* in his ethical theory. Although both thinkers accept the idea of the separateness of persons as the basis for the liberal respect for individuals, Kant pays that respect to the person as a rational being, while Rawls (like Mill) values the individual as a self-originating agent of goals and life-plans, and uses "rational" in an instrumental sense.

In that respect, the very term "ideal" serves Kant and Rawls in different ways: ideals for Kant have regulative power and efficacy in the direction of human behaviour both on the individual and on the collective-historical levels. Kant believes that human beings can gradually discipline their empirical nature and get closer to the ideal of the Kingdom of Ends, at least in the world to come. In contrast, "ideal" in the Rawlsian context is no more than an adjective describing the abstract model. This model has an important explanatory power and indeed serves as a theoretical justification for substantive normative principles, but it does not move people to act on these principles.

We should however note that although Kant does not separate the rational and irrational powers of human agents in a constructivist way, he demands a very strict isolation of the essential nucleus of reason as the only basis for morality. Rawls, on the other hand, who artificially stipulates pure or "ideal" rationality and reasonableness in the original position, believes that as a matter of fact persons will never be able to overcome their idiosyncratic nature and that this should not be the aim of a moral system. Thus, his idealization is less strict than Kant's and allows general empirical truths of human psychology into the model. Rawls leaves much more room for individual variation within morality than the monolithic ideal of a Kingdom of Ends.

So it seems that by refusing to subject morality to any empirical constraints, Kant is led to view the moral system as a metaphysical ideal which can be realized only in eschatological time. Rawls, for his part, by taking into account psychological and sociological facts, can view his system of justice as realizable in this world.[2]

Morality versus Political Theory

The difference in the conception of the person reflects the difference in the underlying theoretical tenets of the two philosophers. While *A Theory of Justice* created what the author saw as a misleading impression as to the *ethical* nature of the theory, in his later writings Rawls is at pains to emphasize the *political* character of the idea of justice as fairness. This typical constructivist move is put in declarative terms in the title of the 1985 article: "Justice as Fairness: Political Not Metaphysical."

I would like to argue that Rawls's constructivism, being based on the Three Model Conception which is circular in structure, inevitably leads to a purely political interpretation of the validity and authority of the principles of justice. For in the absence of any metaphysical anchor in the form of a theory of human nature (and of a system of values), the constructivist has no other alternative but to treat the persons in the original position as *citizens*, i.e., as political figures engaged in the negotiation of political agreement on principles and institutions which would coordinate their behaviour and social interaction. Moreover, Rawls explicitly says that his conception of justice is political, because the very notion of a citizen is relative to the idea of a well-ordered society, and that idea in turn has no independent source of validity and can only be understood "within a certain political tradition" (JF 225). This tradition is of course that of liberal democracy, characterized (since the Reformation) by the pluralism of incommensurable conceptions of the good.

---

[2] This does not mean of course that Kant ignores the dimension of the empirical in his casuistical discussion of ethics and in his philosophy of history which provides the framework for the moral progress of humanity.

Rawls does not wish to deny that such a conception of justice has some moral dimension (OC 8), but is careful not to grant it the status of a "*comprehensive* moral doctrine" (JF 245). A comprehensive moral doctrine could not tolerate a real pluralism about values which is the core of political liberalism. Taking such profound moral pluralism as a given fact, Rawls must devise an alternative to the a priori deductive model of derivation of normative principles. The only way is to start with democratic society as an arena both of individual fights over values and of techniques of negotiation, compromise and agreement.

Rawls is aware of the differences between his and Kant's theory on this point. He mentions Kant's point of departure in the individual conscientiously judging the moral validity of his personal maxims (KC 552-53). However, Rawls does not elaborate the deeper reasons and implications of this difference and specifically ignores the extent to which those reasons would make it hard to call Kant a constructivist.

The fact that Rawls takes social reality as the starting point makes his theory sensitive to historical and social variations and limits it to a more modest scope of application. It also guarantees the theory a higher degree of plausibility, at least (and perhaps only) in the eyes of those belonging to the particular social tradition under discussion. Let us recall that Rawls's ultimate method of verification in moral theory is the doctrine of reflective equilibrium, which rests partly on the agreement of principles with intuitions. The minimum harmony of individual intuitions cannot be guaranteed unless we secure a minimal homogeneity in the basic values of the members of society.

However, for Kant this constructivist political argument is flawed by the hypothetical status of the point of departure. Moral theory is universal and absolute in its requirements. Although its ultimate test is social and coordinative (as in Rawls), the reference group within which it applies is a timeless universe populated by all rational beings. It is not political in the historical and territorial sense as suggested by Rawls (KC 536).

Thus, Kant requires a unique and absolute solution to moral problems while Rawls is satisfied with agreement on what he calls "an overlapping consensus." These constitute two very different standards of normative acceptability: rational *consistency* versus mere *convergence* (KC 561). For Kant reflective equilibrium should not involve intuitions but only a priori examination of the form by which our will is determined.

The political character of Rawls's theory is also reflected in what he calls "the full publicity condition" (KC 538), which prevents manipulation through delusion and ignorance, and ensures the stability of social cooperation without appealing to coercive sanctions. Stability is safeguarded, since beyond the fact that everyone accepts the principles of justice, everyone also knows that the others accept them. Kant, on the other hand, cannot offer his moral principle (acting *from* duty) as a basis for political arrangements (acting *in accordance* with duty), and hence needs the complementary theory of legality. This is because morality is so private a matter that even the individual himself can never be sure whether he has acted morally (from duty). The ultimate standard of morality is conscience and good faith, a standard which can never be subject to public scrutiny. The far-reaching motivational condition of Kant's moral principle creates a harder problem of compliance than is found in Rawls. Yet Kant would say that this problem should not be taken as marring the purity of moral theory and should be dealt with separately on the political and jurisprudential level.

Kant's moral construction is, therefore, based on each individual separately exercising his autonomous will, with the assumption that uniformity of the end-result is secured by the similarity of persons *qua* rational beings. Rawls offers public negotiation as the means of attaining harmony between different individuals. It is instructive that Kant's *Gedankenexperiment* of the universalizability test does not require more than one person, while Rawls's original position essentially consists of many, because it is based on bargaining (though the fact that the contractors lose all their individual character in the original position led some critics to doubt the idea of bargaining, as it could in principle be conducted by one rational person).

This disparity also involves two interpretations of *objectivity*. Both philosophers reject a naturalistic basis for objectivity in morals; yet Kant still expects moral principles to be objective in his technical sense of universal and necessary, namely, a priori justified. Rawls discards these conditions and substitutes for them the consensual condition, the convergence of individual wills. There is something formal about both these constructivist senses of objectivity, but the formal basis of objectivity in agreement is typically political, while Kant's formalism transcends all political boundaries and establishes a purely moral realm. Rawls says that objectivity is acceptability to all from a suitably constructed point of view (KC 554), but the scope of "all" varies — as we have seen — in the two theories, and consequently the criteria of the suitable construction or the right standpoint will vary as well.

It is also typical of political liberalism that it aims at the more modest end, namely a *workable* conception of justice rather than an ideal solution. Liberalism as a political theory takes people as having an indefinite repertory of life-plans and preferences, which are typically incommensurable and thus never fully negotiable. This is Rawls's tribute to the ineliminable empirical element in human nature and its value in constituting one's personal identity as an individual (moral liberalism in Mill's sense). Political theory can never settle all moral issues and should stay outside them as far as possible. But Kant seeks full harmony in the moral realm as well, and believes this search is justified by the metaphysical view of persons as essentially rational and hence able to overcome the empirical differences between one another. Their value as ends in themselves lies in that element which is common to them all, rather than in their individual features.

So although as constructivists both present the practical as opposed to the speculative or epistemological view of the moral world, in Rawls "practical" carries a pragmatic, political meaning of conflict resolution, while in Kant it indicates that aspect in which a person becomes free and attains a glimpse into his real self.

Rationality and Reasonableness

In his later writings Rawls emphasizes the distinction between the rational and the reasonable and claims that the priority of the reasonable over the rational is characteristic of Kantian constructivism (JF 237; KC 528ff). The principles of justice cannot be derived (contrary to the misleading impression created by his *Theory of Justice*) from a theory of rational choice, but must be agreed upon under the conditions of reasonableness. These conditions guarantee the fairness of the model of construction and serve to distinguish it sharply from a Hobbesian model constrained solely by game-theoretic principles of rational choice.[3]

The introduction of the reasonableness condition again highlights the circularity involved in a constructivist argument, since the main import of this condition is to add *moral* constraints on the legitimate rational deliberations of the contractors. The contractors are described as having the two moral powers of the conception of the good (rationality) and the sense of justice (reasonableness); that is to say, they can identify and plan their goals and work out the best way for achieving them, but they are no less motivated by the awareness of the similar pursuit of others and by the wish to cooperate with them out of respect, fairness, and reciprocity. Again, the contractors are not only free (to pursue their ends), but also equal in the exercise of that

---

[3] See Höffe's discussion of this apparently "prudential" element in Rawls's theory of justice. In his later writings Rawls has put his views in a less misleading way, thus trying to avoid the criticism of the type Höffe is articulating in the second section of his article.

freedom. And hence, they are not only driven by the wish to satisfy their natural desires, as in Hobbes, but also by the higher desire to realize their moral powers, rationality being subordinate to reasonableness.

Now, for Hobbes the equality of the contractors was derived from a *naturalistic* view of human nature and from the empirical generalization regarding the equal vulnerability of people in the struggle for survival in the state of nature. For Kant, equality of human beings is not based on any natural fact, but nevertheless it is grounded in the idea of the reality of reason and the equality of persons as rational beings. Only with Rawls do we come to equality as a moral stipulation introduced in the original position and justified in terms of the purpose of the negotiation game.

It is true that Kant's concept of rationality is not economic, Hobbesian, or Weberian (since the latter is typically a hypothetical, means-to-end notion). But unlike Rawls's concept it does not *presuppose* the interest of individuals in social cooperation under fair terms as the basis of morality. It tries to characterize rationality so as to include reasonableness (reciprocity, equality, symmetry), that is to say, as part of what it means to act on reason. In that respect, Kant's conception of rationality is a-political, while Rawls's reasonableness condition is typically political.

The similarities between Kant and Rawls on this point are still instructive: both reject an egoistic interpretation of rationality (in Kant) and reasonableness (in Rawls). Both subordinate the pursuit of personal goals to the formal constraints of reciprocity, but hold that without that pursuit (rationality in Rawls, acting on subjective maxims in Kant) morality would have no axe to grind. Yet, Rawls interprets the subordination of the rational to the reasonable as expressing the Kantian idea of the *unity* of practical reason; but Kant has only *one* notion, that of rationality, and would not treat action on subjective maxims (the analogue of Rawls's rationality) as fully rational.

In more general terms, the unity of reason in Kant is correlated with the unity of the concept of *autonomy*. Rawls offers a two-tier concept of autonomy — the one attributed to the artificial agents of the original position (Rational Autonomy), the other characterizing citizens in the well-ordered society (Full Autonomy) (KC 528-29). For Kant autonomy is always "full," because this is the essence of reason under any conditions. Rawls admits that Kant's liberalism is richer than his because Kant regards autonomy as having intrinsic value (OC 6). Similarly, there is only one sense of freedom in Kant's theory, although only rarely is free action realized; while Rawls distinguishes between the formal freedom of the contractors and the political freedom of citizens in society. The very idea of a two-tier argument for autonomy and freedom is typically constructivist, but not Kantian.

Conclusion

I have tried to point out the problems inherent in the combination "Kantian constructivism," mainly by showing the profound differences that underlie the similarities mentioned by Rawls. The lesson that can be learnt from a critical examination of the extent to which Kant was a constructivist (or the extent to which Rawls is a Kantian) touches upon the most fundamental problems of the justification of a normative system. It seems that once naturalism or rational intuitionism are rejected, we are left with constructivism.

Now, Rawls's strict constructivism has the advantage of being an attempt to offer a model which is entirely free of any metaphysical or psychological assumptions, that is to say, philosophically neutral. This makes the normative system a pure product of the human will. But as, according to Rawls, human will cannot be characterized in any a priori manner, it can only artificially be put under methodological constraints. These constraints are necessarily of a moral nature, having to do with the job this will is destined to perform (namely, arriving at a system of socially agreed principles of justice). This introduces a disturbing circularity which can only be justified in the limited political context.

Kant, on the other hand, holds that moral construction must lead to principles having synthetic a priori validity. This can only be done if certain essentialist, metaphysical, propositions about the nature of human beings and reason are allowed into the theory. Kant's rejection of philosophical toleration makes his system much more controversial — even dogmatic — but leaves the theory with an absolute and universal *claim* for truth.

Rawls's gradual withdrawal from the more comprehensive claims in *A Theory of Justice* to a second line of constructivist defense means going beyond what Kant would agree to. At a certain point, Rawls says that justice as fairness can also be seen as a *moral* conception on its own, but that this is not necessary for establishing the *political* sense of justice as fairness (JF 248). I would like to ask whether Rawls can hold that justice as fairness can be purely a political model of construction without his falling into the trap of a Hobbesian *modus vivendi*, which he is so eager to avoid (JF 247). For, if indeed we do not believe in the idea of fairness as a moral value, independent of the political game which we are playing, why should we adopt it at all? The circular answer "for the sake of the game, or the construction, itself" will not do, because we are now questioning that very idea of social cooperation under fair terms!

Rawls mobilizes the idea of overlapping consensus as the alternative to the *modus vivendi* approach which rests on a "fortuitous conjunction of contingencies." The consensus, on the other hand, is the moral element shared by all people who otherwise hold very different moral and religious views, and hence it guarantees stability (OC 2). But is such a middle way between a comprehensive moral basis for morality and non-moral Hobbesian alternative possible?

I would guess that Kant would have presented Rawls with the following alternative: either take what you call the *higher* desire for justice seriously, that is to say, commit yourself to the belief in the essential role it plays in the human self as such, or be satisfied with a conception of pragmatic solution to a political problem. The constructivist circular model has an appeal only to those who accept it to start with, i.e., decide to play according to the rules, as in a game of Monopoly, in this case those of justice as fairness. In fairness to Rawls we should add that unlike the case of Monopoly, the game of justice is played by rules which gain support by our considered moral judgements or intuitions, i.e., are affirmed by the test of reflective equilibrium. Reflective equilibrium is the only way for the constructivist to avoid the consequences of the circularity of his model. But Kant seeks a more solid anchor than that of moral intuition or shared public culture.

It seems therefore that despite Rawls's attempts to match his theory with Kant's under the notion of constructivism and offer it as a middle ground between a Hobbesian *modus vivendi* approach and a Leibnizian rational intuitionist view, Kant seems to be closer in important respects to Leibniz in his essentialist assumptions, while Rawls is inevitably pushed to a Hobbesian view in his political interpretation of the construction.

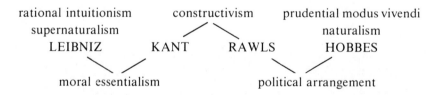

To recapitulate and summarize: Rawls construes justice as fairness as political — not metaphysical; Kant seeks a normative system which will be moral — hence metaphysical. This explains why the basic building block of Rawls's modest construction is the moral concept of a person, while Kant for his grander construction uses a concept of a moral person.

The Hebrew University of Jerusalem

References

TJ   J. Rawls,   *A Theory of Justice* (Cambridge: Harvard University Press, 1971).

KC   _____   "Kantian Constructivism," *Journal of Philosophy* 77 (1980): 515-577.

JF   _____   "Justice As Fairness: Political Not Metaphysical," *Philosophy and Public Affairs* 14 (1985): 223-252.

OC   _____   "The Idea of an Overlapping Consensus," *Oxford Journal of Legal Studies* 7 (1987): 2-25.

Adi Ophir

The Ideal Speech Situation: Neo-Kantian Ethics in Habermas and Apel

Introduction

Two important contemporary philosophical programs have revitalized Kant's critique of practical reason. In the U.S. Rawls has developed his theory of justice as an explicit "Kantian Constructivism." In Germany Habermas and Apel have launched two separate projects whose affinities override their differences and allow one to speak about a shared program. Habermas' "Universal Pragmatics" and its derivative "Diskurs Ethik" and Apel's "Transcendental Semiotics" (or "Transcendental Hermeneutics") and its derivative "Minimal Ethics" are two versions of a new form of Kantian transcendentalism in general and of ethical formalism in particular. Ours is an age whose intellectual predicament seems to be a sophisticated, linguistically informed historicism and relativism; it is an age in which any attempt to utter a universal claim is immediately deconstructed and shown to be something other than what it purports to be; in such an age these two programs are to be admired. Nevertheless, and fashionably enough, I will try to undermine them, and not only because, having no belief in foundations, I rejoice in deconstructionist work, but also because I think the two programs are ill-founded. I will examine the continental program only, trying to reconstruct what seems to me its principal argument. The main concept that I will explicate and criticize here is that of the "ideal speech situation." The focus on this concept — and the limited scope of this paper — is a rationale for the preliminary exclusion of Rawls from the present discussion. Rawls's "original position" can be interpreted as a form of an ideal speech situation or be shown to imply one. If such an interpretation of Rawls is warranted and if my radical criticism of the concept of ideal speech situation is justified, then Rawls's whole program cannot get off the ground.

Y. Yovel (ed.), Kant's Practical Philosophy Reconsidered, 213-234.
© *1989 Kluwer Academic Publishers.*

Neo-Kantian Motifs

Apel's Neo-Kantianism is explicit and straightforward. His call for a "transformation of philosophy" is an attempt to rewrite at least two of the Kantian critiques in pragmatical terms. Drawing basically upon Peirce and the later Wittgenstein, he proposes to replace a transcendental reflection upon the knowing and acting subject with a transcendental reflection upon "communities of communications" and the plurality of language games. In the moral realm Apel claims "to show how Kantian ethics might be reconstructed and transformed in terms of an ethics of consensual communication" (Apel 1981, 33). Notwithstanding the rejection of some important Kantian themes (Apel 1980, 77-92, 267ff.; 1981, ch. 4), the main task of such a reconstruction remains the grounding of a universally binding and a priori valid moral principle.

Habermas' acknowledgement of his own Neo-Kantianism has been more reluctant and elusive. With hesitation he names his attempt to ground the critique of ideology and his concept of progress "quasi-transcendental." The mixture of Hegelian, Marxist, and Weberian conceptual tools that comprise his intellectual background has concealed his Kantian move while still in the making and presents it somewhat dramatically in retrospect. But recently he has reconciled himself to the effects and connotation of his Kantianism. In an interview published in 1981 he spoke about an "obstinate Kantian manner" responsible for his fundamental separation of questions of justice from questions of truth and a "Neo-Kantian jargon" to which he has accustomed himself in the last fifteen years (Habermas 1981a).

The Kantian elements in the ethically relevant works of Habermas and Apel seem easy to discern. In fact, these elements are so conspicuous that it is redundant to argue for them interpretively; I will simply sort them out.

Habermas and Apel follow Kant in distinguishing three competences of reason, interpreted as separate interests of reason, each constituting its own domain of application, and each deserving its own critique (Habermas 1971, Appendix; 1973, Introduction; 1973a; Apel 1977). They claim that the very "fact of reason," when properly understood, entails the moral imperative. They argue for this imperative through a form of transcendental reflection which anyone who philosophizes (Apel) or merely speaks (Habermas) should acknowledge as valid. They reject hypothetical imperatives as a possible basis for a moral theory. Like Kant they try to formulate their categorical imperative in purely formal terms with the consequence that ethics becomes a theory of right or justice while the theory of the good assumes a rather marginal and derivative role. As in Kant, certitude in moral matters is achieved on a *procedural* level only; conversely, the right procedure in arguing a moral claim should delimit the content of such a claim. On a par with the delimitations of hypothetical imperatives by a formal, categorical one, Habermas and Apel are looking for a delimitation of strategic-instrumental rationality by a form of rationality that presupposes a recognition of the other as "an end in itself," not only as a means towards one's selfish ends. Contrary to Kant, they find that form neither in duty and the purity of a good will nor as a basis of human solidarity in the counterfactual "kingdom of ends," but as a norm implied in every serious discourse.

The structural similarities between Kant and his modern heirs can be followed even when turning from the analytics to the dialectics of practical reason (especially if one follows the historical interpretation of the moral imperative in Kant, in e.g., Goldmann 1971 and Yovel 1980).[1] The unity of reason's theoretical and practical interests, which Kant postulated dogmatically through the primacy of practical reason (KpV 143), is a main intellectual preoccupation for both Habermas and Apel (e.g., Habermas 1973, Introduction, ch. 7; 1981, ch. 8; Apel 1977, 429ff.). I will not go into this problem here but note only two of its more visible Kantian motifs.

Rational moral agents should impose the moral imperative upon history in order to constitute its telos — an enlightened and free community of moral agents who recognize each other as ends in themselves — and they should act in the political realm in accordance with the criteria of progress this telos entails. Moreover, history may be reconstructed as the story of the realization of freedom and rationality (esp. Habermas 1979, ch. 4 and 1981, vol. II, viii). If this sounds Hegelian one should remember that in the Kantian and Neo-Kantian versions progress is not guaranteed; it may only be rationally hoped for. Therefore there is a reason, in fact a duty, for political intervention in progress's name. Finally, the present historical moment deserves careful attention and insightful interpretation for not only does it contain indications for the direction history actually takes but also a powerful educational import. The present historical moment is capable of raising consciousness and transforming people from passive into active historical agents. If this sounds too Marxian one should remember that we are concerned here only with certain specific events, not with an inevitable historical process. I will say more about this later; for the time being, let me only name the analogy I have in mind: it is an analogy between the way Kant dealt with the French

---

[1] While exposing an antinomy in the Kantian system, the historical interpretation rightly emphasizes reason's interest in the realization of an ethical world in history and through the historical works of humans.

revolution and the modern German discussion of ecological questions and the nuclear arms-race.

If this parrallelism with Kant holds, then what's new? The new element, in a word, is language. At long last German thinkers have discovered the merits and dangers of Wittgenstein and Austin, of Searle and Grice, of Quine and Dummett, and triumphantly they have drawn Kant into the linguistic turn. (Rawls, by the way, draws Kant into the spheres of Anglo-American formalized social sciences). More specifically, reason is replaced with discourse and argumentation within a community of sign-users, speakers and interpreters; its transcendental analysis gains the form of so-called "universal pragmatics" or "transcendental semiotics" of the communicative interaction; the a priori structure of transcendental consciousness gives way to the a priori norms of the ideal speech situation.

Such a formulation does injustice to Apel who, long before adopting the later Wittgenstein, wrote major works on Humanist rhetorics and on Peirce (Apel 1963, 1967, 1970), as well as to Habermas, whose interest in linguistic interaction was the main focus of his discontent with the Hegelian and Marxist traditions within which he was raised (e.g., Habermas 1973, Introduction, ch. 4). Nevertheless, despite the biographical distortion, I think the formulation is accurate as far as the moral argument is concerned. More precisely, in both thinkers the earlier interest in language could not be integrated into the strucure of a philosophical theory, let alone serve in its grounding, without the encounter with the later Wittgenstein and the philosophy of ordinary language. If this causes the continental philosopher some embarassment I may add that on his part, Habermas, at least, has drawn the somewhat arid philosophy of ordinary language into the inspiring speculative spheres of a new Grand Theory. His is a theory that, against all odds, does dare to encompass epistemology and ethics, philosophy of history and cognitive psychology, without forgetting for a moment the theorist's *engagement* and the theory's "practical intent."

The Grounding Argument

A widespread conception of language which has become a commonplace of our intellectual age lies here at base. Private language is impossible; the positivist search for a pure descriptive language, isomorphic with the reality it describes, is a dream; no theory of meaning can exclude pragmatical considerations. From the German Hermeneutic tradition, especially from the work of Gadamer, both Habermas and Apel accept a soft version of the hermeneutic claim to universality. Language, according to this claim, always mediates our encounters with nature and with our fellowmen; there is no way to describe or prescribe these encounters except in terms of a linguistic community that looks into its own and other communities' life-worlds. Most importantly, the search for truth or justice must be conducted as a process of argumentation, an exchange of validity claims, within the context of a certain linguistic community. Argumentation can never start or end meaningfully outside such a community; the starting point is always rooted in some tradition, always constrained by the rules of some language game, and the absolute end remains forever a promise. In short, reason is embodied in language and determined by its constraints: historical, cultural, and structural. But instead of following the trendy line of argument here straight into historicism or relativism, both Habermas and Apel insist upon a transcendental reflection on the very possibility of language games in general and argumentation in particular.

This reflection shows that argumentation is a special kind of a human "given," an "is" with a claim to universality that contains an "ought" with a similar scope. Apel emphasizes the very existence of a scientific community or a community of scholars; Habermas stresses the coordination of actions in society as an element of human facticity and the special institutions for legitimation of norms that such coordination contains. The institutionalized search for truth and the institutionalized legitimation of norms are presupposed by any dispute over truth claims or normative claims. Recourse from dispute to argumentation is a real option open for any such dispute. Our relevant "is" consists of those special institutions for argumentation that any society contains. The neo-Kantian formulation of the "fact of reason" posits the existence of the linguistic and social institution of argumentation as both an empirical given and a condition for the possibility of morality and knowledge. When this fact is properly analyzed, the "ought" implied in it is exposed. I will follow this exposition through a reconstruction of the set of normative principles that argumentation presupposes and that constitute the so-called "ideal speech situation."

The ought of the ideal speech situation is not *derived* from the "is" of argumentation. Rather, reflection grasps it as a normative claim that "always already" exists (Apel 1980, 273-76 and note 96) wherever argumentation takes place or even when its possibility is implied by a non-argumentative quarrel over conflicting claims. The claim becomes a valid "ought" once a speaker prefers argumentation over other means of solving conflicts. Discovering the Heideggerian dimension of the ought as being "always already" contained within a universal "is" saves Habermas and Apel from a naturalistic fallacy, and gives them, so Apel claims, an edge of advantage over Kant.

But they still have to prove that argumentation's claim to universality is indeed justified; i.e., they have to show that recourse to argumentation is always to be preferred. In other words, in order to show that the linguistic embodiment of reason — argumentation — is morally and universally binding, that this special kind of human facticity not only contains a moral principle but is also required by one, and that science not only presupposes ethics but is also justified by it, a separate normative justification is required. In order to do this an auxiliary argument is advanced, especially by Apel. It is based upon the interpretation of the historical situation of humanity as being on the verge of self-destruction. I will present this argument, which I call the "doomsday argument," shortly.

The Ideal Speech Situation

An army of distinctions, linguistic theories, and pragmatic concepts is drawn into the fold (Habermas 1979, ch. 1; 1984, iii; Apel 1980, chs. 5, 7). Apel's discussion remains interpretive and somewhat schematic but Habermas enters into detailed debates with, and borrows critically from, Searle and Toulmin, Grice and Tugenhadt. The basic linguistic unit is the speech act, the basic unit of argumentation is the specific "validity claim" or claims a speech act expresses. Validity claims are classified according to their domains: truth claims in theoretical discourse, claims of right in moral or normative discourse, evaluative claims in aesthetic discourse (that judges a work of art according to the norms of its genre), sincerity claims implied in any expression of a serious validity claim ("I really mean that..."), and finally, the claim of comprehensibility implied by any attempt to communicate.

Presupposing this theoretical apparatus, the grounding argument for ethics has its point of departure in the definition of argumentation as a procedure for the exchange of validity claims, their thematization, problematization, and justification (Habermas 1984, 18ff.). Argumentation has three inseparable aspects for which the theory of argumentation should account: (1) Thematization of validity claims means a continuation of a dispute by refining the linguistic exchange and suspending other types of actions in favor of pure communicative activity, bracketing praxis for the sake of discourse. (2) Within the realm of discourse itself there must be rules of conduct that determine varieties of possible exchanges, order of thematization and problematization, strategies for giving reasons, and criteria for reaching understanding. This is the procedural aspect of argumentation that determines argumentation as a special kind of a language game. (3) Finally, there are rules that determine what counts as a valid argument, i.e., the form of the "product" each participant tries to produce.

Logic deals with the third aspect. A Platonic dialogue calls our attention to the second aspect, to argumentation as a competition for the prize of the better argument. This is also the aspect into which modern pragmatics and the dialogical logic of Lorenzen and others have gained new insights (Lorenzen 1969). All this is still beside the point. The main point here is Habermas' and Apel's insistence on an explication of the first aspect, which both logic and pragmatics (dialectics) have assumed as given. They ask about the conditions of possibility for argumentation as a competition — whose rules are determined by dialectics — between arguments — whose structure and validity are determined by logic. Oddly enough, Habermas calls this transcendental aspect the aspect of "argument as a process," for he is actually asking about the *moment* of entering argumentation; he is asking what a participant must presuppose at the moment he suspends other types of action for the sake of discourse.

Real suspension of goal oriented activity is — by definition — the *first condition*. This is also implied by the typological distinction between strategic speech act and purely communicative acts, which Habermas and Apel posit against Weber's conception of instrumental rationality. The strategic speech act uses speech as a means towards an end that is not determined within discourse and is not subject to its constraints. The whole argumentative speech situation may be such a means, e.g., when disputing conflicting truth claims in technology or economics. But within the context of argumentation, even for its very success as a means, the external end should be bracketed in favor of the internal end that the argument posits: finding the truth about the subject matter, e.g., the effect of a certain nuclear reaction or of a certain form of taxation.

The *second condition* is that in argumentation all force has been excluded from the speech situation. This follows from the definition of the situation as a competition for the prize of the better argument. Ideally, in such a competition results should be determined by the power of the better argument alone. Hence authority of all kinds, traditional as well as professional, is subject to the same procedural rules as the layman; manipulation of participants through the use of power, money, or even rhetoric is strictly controlled in order to be entirely excluded.

A *third condition* follows immediately: if the special status of authority has been erased, all participants in argumentation are equal vis-à-vis the procedural structure. This means that the argumentative situation presupposes mutual recognition of subjects (participants) as holding equal rights to thematize, problematize, and give reasons. In other words, a participant in argumentation can never become a means only, he or she is always also an end in itself.

A *fourth condition* is articulated through a better formulation of the third. Actually, all participants serve equally as means towards a common end: finding the truth about the matter at stake.[2] Since revelation and other kinds of proclaimed absolute truth need authority and authority has lost its special status, all the participants can hope for is agreement about the truth of the matter. The real goal of the speech situation is therefore consensus among rational participants who follow the force of the better argument alone. But even if force is strictly excluded participants are obviously limited by the state of their knowledge, the constraints of their language, and the horizons of their historical situation. Hence the consensus looked for is ideal in one more sense (which Apel, following Peirce, stresses more than Habermas): it is a consensus within an unlimited community of communication, i.e., one that contains the wisdom and good reason of all speakers to come. Backing my validity claim in argumentation I am actually "always already" trying to convince and gain approval from the unlimited community of all free and equal rational speakers.

A *fifth condition* is called for by the fourth. If an ideal consensus regarding the subject matter is the goal, a consensus regarding the language of argumentation is a necessary means to achieve it. A transparent language — at least a transparent common ground from which interlocutors depart — is a precondition for a meaningful agreement. (Although Habermas' definition of the communicative act as an act aiming at "reaching understanding" ambiguously captures both mutual understanding of the meaning of a validity claim and a shared view regarding its validity, the two aspects should be kept apart.[3])

---

[2] There is an interesting and significant agreement here between the historicist hermeneutics of Gadamer and the transcendental hermeneutics of Apel and Habermas. Cf. e.g. Gadamer 1975, 325-33.

[3] Two parties may reach an agreement without necessarily fully understanding each other — too often margin of ambiguity eases an agreement. On the other hand, an understanding between two parties may still result in a disagreement regarding the matter at stake — too often a better understanding leads to diminishing agreement. It is only within a community of purely rational subjects, each equally equipped to represent reason's pure interests, that reaching understanding can be equated with reaching an agreement. But such a convergence between agreement and understanding is not something presupposed by the actual speech situation; at most it is a utopian projection out of what is conceived as the actul situation's limitedness or deficiencies.

The *sixth condition* is also contained in the fourth: participants in argumentation have at least one common interest: the interest of finding the truth of the matter. This point is crucial, for it is exactly what stands between communicative and strategic action, what suspends praxis for the sake of discourse. At the moment one's interest in an extra-discursive goal overrides one's interest in finding the truth there is nothing to prevent one from pretending seriousness in argumentation in order to manipulate other participants.

There is a corollary to this condition that, together with the third condition, may remind one how Kantian the whole situation is: the distinction between serious and manipulative interest in argumentation is a matter of pure intentions, it cannot be read out of the overt behavior of participants in actual argumentation. But a serious participant in argumentation always takes her interlocutors seriously, that is, she always assumes their pure intentions, i.e., their sincerity. Hence the *seventh* condition.

What I have just described is the ideal speech situation. I have tried to reconstruct it discursively for didactic purposes alone; actually, this whole set of presuppositions is intrinsic to the very concept of argumentation; thus its articulation is dependent on its context of explication.

The ideal speech situation has a dual status; it grounds argumentation on the one hand, and serves as its regulative idea on the other. No actual argumentation is possible without presupposing an ideal speech situation and no actual speech situation will become argumentative if the ideal one does not serve as its regulative idea.

The ideal speech situation is not merely a utopia of rational discourse. The force of Apel's and Habermas' arguments lies in the claim that the norms described under this title are actually implied by any impure communicative act. Even distorted communication cannot go on without assenting to these norms; the strategic character of the assent does not change its commitment to the norms. The "fact of reason" to which Habermas and Apel appeal is not the actual existence of pure discourse, but the existence of pure intention[4] to find the truth through discourse (at the very least the truth about what the other actually means) *and* of the appropriate institutions that regulate argumentation in order to realize that intention.

The argument that advances this point has two basic forms that are actually

---

[4] More accurately, the transcendental analysis of the actual speech situation should push even the existence of pure intention into a phenomenological *epoche* and be committed to the belief in the existence of such intention only. An actual speech situation implies only the belief that pure intention is possible, but it really does not matter, for it all remains in the innermost realm of the heart.

versions of a classical argument against the sceptic. According to one version, the sceptic cannot cast reason in radical doubt without doubting the validity of his own doubting; the one who doubts already presupposes the logic which makes his scepticism possible. Similarly, Apel claims that the rejection of consensus or mutual understanding as the goal of any serious argumentation is doomed to failure. One who justifies such a polemical move elicits or fails to elicit approval by his very act of justification; but he cannot try to justify without anticipating a desired agreement with at least some of his actual or imaginary interlocutors, as well as with the whole community of ideal-rational speakers (Apel 1980, 110-27).

Wittgenstein gave the classic argument a linguistic turn and extra force when he claimed that a community of all-time liars is impossible; lying too is a form of communication and it presupposes the serious intention which underlies the communicative act to transmit true messages (Apel 1980, 258-59).[5] In the same way that the sceptic is parasitic on rational discourse, the liar depends upon sincere speakers. Similarly, Habermas argues that all distorted forms of communication are parasitic on serious and sincere communication (Habermas 1984, 307ff., 332). Or, viewed from a different angle, the very existence of language consisting of speech acts capable of becoming explicit validity claims presupposes a certain procedure "to redeem" validity claims, which means argumentation, which in its turn presupposes the norms of the ideal speech situation. I will stop short of a systematic reconstruction of the move from everyday communication to the universal norms of argumentation, for even if this argument were faultless, the very idea of an ideal speech situation, I will argue below, is empty.

The Doomsday Argument

An ideal speech situation is normatively binding whenever people argue about something. It becomes morally relevant, however, only when disputed moral matters are at stake, e.g., the good way of life, or the just society, and, at any rate, when a common interest of members in a community dictates the

---

[5] Apel seems to overemphasize Wittgenstein's remark that "lying is a language-game that needs to be learned like any other one" (*Philosophical Investigation* [Oxford: Blackwell, 1967] 249), and never to consider Eco's: "semiotics is in principle the discipline studying everything which can be used in order to lie. If something cannot be used to tell a lie, conversely it cannot be used to tell the truth; it cannot in fact be used 'to tell' at all" (*A Theory of Semiotics*, 7).

solving of conflicting interests through argumentation. At this stage of the argument there is still nothing that would censor, say a scientist, from accepting the norms of the ideal speech situation while working with her team in the laboratory and rejecting them while doing business in the marketplace. In the same vein, the normative basis of argumentation may be presupposed by a certain community whose members have a shared interest in the preservation of their society and therefore always prefer argumentation to civil strife. But such an argument that assumes some basic solidarity, and which may serve as the normative foundation of a democratic way of life, cannot be applied to conflicts between communities with radically different language games that do not acknowledge any shared interest whatsoever. In order to argue for such a shared interest and for the sincere dialogue it prescribes, an a priori commitment to one of the competing language games is required. One does not have to show here that language games are, in principle, commensurable, but that bridging seemingly incommensurable language games, or interests for that matter, is a moral duty indeed. Argumentation is normatively binding but its normative ground cannot ground its *universal* applicability.

This is the other side of Apel's argument against the sceptic. You cannot dismantle the normative ground that argumentation presupposes without entering discourse and thus tacitly assenting to its implied norms, says Apel. In the same vein, however, if I may inverse the argument, you cannot justify these norms or claim they are binding on someone who refuses to enter an argument with you. The ideal speech situation may be the transcendental language game of argumentation; this fact by itself, however, cannot bridge what seems to be incommensurable moral languages of communities with conflicting interests. The minimal ethics implied in argumentation has a justified universal claim only if argumentation can be shown a priori — or at least for the present historical moment and for humanity as a whole — to be the best means for solving conflicts. Put in Kantian terms, Apel's and Habermas' discursive transcendentalism forces them to answer a question Kant never dreamt to ask: why should one *always* act morally?

I call the argument that does precisely this, i.e., that attempts to justify the universal claim of argumentation, the doomsday argument. It was already anticipated by Habermas' second thesis in the Appendix to *Knowledge and Human Interests* (Habermas 1971, 313) and has been recently exemplified in Apel's paper bearing the impressive title: "The Situation of Humanity as an Ethical Problem" (Apel 1985). Using quasi-anthropological language, Apel says that in order to survive, "homo faber" needs *phronesis*, not merely *techne*. In other words, "homo sapiens" cannot be reduced to a tool-making-animal or a problem-solving-machine. Humans invent and produce tools in order to control nature and manipulate others. But tools are not always used according to the intentions of their originators. Successful tools may even turn the ends they serve into powerful new means towards new ends, unforeseen and undesired by the original intention. In short, possible abuse and misuse of tools require that the use of tools be socially coordinated and subject to a system of constraints. Generally speaking, morality is that system of coordination and constraints over the use of tools or, more precisely, means, within a given community. Such a system cannot be reduced to a simplistic instrumental calculation of relations between means and ends, for it involves coordination among conflicting ends. In fact, the rationality of coordination and constraints is supposed to delineate the legitimate field of application for instrumental rationality.

The Aristotelian notion of *phronesis*, however, does not capture this type of rationality for it lacks the distinction between *poesis* and communication. Hence a communicative ethics must transform the old notion of practical reason. But the "ethics of community" which Aristotelian *phronesis* and its modern heirs[6] represent is lacking on another, much more crucial ground: it is limited to a specific, well-defined community; *phronesis* has many and various forms and each is responsible for one particular *polis* only. In order to found the universality of the ethical claim, not only *phronesis* has to be transformed into communicative ethics but its realm of accountability must be shifted from the particular *polis* to universal history.

Moreover, the invention of tools has grown so rapidly in modern times that it has long transcended the evolution of the moral system. As the old Frankfurt school has argued correctly, instrumental rationality has transcended the limits of the individual national state, monopolized all areas of life, and turned moral reasoning into ideology in the service of a technological-capitalist social order. But much more important is the fact that the gap between the invention and production of tools on the one hand, and the state of the constraining moral system on the other, has become so great that it endangers not only this or that community but the entire human race. This danger is the basis of a new universal solidarity, which for the first time (since

---

[6] For the modern heirs of Aristotelian ethics, or at least some of its main motifs, see e.g., Gadamer, *Truth and Method* (especially part II, 2,b); H. Arendt, *The Human Condition* (University of Chicago Press, 1958); A. MacIntyre, *After Virtue* (University of Notre Dame Press, 1981) and *Whose Justice? Which Rationality?* (University of Notre Dame Press, 1988); or M. Walzer, *Spheres of Justice* (New York: Basic Books, 1983).

its abstract proclamation by Christ) has been called down from heaven to earth and embodied in real social institutions (Apel 1981, 33-44; 1985).

Every human being should become conscious of this gap for it concerns his or her own survival. Doomsday consciousness is the basis of a new form of solidarity and a new common interest upon which the argument for the monopoly of argumentation rests. In liberal democracies, the fear of self-destruction of society has long been an argument for the monopoly of argumentation over the use of power; similarly, the fear of the self-destruction of humanity is the argument for such a monopoly of argumentation in the international sphere. In our present era, and at least as far as the super-powers are concerned, no recourse from negotiation to war can be envisaged which would not result in the annihilation of the human race. Therefore it does not matter how strategic and manipulative these negotiations are, in principle they commit their participants to the minimal ethics of argumentation (Apel 1985, 256-64). It is not hard to see how this line of argument is extended to solving international conflicts in general and then to solving conflicts in general. In any disguise, the doomsday argument could supply the rationale for a common interest in argumentation wherever it is still lacking. When this interest exists minimal ethics is binding, and since such an interest should exist universally, minimal ethics is universally binding.

Moreover, the gap between actual institutions for argumentation and the ideal speech situation should not only concern scientists but should serve as a guide towards the reform of society at large; a critical work should be directed at the whole system of institutions in which conflicts of interests are settled through argumentation, in order to bring them somewhat closer to the state of an ideal speech situation.[7] Perhaps the ideal speech situation would even give history its regulative idea, thus endowing universal history for the first time with a meaningful telos. Marxist and Hegelian motifs fall back here upon Kant. An awakened consciousness of a real universal solidarity constitutes a moral-historical imperative which must be strived for although lacking the guarantee of a real historical process, otherwise humanity is doomed.

The moral argument should therefore take a close look into the present historical moment. What is required is a historical interpretation that com-

---

[7] Recently, Habermas has backed off this idea. Accepting some of his critics' counter-arguments (see e.g., Thompson & Held 1982, 227-28), he claims that the ideal speech situation is not a guide for progress towards "the good life" but merely a criterion for the reconstruction of the evolution of normative systems. But it seems to me that the evolutionary argument implies a norm and a telos, which are logically binding even if one wishes to stop short of giving them explicit articulation.

prises the Holocaust and Hiroshima, ecological catastrophes and world-hunger. There are certain contemporary, traumatic events that play here the role Kant ascribes to the French Revolution: "signum rememorativum, demonstrativum, prognostikon." What the French Revolution recalled, demonstrated and foretold was "the constant human tendency to progress." Kant needed that "tendency" in order to protect his moral imperative from its cynical, naturalist despisers. He had to complement his theory of the highest good and show that, indeed, man is capable of the behavior the categorical imperative dictates. In the same way, modern traumatic events signify the human "tendency" to self-annihilation. Modern thinkers need this tendency in order to protect their categorical imperative from its relativist despisers. They have to complement their theory of an ideal speech situation and show that indeed man should always behave according to the moral guide it dictates.

There is, however, an important difference in this parallelism: Kant turns to history after securing the universality of the moral imperative through a transcendental reflection; his turn to history is an attempt to bridge theory and practice. The problematic relation of theory and practice is (at least) Habermas' point of departure; his is an attempt to rewrite "a philosophy of history with practical intent" (Habermas 1973, 212ff.). In order to save room for the idea of progress in such a philosophy of history he then turns to a transcendental reflection upon a linguistically embodied reason. What he discovers is that "the fact of reason" indeed presupposes a normative principle, but that he needs a philosophy of history in order to make good the universal claim of this principle. Whereas the Kantian turn to history simply contradicts a basic presupposition of the whole system — the radical separation of reason and nature — the Habermasian re-turn to history renders his whole philosophical move circular through and through.

There is still much more to be said against the consequences of the doomsday argument. The monopoly of argumentation, within the scope of both the national state and universal history, extracts a heavy price. Any form of life, any community of communication should be made subject to the requirements of argumentation whenever it has a conflict of interests with other communities. It must justify its normative claims regarding the interests it rightfully pursues as well as its truth claims regarding what counts as its real interests, and it must do so with no regard to its own system of authority, set of traditional beliefs, or personal tastes. Indeed, not only is traditional community made transparent through argumentation, but the same goes for the individual whose private sphere is always endangered by new normative claims that question its limits. In fact, arguments for some form of moral-cultural relativism, for incommensurability of belief systems or language games, or for a sacred private sphere, are, in a sense, made immoral by the very act in which they are uttered. Arguments of this kind put limits upon argumentation; they may thus contribute, willy-nilly, to the coming catastrophe.

All this is based upon Habermas' and Apel's assumption that argumentation is instrumental to survival. In the name of this assumption instrumental reason should accept the logic of non-instrumental, dialogical reason and be subject to its constraints. If the radical distinction between instrumental and dialogical reason upon which the above argument rests is valid, this formulation seems paradoxical. If the distinction needs qualification, let alone if it is faulty, the grounding argument as a whole loses its universal ground.

Against the Very Idea of an Ideal Speech Situation

Rejecting the doomsday argument, one may still claim that the ethical principles derived from the ideal speech situation are binding on all members of a community that share an interest in solving conflicts through argumentation. This is more or less the scope of application that Rawls's theory of justice claims for itself (Rawls 1971, chap. 1). My main criticism is directed against this more modest, much more plausible, claim. The ideal speech situation cannot serve as a basis for moral criticism and as a guide for moral politics even on these restricted terms, I argue, for what the idealized conditions really imply is not the rationalization of communication but rather its very elimination.

First we should qualify the presentation of the ideal speech situation to fit more appropriately the case of normative argumentation. In normative argumentation another condition must be added to the ideal speech situation that cannot be articulated through a further explication of argumentation in general. The condition lacking is that of a disinterested representation of interests of all those affected by a disputed normative claim.

In general, the goal of the ideal speech situation is supposed to be a consensual agreement. This means that a claim is taken as valid only if all speakers would assent to it were they free of all external or internal constraints. And here lies an important difference between matters of truth and matters of right. Laymen or irrational speakers do not have to be represented in theoretical discourse, nor could they be; the ideal speech situation means their formal and final exclusion. But the layman, the non-competent speaker, and the insane — all these have interests and implied claims of right whose a priori exclusion from normative discourse would not ground ethics but destroy its very possibility. Precisely because the ideal speech situation implies such a sophisticated mechanism of exclusion,[8] even if a counterfactual one, it requires a complementary, valid mechanism of representation. When a normative claim is disputed, all interests of those who are affected by it should be represented in the speech situation, and they should be represented disinterestedly (Apel 1980, 277ff.; Habermas in Thompson & Held 1982, 250-263).

However, such a concept of representation does not follow at all from the idea of an ideal speech situation and it cannot be grounded through an explication of the concepts of argumentation or communication alone. Actually, disinterested, transparent representation is brought into the course of the argument by a moral consciousness that has been Kantian all along. Not only does participation in an ideal speech situation require mutual recognition of interlocutors as subjects with equal rights, it also demands that such a recognition be carried over beyond the scope of the speech situation to the public sphere at large; any subject that may be affected by the discussion, which means, in principle, any other human being, must be included. In short, participants in the ideal speech situation should bring the Kantian categorical imperative into the speech situation; rational speakers in moral argumentation are simply Kantian moral beings engaged in a polite debate about the appropriate conduct of the rest of mankind.

Rejecting both the doomsday argument and the principle of disinterested representation, communicative ethics is applicable only to those actually involved in argumentation; also, the responsibility and accountability of those involved in argumentation is confined to the communication community alone. But the very idea of an ideal speech situation has still been left intact. Concluding this paper I will outline a sketch of a critique against the very idea of ideal speech situation.

The ideal speech situation is a theoretical, counterfactual construction as well as a regulative idea for praxis. Two distinct, though related, questions seem appropriate at this junction: (1) What is the nature of that possible world in which the counterfactual fantasy is realized? (2) What are the consequences of the attempt to counter the facts and change that possible world which happens to be ours by using this counterfactual as a regulative idea?

The suspension of non-discursive interests and the ultimate exclusion of force (conditions 1 & 2) are the two cardinal conditions of an ideal speech

---

[8] Of exclusion as a mechanism of power, among other such mechanisms operating in discourse, see Foucault 1980.

situation. Regarding these, one may imagine three kinds of possible worlds: a world entirely devoid of power relations; a world in which interest in discourse is a magic for the ultimate suspension of power; a world in which truth and justice are so powerful that their triumph over non-discursive interests means a final dissolution of the struggle between reason and all its "others." One thing is common to the three worlds. Once speech has set forth its ideal conditions, there is no more need to use power other than that of the better argument. Otherwise, rational speakers would be dependent upon the guardians whose behavior they are supposed to regulate, strategic negotiations would constantly mingle with acts of pure communication, and the schism of reason into instrumental and dialogical domains would penetrate the dialogical domain itself.

What kind of language can be spoken in a situation so completely devoid of power? It is an arid language whose texts prepare and maintain no place for authority, whose language games constitute no privileged roles, and in which communicative means lack any rhetorical device; communication consists of simple assertive statements and questions that directly appeal to reason, using reasons only. The statements used in such a language describe the world rightly or wrongly, but always transparently, i.e., with no evaluative implicatures. Communication is transparent from the very beginning both in regard to the meaning of what is uttered and the interests any utterance may serve. This means that the classification of the world and organization of experience — implied by even the most fragmented section of speech or writing — are never disguised. At least one alternative way to classify the world and organize experience is already presumed, and the advantage any party may gain by adopting one way or the other can be clarified easily and completely at any turn in the speech situation. All this is necessary because language and the reality it pertains to are not isomorphic; we have come all too close to the positivistic image of ideal language anyway, and we cannot go so far with our purified communication. The competing descriptions of the world must therefore be wholly transparent in regard to the kinds of world and experience they allow and those they exclude. Accordingly, speech acts must be wholly transparent in regard to the effects they are trying to elicit. In short, the language of the ideal speech situation is one devoid of any hermeneutic or pragmatical dimension — what an ironic consequence for an approach that has pragmatics and hermeneutics as its principal points of departure!

One can hardly imagine what it means and what it takes to communicate in such an ideal speech situation. It is questionable whether "ideal communication" maintains even a minimal family resemblance with "communication." One thing is clear, however: it is impossible to communicate what the "ideal communication" means without falling prey to the pragmatical constraints and hermeneutic limitations of ordinary language. This ordinary language, and not the ideal speech situation, is the meta-institution of all theoretical, artificially constructed language games, as Apel himself notes (Apel 1980, 119). It is impossible to construct a possible world for the ideal speech situation without using rhetorical devices, employing some authority, and appealing to sensitivities other than that of pure reasoning. Already Plato, that master of ideal speech situations, knew how much rhetoric, dramatic effects, and writing competence is necessary in order to construct such a situation in discourse. The dramatic prelude to a Socratic conversation is a reminiscence of that understanding, that self-awareness of the path language must traverse in order to purify itself, and of the constant rhetorical price one must pay for keeping the fantasy alive.

So the question, really, is not what is the nature of the possible world in which an ideal speech situation can be realized, but whether we are capable of realizing the meaning of such a world without contradicting the very idea of an ideal speech situation. The answer, I think, is that we cannot, and that in order to fully understand the idea of an ideal speech situation one should have already lived in such a situation. Otherwise, and this is the case with both Apel and Habermas, the philosophical move from ordinary to ideal argumentation can neither explicate universal presuppositions nor lay foundations for ethics; such a move can merely produce the ideology of one particular form of discourse, one special kind of family of language games, the discourse of Western philosophy, the language games of modern sciences.[9]

Things become even more problematic considering the status of the ideal speech situation as a regulative idea. Here as well we may start with suspension of external interests and exclusion of force (conditions 1 & 2). In our actual world, these two conditions require an elaborate mechanism of power. And here, too, Plato is an excellent teacher. He knew well that the ideal speech situation is a fiction and that even as a fiction its story can hardly be told without telling the story of the forces that sustain it. For example, in the first book of the *Republic*, the conditions of an ideal speech situation are gradually set through a step by step elimination of all kinds of authority and sources of legitimation for validity claims. Exclusion proceeds from old pious Cephalus through the reverend poets to violent Thrasymachus, the rhetorician. But Plato makes it very clear that without the active cooperation of the interlocu-

---

[9] For a systematic critique of linguistic intellectualism and the priority given to purely discursive rationality in Western society see Bourdieu 1977; cf. Ingram 1982.

tors and their willingness to use power, even physical force, to impose the rules of the dialogical game and maintain its suspension from everyday life, Socrates, the ideal speaker, could not have won the competition of arguments.[10] Similar points are made by other dramatic preludes and interludes in many of the dialogues. They all portray or allude to the fact that suspension requires a delicate system of power relations between the suspending game and its suspended environment, and that exclusion of force for the sake of discourse rests on powerful threats.

In short, the force of the better argument involves other kinds of force and other kinds of non-discursive power relations. Our islands of hope, those institutions in which argumentation is actually embodied, counterfactual as their regulative idea may be, are doomed to remain engulfed by the cruelty of everyday life. The efficient use of power, of strategic communication, and of instrumental actions are preconditions for the possibility of the strive for pure communication.

Another, relatively minor, problem, noted by many critics, is the tension, if not real contradiction, between the effacement of authority (condition 3) and sincerity (condition 7). The seventh condition of the ideal speech situation requires mutual recognition of interlocutors as sincere speakers. In an ideal speech situation there is no place for charlatans and impostors. But the effacement of authority and the right to problematize any validity claim makes everybody suspect. Without the presence of any other authority, reason itself should play the policeman and act as a censor — i.e., reason should produce its own disciplinary system. It should do so, however, while using the power of the better argument alone, applying its power among sincere speakers only, suspect the unsuspectable, and coerce with no means of coercion. Not a small job for the knights of coherence and consistency! But what is paradoxical in the ideal world becomes a dangerous parody in the real one. Here, when the knights of reason strive towards purified communication, they do have their own, quite practical and all too material policing strategies and censorship devices. Here, problematization of validity claims is always a political act and thus always related to this or that power struggle. In the name of universal ethics very particular battles are fought. And in these battles it is impossible to distinguish exclusion and delegitimation strategies based upon the universal claim of communicative ethics from ethical claims employed as delegitimation strategies.

---

[10] For a detailed presentation of the Platonic dialogue as an attempt to create an ideal speech situation see Ophir 1986.

Truth and justice are meted out with power and won through struggle. Both externally and internally, argumentation is embedded in systems of power relations, itself being one form of power among others. As such it must be constantly sustained through interaction and exchange with other forms of power. If this account of argumentation is truer to the "facts of reason" than the account given by Habermas and Apel, then the presupposition that lies at the heart of the ideal speech situation must be critically and crucially amended: one never seeks the *agreement of an unlimited community of communication* that consists of ideal speakers. Claiming the validity of a statement is a polemical act directed at a very specific community of communication; agreement is sought against a background of disagreement with other communities of communication; and the consensus sought is always a means for silencing dissenting voices within the assentient community.

This general characterization is true not only regarding the given plurality of discourses and communities of communication; it is true regarding the isolated, ideal, dialogue itself. It is possible to imagine the ideal speech situation as consisting of a series of dialogues in which interlocutors switch positions while maintaining the dual structure of the situation: on the one hand a speaker who thematizes, problematizes, or justifies a validity claim; on the other — the rest of the community whose consent is being sought. Each dialogical event aims at reaching understanding between two partners, but always at the expense of a third one, whose exclusion from the speech situation, as Michel Serres has rightly noted (Serres 1983, 13), is one of the dialogue's preconditions. Consent and dissent, *consensus* and *polemos*, are complementary concepts that imply each other dialectically. Universal consensus, a consensus that has terminated the dispute and overcome all dissension, is the real *end* of communication. As Mill already noted, it is a state of mind and discourse in which the very meaning of the agreed upon statement is doomed to oblivion.

Of the seven conditions of the ideal speech situation I would leave intact four as valid presuppositions of argumentation: sincerity, discursive solidarity (real interest in finding the truth of the matter), suspension of nondiscursive interests, and exclusion of non-discursive forces. I would amend the conditions of consensual agreement to meet the above objection and reformulate it as a consensus within *polemos*. The effacement of authority and the transparency of communication, even only in its initial stage, have to be rejected; they are not presupposed by any real argumentation, at the most they are postulated as its legitimating ideology.

This amended ideal speech situation contains indeed a minimal ethics. But it is an ethics whose principles are binding only on those who freely express an interest in argumentation. The short-winged ideal is not capable of carrying the moral argument beyond the scope of the initial consensus that allows argumentation, let alone grounding a critique of actual consensus and questioning its legitimacy. Authority, *polemos*, and strife invade the speech situation even when ideal, for they are intrinsic to the very idea of a speech situation, of language and communication. Therefore, crutches in the form of a principle of disinterested representation, dogmatically postulated, and a doomsday argument — in which history is problematically interpreted — would not help. The transcendental strategy is faulty from top to bottom. However, I do believe that philosophical ethics is possible and I do accept a hermeneutic-pragmatical conception of language as both correct and morally relevant. But I think the two have to meet some place other than at the utopia of the ideal speech situation.

Tel-Aviv University

Bibliography

Apel, Karl-Otto, 1963, *Die Idee der Sprache in der Tradition des Humanismus von Dante bis Vico*, Archive für Begriffsgeschichte, 8, Bonn.
    1967, Introduction to S. C. Peirce, *Schriften I*, Frankfurt.
    1970, Introduction to S. C. Peirce, *Schriften II*, Frankfurt.
    1977, "Types of Social Science in the Light of Human Interests of Knowledge," *Social Research* 44, no. 3.
    1979, "The Common Presuppositions of Hermeneutics and Ethics: Types of Rationality Beyond Science and Technology," in J. Barmark (ed.), *Perspectives in Metascience,* Gothenburg (Sweden).
    1980, *Towards a Transformation of Philosophy*, London (*Transformation der Philosophie*, Frankfurt, 1972).
    1981, "Normative Ethics and Strategical Rationality: The Philosophical Problem of a Political Ethics," *The Third Hannah Arendt Memorial*, New York.
    1985, "The Situation of Humanity as an Ethical Problem," *Praxis International.*
Bourdieu, Pierre and J.-C. Passeron, 1977, *Reproduction, Society and Culture*, London.
Eco, Umberto, 1976, *A Theory of Semiotics*, Bloomington, Indiana.
Foucault, Michel, 1980, "The Order of Discourse," in Robert Young, *Untying the Text*, New York (*L'Ordre du discours*, Paris, 1971).
Gadamer, Hans-Georg, 1975, *Truth and Method*, New York (*Wahrheit und Methode*, Tübingen, 1960).
Goldmann, Lucien, 1971, *Immanuel Kant*, London (*Introduction à la philosophie de Kant*, Paris, 1967).
Habermas, Jürgen, 1971, *Knowledge and Human Interests*, Boston (*Erkenntniss und Interesse*, Frankfurt, 1968).

1973, *Theory and Practice*, Boston (*Theorie und Praxis*, Frankfurt, 1971).

1973a, "A Postscript to Knowledge and Human Interests," *Philosophy of Social Science* 3: 157-189.

1979, *Communication and the Evolution of Society*, Boston.

1981, *Theorie des Kommunikativen Handelns*, Vols. I & II, Frankfurt.

1981a, "The Dialectics of Rationalization," an interview with Axel Honneth, Eberhard Knodler-Bunte, and Arno Widmann, *Telos*, no. 49.

1984, *Theory of Communicative Action*, Boston (*Theorie des Kommunikativen Handelns*, Vol. I).

Ingram, David, 1982, "The Possibility of a Communication Ethic Reconsidered: Habermas, Gadamer, and Bourdieu on Discourse," *Man and World* 15: 149-161.

Lorenzen, Paul, 1969, *Normative Logic and Ethics*, Mannheim/Zurich.

Ophir, Adi, 1986, "Plato's Republic: Philosophy as a Serious Game" (Hebrew), *Iyyun* 35: 3-29.

Rawls, John, 1971, *A Theory of Justice*, Boston.

Thompson, J. B. & D. Held (eds.), 1982, *Habermas: Critical Debates*, Cambridge.

Serres, Michel, 1983, *Hermes: Literature, Science, Philosophy*, Baltimore.

Yovel, Yirmiahu, 1980, *Kant and the Philosophy of History*, Princeton.

Victor J. Seidler

Kant: Respect, Individuality and Dependence

I. Respect, Hierarchy and Individuality

In elucidating a notion of respect in terms of the distance we want to maintain from others, we are not simply clarifying an aspect of moral language which helps us understand the nature of our moral lives. To analyse a particular notion such as respect, we have to become clearer about a particular form of social relations within which this notion is embedded and comes to life. It can be misleading to think that we can give a neutral and impartial account of a concept we involve in our moral understanding of ourselves, without bringing into focus the form of life of which it is an integral part. It is not enough for us simply to work out the different contexts within our everyday lives when we might say that we respect someone, though this might be an important aspect of our analysis. This can never be the whole story. In acknowledging the ways in which a notion such as respect is embedded in a particular form of life, we are acknowledging the dangers of analysing a concept as if it were not an essentially historical formation. Forms of life are essentially historical, involving particular relations of power and dominance, even though particular social theories often do their best to hide their historical character.[1] Rather we need to understand the different ways in which moral theory so often presents itself in universal terms. To recognize the historical character of our moral conceptions does not have to concede to a form of historical and sociological relativism, though it does raise new questions about the nature of moral theory.

As long as moral theory presents itself as being solely concerned with the decisions individuals make about how to live a moral life, this encourages us

[1] I am drawing upon the notion of a 'form of life' which can be found in Wittgenstein's later writings. Somehow I think that it has to involve more of a developed social and historical dimension if it is to be illuminating within moral and political philosophy. I am not suggesting that Wittgenstein would have been sympathetic to this approach.

Y. Yovel (ed.), Kant's Practical Philosophy Reconsidered, 235-254.

to give a particular meaning to our 'moral lives' as a particular realm of our experience. This makes us think that our moral decisions have to do, for instance, with those decisions that relate to an individual's relationship to the moral law. Morality becomes essentially an individual quest in which, for Kant, the individual has to prove his or her moral worth. This hides and mystifies the fundamentally moral character of the decision about *how* I am to live a moral life living in an unjust society. It is this fundamentally individual-istic ethic that is challenged by Greek thought, particularly by Plato, where it was recognized that it was not simply a question of individual choice and decision, whether an individual could live a moral life.[2] There was an impor-tant recognition of the social and political nature of morality, so that it could no longer be simply assumed that it is up to the individual to choose whatever relationships with others he or she wants to have. This is to conceive relation-ships as the outcome of individual decision and resolve, and so to abstract them from the character of the social relations of power and dominance within which they take place. Plato recognized that it was only in the context of a society that was organized in a just way that we *could* individually choose to have just relations with others. This is to challenge moral traditions of thought that assume it is simply a question of the moral qualities of an individual whether they choose to act morally. For Kant it is a question of individuals living up to the moral law, regardless of the social situation they find themselves in. As long as I am acting out of a sense of duty then the moral worth of my actions is guaranteed. As long as my life is full of moral actions then I am guaranteed the moral equivalent of salvation. This tradition has enormous moral strengths in the support that it can give to individuals to stand up for their beliefs and to resist relating simply to the consequences of their actions. At the same time this clarity is often given at the cost of simplifying the moral situations people are in because of the prevailing inequalities of wealth and power in society. Kant came to the edge of consid-ering these difficult issues in his consideration of the relations between rich and poor. It is important to highlight these difficult moments because they can throw into relief important contradictions within the moral conscious-ness of liberal society.

---

[2] I want to come to a recognition of the strengths of this tradition and so to an awareness of the centrality of social and political philosophy. I think this makes a difference to the place that epistemology should have. I want to show this through showing contradictions which emerge within individualistic moral theory when con-fronting questions of inequality and dependency. This becomes a way of recognizing the philosophical importance of Hegel's recovery of this tradition.

Setting out the implications of growing up to respect others, through distancing ourselves from others, can help us clarify a certain form of social relations we grow up to take very much for granted. But we also learn something about the formation of 'character' and 'personality' within a particular moral culture. So Kant's ethical writings can serve to reconcile us to a certain distance in our relations with others, and to thinking that the meaning of our lives is not going to come from our close relations with others, but rather from achieving the goals we have set for ourselves individually. We will often be left assuming that we should not really need the help and support of others, and that we will prove ourselves all the more if we are able to do things ourselves. We will also come to take for granted a rationalist conception of morality in which very little can be learned from our emotions and feelings. Rather at some level we will learn to subordinate our own wants and desires so that we are ready to do what is required of us. In its own way this will work to suppress our individuality, which we will too easily identify with achieving the goals we have set ourselves, rather than with the fulfilment and nourishment of our capacities, wants and needs.

This can potentially introduce us to new terms of moral criticism as we can begin to sense the source of some of the limits and frustrations we feel in ourselves and in our relationships with others. Rather than assuming that these simply indicate our own individual inadequacies and lack of resolve and dedication to the goals and ends we have set ourselves, we will have more sense of *how* our 'moral characters' have been influenced and organized within a particular moral culture, within a particular pattern of social relations of power and dependency. Through a deeper grasp of the tensions Kant identifies in his later ethical writings we can have more sense of some of these *processes of reconciliation* we have been brought up to take very much for granted within our moral culture. We become more aware of the *costs* to our individualities and emotional selves involved in this implicit denial of our needs, desires and emotions.[3]

Kant tends to assume that our characters simply express whatever individual qualities we have, so he never has to understand the ways these are influenced by the character of social relations people grow up to take for granted. It is partly because you can judge a person's 'character' by whether

---

[3] It has been an aspect of the importance of the history of psychoanalysis that it has given us a start in thinking about these 'costs.' This would involve a serious investigation of our implicit conceptions of the relationship between psychology and philosophy. See Sigmund Freud's *Introductory Lectures on Psycho-Analysis* (London: Allen and Unwin, 1929).

or not they act morally, that a person's moral life can be conceived more or less as a series of discrete moral actions. This has a deep influence upon the conception Kant develops of human relationships. In *The Doctrine of Virtue* Kant sometimes sketches a deeper recognition of the ways people need to reveal themselves to others, though he also recognizes that others can take advantage of us. He tends to assume that this is a necessary feature of social relations, rather than something which becomes particularly threatening within a particular form of social relations, as say, for instance, when we are brought up within competitive institutions to prove ourselves to gain our very sense of individual identity. This can easily make the fear we have of the use others will make of what we share with them 'rational.' It will also be influenced if we are brought up to assume that needing to share ourselves with others is already a sign of weakness. Kant might have felt this himself in his earlier writings:

Man is a being meant for society (though he is also an unsociable one), and in cultivating social intercourse he feels strongly the need to reveal himself to others (even with no ulterior purpose). But on the other hand, hemmed in and cautioned by fear of the misuse others may make of this disclosure of his thoughts, he finds himself constrained to *lock up* in himself a good part of his opinions (especially those about other people). (DV 471)

Kant does not think through the consequences of locking up in ourselves a good part of our opinions, especially when he also acknowledges that "he feels strongly the need to reveal himself to others." This is a contradiction within our experience that will inevitably have implications for the formation and development of our 'characters.' This was difficult for Kant to develop within the framework of a rationalist conception of ethics. It was Freud who gives us the understanding to make sense of this experience. But it was particularly difficult for Kant even to acknowledge this, since there is a deep tendency within his thought to regard the subordination of our needs and desires, our self-denial, to be near to the core of our moral experience. Acting morally can be very much a matter of learning to deny whatever thoughts and feelings we have personally, so that we can do what is required of us by the moral law. This is connected to the notion that we show our respect for others through keeping our distance from them. This can make it easy for us to grow up within a moral tradition which systematically denies the need, which Kant partly recognizes here, to be able to share ourselves with others. It only seems to be in Kant's later writings that he worries about the kind of limitations this puts on our relations with others, and sometimes about the ways this denies our need to reveal ourselves to others.

It is also because Kant tends to assume that we are equal before the moral law that Kant can think we are equal in what really matters in our lives. This makes it easier for him to discount the workings of the inequalities of wealth and power. He is forced to rethink the assumption he makes about autonomy of morals, about the equality he assumes within the moral realm for us to live moral lives, when he thinks about the relations between rich and poor. Since we often assume that structures of social inequality and class power belong solely to the empirical investigations of sociology, we are barely sensitive to the moral questions which they can raise. This deep separation of morality and politics was unknown to the Greeks, but it has become almost definitional to the individualistic moral traditions we grow up to take very much for granted. It was also at the centre of Hegel's critique of Kant's moral writings. It is not simply that it is easer for those with wealth and power to live moral lives through doing good for others, it is also because the relations of class, sexual and racial power form and influence our personal and social relations with others. When Kant talks about the "fear of the misuse others may make of this disclosure of his thoughts," he cannot assume that he is dealing with a relation between equals. This fear is deeply mediated through the social relations of power. It is harder to share myself with someone who has power over me, since it is easier for them to abuse this knowledge.

These issues are also keenly present in how we interpret the respect we owe to others. If we can assume that we are equal as 'moral beings,' then it is easier for us to think that it is simply a matter of individual choice whether we respect others in our relationships with them, since this will depend upon the attitude we individually choose to take up. It can be said that we are 'free' to take up whatever attitude we want towards others. Similarly it might be said that we are always 'free' to show respect to others by adopting "the maxim of not abasing any other man to a mere means to my end (not demanding that the other degrade himself in order to slave for my end)" (DV 449). But does this 'freedom' rely upon our being able to abstract from the social relations of power and inequality? Is not the attitude we want to take up towards others sometimes *contradicted* by the nature of the relationship we are involved in with others? Is simply enough for us to adopt individually a certain maxim in our relations with others? Does not the relationship itself sometimes have to be *transformed*, since there might be no way within a certain kind of relationship for us *not* to use a person as a "mere means to my end"? If this is not simply a question of individual intentions but relates to the very character of the relationship, how is this to be thought about?

We can only become aware of some of the issues involved if we begin to bring out the central tension in using the notion of respect to articulate both our sense of human equality and our sense of hierarchy and inequality. This is already reflected in the ways we think about 'distance,' both in terms of the respect that is due to but also in the 'distance' that is experienced, say, between parents and children, teachers and pupils. We learn to respect our parents and teachers through learning to 'look up to them.' We acknowledge this respect by being careful to keep a certain distance from them. This can involve learning only to speak when we are spoken to, learning not to be too familiar or personal with someone we respect. In this hierarchical notion of respect there is a sense of maintaining a certain 'social distance' between people. Often it is in these contexts that we think most easily about the nature of respect. Kant also talks about 'distance' when he talks about the respect we owe to others as equal human beings. In doing this, there is a danger of trading upon our understanding of what is going on in 'unequal relationships' between, say, parents and children, teachers and pupils. The character of the 'distance' within these relationships is different from the 'distance' we keep from others when we are careful not to infringe upon their rights. It is left unclear how much Kant wants to include a sense of deference within the sense of respect due to each person.

Sometimes it seems as if Kant is trading upon the hierarchical sense of respect, in clarifying the respect due to others as human beings. This is because he is often thinking about respect for the moral law. This could argue that we should give priority to this hierarchical sense of respect. But it also helps us understand the *abstract quality* of the respect that is given equally to others. It does not involve a personal understanding of someone's needs and wants, emotions and feelings. Often it threatens to become an abstract acknowledgment of others, even though it seems to promise much more. In the very distance we have to maintain from others, it is easier for our acknowledgment of others to become purely *formal*. This relates to the notion of abstract rights which are so central to a liberal conception of an individual's relationship to social life. Rather than existing as individual men and women who have individual wants, needs and desires, we exist as the abstract bearers of these rights. Our individuality is defined very much in these terms. It is as if we are almost encouraged to abstract from the personal qualities that people have, in the respect we owe them as human beings. It is almost as if we do not want to know too much about them, since this respect is due to them regardless of the particularities of their history, experience and background. It is as if knowing more will serve as a temptation to discriminate, and can easily be interpreted as a form of interference. It is as if saying that it is the 'individual' who is owed respect is *already* to abstract someone from their personal, sexual and class histories. This is something that Sartre notices in *Portrait of the Anti-Semite:*

He has no eyes for the concrete syntheses with which history confronts him. He recognises neither Jew, nor Arab, nor Negro, nor bourgeois, nor worker, but only man — man always the same in all times and in all places. He resolves all collectivities into individual elements... And by individual he means the incarnation in a single example of the individual traits which make up human nature.[4]

It is this conception of an 'individual' which has powerful influence upon liberal social thought. In its own way it can serve to *depersonalize* our conception of others whom we implicitly see as clusters of abilities, qualities or capacities. If this reminds us we owe respect to people whatever their social background, and whatever social position they have, it also makes us think these are incidental to our understanding of others. This is supported by the recognition that, for instance, if we get to know that someone is a cleaner in a building, rather than a professor, this can make a difference to the respect we give them, so it is better if we know very little about others if they are owed equal respect.

It can be argued that we are concerned with giving others the respect due to them, rather than with fully understanding them as people. To make sure that we are not discriminating between people we ofter prefer to know little about them, like the teacher who thinks he is showing respect to the pupils in the class by being careful not to be too aware of their backgrounds. He is anxious to relate to them equally. But this does not necessarily help the pupils to a sense of their own individual identities and histories. Rather it can encourage children to discount their class, cultural and sexual backgrounds, secure in the knowledge that these will not count against them within the social relations of schooling. So pupils are encouraged to think of themselves as individuals with particular abilities and talents. This is what it means to define our individuality within the liberal school. It provides us with the ways in which we can prove ourselves as individuals. In its own way this can unwittingly work to make children, say of Jewish or Black background, feel almost ashamed of their background, even though this is no part of the conscious intention of the schooling. Even if the school openly encourages pupils to be proud of the background they come from, the social relations of schooling can work in a way that makes people *discount* their culture and history. At least it becomes no part of a person's recognized identity and sense of self. It can easily become threatening to the sense of individuality which is encouraged within the school. As an individual with a discrete set of abilities, it is taken to be almost contingent that I happen to have a certain cultural background. Since this is

---

[4] See Jean Paul Sartre, *Portrait of the Anti-Semite*, tr. E. de Mauny (London: Secker and Warburg, 1948), p. 55. (Eng. tr. of *Réflexions sur la question juive.)*

242   *Victor J. Seidler*

not supposed to affect the ways others relate to us, since they would be discriminating, so it is not supposed to influence the ways we think and feel about ourselves and our 'identities.' Our individual identities are to be given to us by the inner qualities and abilities we have. This can encourage a Jew to discount his Jewishness, as Sartre clearly understood:

The democrat, like the scientist, fails to see the particular case; to him the individual is only an ensemble of universal traits. It follows that his defence of the Jew saves the latter as a man and annihilates him as a Jew... he fears that the Jew will acquire a consciousness of the Jewish collectivity — just as he fears that a 'class consciousness' may awaken in the worker. His defense is to persuade individuals that they exist in an isolated state... wishes to destroy him as a Jew and leave nothing to him, but the man, the abstract and universal subject of the rights of man and the rights of the citizen.

Thus here may be detected in the most liberal democrat a tinge of anti-Semitism; he is hostile to the Jew to the extent that the latter thinks of himself as a Jew. (*Portrait of the Anti-Semite*, p. 57)

So our individuality is thought about very much in terms of "the abstract and universal subject of the rights of man and the rights of the citizen." Learning to think and feel about ourselves in this way is taken as a sign of cultural maturity. In this way a person's Jewishness can only be a matter of the individual beliefs he happens to hold. It can be no part of his or her individuality. So in claiming his or her individuality they learn to renounce tacitly their Jewishness. It is this very universalism which is taken as a sign of moral maturity. This is embedded in the ways Kant conceives us to be individually subject to the moral law. This is partly why the "defence of the Jew saves the latter as a man and annihilates him as a Jew." In learning to prove ourselves individually, we learn to distance ourselves from a cultural and historical heritage. Since this is no part of our individuality, it cannot be anything that we draw our strength and identity from. It is an individual's relationship to the moral law which, in Kant, works "to persuade individuals that they exist in an isolated state."

Even though Marx was critical of this tradition of abstract rights and the notion of the universal subject of the rights of man, this has also remained a very powerful influence within the Marxist tradition.[5] It has been too easy to dismiss abstract notions of 'bourgeois individuality' in contrast to notions of class solidarity and collectivity.[6] Often these oppositions just show that the

[5] Some of Marx's own deep ambiguity about these issues that he never really resolves are to be found in his discussion "On the Jewish Question" which is reprinted in Karl Marx, *Early Texts*, tr. David McLellan (Oxford: Blackwell, 1971), pp. 85-114.
[6] See "The Emancipation of Women," in *The Writings of V.I. Lenin* (New York: International Publishers, 1966), p. 104.

critique has not gone deep enough. Crucial issues about the notions of individuality which have taken into consideration notions of class, ethnic, and sexual formation have barely been thought about. This is hardly something that we can do justice to within this work.[7] Hopefully our investigations in Kant will throw some light on the broader issues involved. At some level this involves challenging a rationalist conception of morality which identifies our capacity for morality and our sense of individuality with our rationality, and sets this in sharp opposition to our needs and desires, our emotions and feelings.

When Kant says that respect is not to be taken "merely as the *feeling* that comes from comparing one's own *worth* with another's" but is to be taken "in a practical sense" as "a maxim of limiting one's own self-esteem by the dignity of humanity in another person" (DV 448), he wants to make sure that it affects the ways we relate to others, not simply the ways we feel about them. He makes his point by giving as an example of the feeling that comes from comparing one's own worth with another, the "mere habit" that "causes a child to feel [respect] towards his parents, a pupil towards his teacher, a subordinate in general towards his superior." It can seem as if the deference that we have felt in these relationships is "mere habit" that will have to be replaced by adopting the maxim. In its own way this is to mystify the relations of power and authority which exist between parents and children, pupils and teachers, especially if we think it is simply a question of the personal qualities of the individuals concerned. This is something that Kant was to learn more about in thinking about the relations between rich and poor. He was to come to terms with the difficulties in the hierarchical senses of respect. He was to learn that the sources of inequality cannot simply be located in the qualities of individuals. This is particularly important, since it challenges the notion that social inequalities of wealth and power can be assumed to reflect individual differences in abilities, talents and qualities.

But it also involves learning that "the dignity of humanity in another person" cannot simply involve abstracting from social, cultural and historical distinction. Sometimes it involves a deeper analysis of their sources. This was something that Kant was to recognize in his discussion of the relations between rich and poor. He faces the difficulty of treating someone not as rich

---

[7] See, for instance, Sheila Rowbotham's discussion in *Woman's Consciousness, Man's World* (Harmondsworth: Penguin Books, 1973), and in *Dreams and Dilemmas* (London: Virago, 1986). See my discussion in "Trusting Ourselves: Marxism, Human Needs and Sexual Politics," in *One-Dimensional Marxism*, ed. S. Clark, T. Lovell, K. Robbins and V.J. Seidler (London: Allison & Busby, 1980).

or poor, but simply as a person in his or her own right. In this context he faces the difficulties of abstracting from the social relations in which people relate to each other. This does not mean that Kant is not acknowledging something important when he recognizes "the dignity of humanity in another person," but it does challenge the ways he has thought about this, and so also the moral culture we are brought up within liberal society to take very much for granted.

II. Dependency and Individuality

1. Freedom and Independence   Kant was always acutely aware of the dangers of dependency. He understood the ways that dependency could so easily undermine people's sense of themselves. This is very much how he understands the workings of traditional forms of authority. Individuals had to learn to listen to the voice of the moral law, not to the blind instructions of traditional authorities. So the struggles against traditional forms of authority became the struggle against forms of dependency and the assertion of the necessity of individuals making decisions for themselves. It was part of the emphasis upon the rational powers of each individual to undermine the grounds people have for controlling and dominating the lives of others. This is an expression of the egalitarian strain in Kant's thinking. It also helped Kant voice his scepticism about the legitimacy of traditional forms of authority. This is clearly expressed in Kant's essay on "What is Enlightenment?" where he explains how easy it is for people to be dependent upon others, rather than learning to make decisions for themselves:

It is so convenient to be immature. If I have a book to have understanding in place of me, a spiritual advisor to have a conscience for me, a doctor to judge my diet for me, and so on, I need not make any effort at all. I need not think, so long as I can pay; others will soon enough take the tiresome job over for me. The guardians who have kindly taken upon themselves the work of supervision will soon see to it that by far the largest part of mankind (including the entire fair sex) should consider the step forward to maturity not only as difficult but also as highly dangerous. Having first infatuated their domestic animals, and carefully prevented their docile creatures from daring to take a single step without the leading-strings to which they are tied, they next show them the danger which threatens them if they try to walk unaided. Now this danger is not in fact so very great, for they would certainly learn to walk eventually after a few falls. But an example of this kind is intimidating, and usually frightens them off from further attempts. (WiA 54)

Kant recognizes something crucially important about the nature of individual responsibility. At some deep level we have to make our own decisions about the kinds of lives we want to live. These decisions often express our deepest wants and needs which we want to give expression to in the ways we live our lives. Others cannot make these kinds of decisions for us, even though it is often easier to give this kind of power over our lives to others. These are crucially important areas of our lives in which we have to learn to trust our own judgement. A crucial issue is whether the very presuppositions of Kant's moral theory which often involves the subordination of our neeeds and wants, feeling and desires, actually prepare us to take this kind of control over our lives. At some level it can be argued that Kant unwittingly undermines the very conditions he wants to create for people's sense of independence and autonomy. This is deeply contradictory within the very relationship we are to have to the moral law. In one sense we legislate for ourselves, but at another level we cannot help experiencing the moral law as having an essentially external voice, since it has little to do with our individual perceptions of our wants, needs and desires.

Kant is aware of how easy it is to accept the authority of others rather than to develop our own understanding. But he does not grasp the ways that the very subordination of our 'animal nature' can make it difficult for us to listen and respect the signs that our body gives us. It makes it easier for us to assume for instance that "the doctor knows best" and to assume that our respect for his knowledge involves us accepting the truth of what he says, regardless of the indications that our bodies might otherwise be giving to us. It is the very distrust of the body that is a deep presupposition within the Kantian inheritance in our moral culture. The body is a place of temptation. It cannot be trusted to offer us a knowledge of its own. Rationalism tends to undermine our trust in different sources of knowledge and understanding. This can make it difficult to develop a different kind of relationship to our health, which involves taking more control over our lives by understanding much more of what is happening to us. But this in itself provides a certain kind of critique of the medical practices we take very much for granted. This is not simply embedded within a particular conception of medical knowledge, it is also an aspect of the social relations of health care.

In a very real sense "It is so convenient to be immature" since trusting our own judgements and learning to listen, say, to the indications of our bodies is bound to be a challenge to the prevailing relations of power within health care. This is not to undermine the importance of a doctor's training and understanding, though it is to suggest that this understanding has to find a different, more cooperative relationship with the person who is being treated. In this sense it involves a different conception of medical knowledge. But this is not to identify 'maturity' with making our decisions without the help and understanding of others, even if it is to recognize that often in the end we have to take the responsibility for the decisions. Taking more control over our health will mean a challenge to traditional conceptions of medical knowledge and the conventional relationship between doctors and patients.[8] It will mean learning much more about ourselves. It will mean learning to listen to our bodies. In this sense it involves challenging some of the very presuppositions of Kant's rationalim.

It is important to distinguish the individualism that makes us aware of the need to make decisions for ourselves and for us to take greater control over our lives, from the individualism that assumes that it is always of greater 'moral worth' for us to do without the help and support of others. There is a balance here that a strict opposition between 'individualism' and 'collectivism' has generally failed to appreciate. In its own way it has sometimes been captured in notions of solidarity and community, when these notions have not become mechanical. Learning to walk is a good example. In the end we have all had to risk taking the first step. Others could not take this step for us, however much they have wanted to ease this difficult moment. Others have to accept that we are likely to make a few falls before we eventually learn to walk on our own. But there is also the right moment for our walking. This is something we have to be ripe for. The moment will come in its own time. It cannot be rushed. It is by no means true that the earlier we walk the better. It is possible for people to be made to walk too early. If we see human development as some kind of race, in which we have to prove that our children are more 'advanced' than others, we will be tempted to push them to 'stand on their own two feet' earlier than is right for their own individual process. It is part of a deeper notion of individuality to recognize that, as individuals, we have our own processes and rhythms.

We need the loving support of others to learn to walk. We need to know we can depend upon others being there for us. This will make all the difference to the quality and ease with which we learn to walk. It will make a difference to the ways we trust others and the ways we trust ourselves. There is a certain important emphasis within Kant which has fed a tradition of individualism as *self-sufficiency*, which assumes that it is best for us to do things ourselves without needing the help of others. With this doctrine children have to learn to walk on their own, since the sooner they learn through falling the better it will somehow be for them. It is an integral part of this that we have to learn that we *cannot* trust others, and that it is always much better for us to do things without needing the help and support of others.

[8] See Ivan Illich's discussion of some of these issues in his *Limits to Medicine* (Harmondsworth: Penguin Books, 1971).

Kant is aware of how easy it is to undermine the confidence of people in their ability to think for themselves. He thinks that this can be prevented and our individual judgement safeguarded if we avoid becoming dependent upon others. In this way he tends to identify our 'independence' with a notion of 'self-sufficiency,' which relates to his notion that our actions have greater 'moral worth' if they are done without the assistance and help of others. But if Kant is aware of the dangers of dependency, he tends to explain this in terms of people's individual qualities — our laziness and cowardice — rather than explain how the nature of dependency is reproduced within particular kinds of personal and social relationships. So he tends to think that it is simply a matter of individual weakness if, say, John cannot take more control over his health. We very much inherit this notion within our individualistic moral culture, so that it is easy to feel it is simply a question of individual will. This can make John feel that it is simply a question of collecting himself so that he can share more of his insight and understanding with his doctor. This gives him little sense of what he is up against. This makes it hard for him to understand how to respond to his doctor when she says quite straightfor-wardly that it would not be 'professional' if she let him read the case notes she has made. He can be left feeling that he is simply 'interfering' in her busy schedule, so that there is almost something wrong with him if he cannot trust her, since her other patients never seem to want to question her in this way. This is a situation we need to understand.

Kant is aware of how easy it is for people to accept a situation of depen-dency as "second nature," so that people are barely aware that they are not thinking for themselves. He has a deep sense of the ways in which our understanding can be crippled, though he tends to explain this in terms of individual qualities. In expressing this he captures an important truth about the need for us to take certain steps in our lives which others can never take for us. But at the same time he makes it hard for us to realize the social relations of power we are up against, so that it is very easy for us to blame ourselves even more. This is not simply a question of individual psychology. It is a question of the moral culture and the social relations of power and dominance we are brought up to accept as "almost second nature":

Thus it is difficult for each separate individual to work his way out of the immaturity which has become almost second nature to him. He has even grown fond of it and is really incapable for the time being of using his own understanding, because he was never allowed to make the attempt. Dogmas and formulas, those mechanical instru-ments for rational use (or rather misuse) of his natural endowments, are the ball and chain of his permanent immaturity. But if anyone did throw them off, he would still be uncertain about jumping over even the narrowest of trenches, for he would be unaccustomed to free movement of this kind. (WiA 55)

This conception of "second nature" is crucial. It helps us understand the ways that people "even grow fond" of their dependency, so that someone is "really incapable for the time being of using his own understanding." But this notion of learning to use our own understanding is complicated when we realize the ways we have been brought up to silence ourselves in front of doctors in the secure knowledge that they "know best." We are not assumed to have any kind of privileged knowledge and understanding of our bodies. We are assumed to be radically ignorant, and we are *made* radically ignorant, through the ways we are brought up to think and feel about our bodies. In trusting our own judgement we are already challenging not only the prevailing definitions of medical practice, but the social relations of power which maintain them.[9]

But why is it so "difficult for each separate individual to work his way out of the immaturity which has become almost second nature to him"? Can it be that people have simply become too lazy to think things out for themselves? Kant helps people question an obedience to traditional authorities. In this way he helps people trust their own intelligence and understanding, even if he tends to assume a rationalist conception of this, which already subordinates any understanding coming from our desires and emotions. At some deep level Kant acknowledges that each individual has to discover his or her own powers of understanding. But there are profond questions concerning Kant's assumption that this is somehow more important for men than for women. There are also critical issues about the areas of our lives in which we can be expected to enjoy this understanding. The very conception of the 'body' as part of the 'natural world' governed by similar laws makes it easy for us to discount whatever understanding our bodies might otherwise give us. This is deeply embedded in Kant's presuppositions.

Kant tends to see dependency in terms of the power and authority of one individual over another. If he helps us face some of our complicity in the ways we interiorize and accept a position of subordination, he makes us think we can free ourselves through releasing the chains to our understanding. Kant shares this conception of freedom with other thinkers in the Enlightenment. This was to place enormous confidence in individuals learning to use their independent powers of reasoning. But this does not help us fully understand the forces we are up against. It tends to make this a matter of individual

[9] Some of these issues are discussed in *Our Bodies, Ourselves* by the Boston Women's Health Collective (Harmondsworth: Penguin Books, 1978).

resolve and decision. We inherit this notion of freedom in our moral culture, though it barely helps us grasp the issues about the ways subordination and dependency become "second nature":

> For enlightenment of this kind, all that is needed is *freedom*. And the freedom in question is the most innocuous form of all — freedom to make *public use* of one's reason in all matters. But I hear on all sides the cry: *Don't argue*. The officer says: Don't argue, get on parade. The tax-officer says: Don't argue, pay. The clergyman: Don't argue, believe. (WiA 55)

This conception of 'freedom' as the "public use of one's reason" has deep currency within our moral and political culture. But this barely helps us understand the sources of power which, say, the army, state bureaucracy and church have over our lives. If a young private questions the orders he is being given, he is usually punished for disobedience. He will soon find himself out of the army. At some time he might be told that "it isn't your job to give orders only to obey them." So it is one thing to have an acknowledged right to our own individual political and moral opinions, but quite another to think we should question the doctor, manager or officer. In some sense this is contained in the ambiguity of the notion of the "freedom to make public use of one's reason." In its own way this has been limited to the use of our 'freedom of thought' within the public realm of political discussion. But this has served to limit the realms of social life in which we are supposed to be capable of using our own understanding. This has also limited the notion of democracy. It is used to control the power we can expect to have over our own lives at work, or even at the doctors. It is too easily assumed that an involvement in the institutions of representative democracy somehow gives us effective control over all areas of our lives. This has been a powerful myth. It has an important source in Kant. It means that if we acknowledge the problems that Kant begins to identify we can also be forced to contest the solution that "all that is needed is freedom... to make public use of one's reason."

Kant is aware of the ease with which we give up our own understanding within relations of dependency, so that this becomes "almost second nature." The effectiveness of the solution he offers to "make public use of one's reason" has to be evaluated historically. In societies where this kind of freedom is available, do we find that the forms of dependency Kant highlights disappear? Is it possible for each individual "to work his way out of the immaturity" simply through invoking this freedom? Does this begin to explain the difficulties Kant acknowledges in trusting our own understanding? Kant should have more to say which could help us explain *why* it is so difficult to jump "over even the narrowest of trenches."

At one level it can be deeply mystifying to reproduce the common sense notion of liberal culture that we are "always free to use our freedom in questioning others." This can make us assume that if we do not question doctors, say, then we only have ourselves to blame. It becomes easy to blame ourselves. This becomes one of our easiest impulses within liberal society, especially when we are told we already have whatever "freedom" we might otherwise claim. This is to separate questions about the "public use of one's reason" from questions of the social relations of power. At one level it might remain true that we collude in giving doctors enormous power over our lives. It is important to understand the cultural and psychological reasons for doing this. But we can hardly understand this without understanding the power which doctors, medical institutions and medical knowledge come to have in society. It is not simply that we do not take responsibility to learn more about our own health. It is not simply that we are lazy. It is also because of the ways we are brought up to assume that the doctor has a knowledge that is privileged and that this will only be revealed if we are ready to completely submit to his or her power. This can make it difficult to think that it is even possible to learn much about ourselves.

The point is that it is not simply our individual laziness that prevents us taking more control over our own bodies. It is also very much a question of the relations of power we are brought up to accept as "second nature," as we learn of the respect due to the doctor. Our bodies become the passive objects organized according to the laws of medical knowledge. We learn to lie in respective silence ready to "talk only if we are spoken to." It is not simply that we give up our power to doctors, but that this is very much taken for granted in our relationship to medical knowledge. It is difficult to begin developing a different relationship to our bodies without recognizing the institutional powers that we thereby question. This is not simply a question of asking an individual doctor to be patient enough to explain the diagnosis, though this itself can challenge the very sense of the doctor's professionalism. This raises far deeper questions about the historical development of medical knowledge and the development of the professionalization of medicine. This gives us more sense of the powers we are questioning. It can also make us aware of the kind of support we need from others, since it is so easy to be made to feel 'silly,' 'idiotic' and 'stupid' in our questioning.

Even though we are talking about our individual health and well-being, it is easy for the power of doctors to make us feel that we are 'interfering' in their professionalism. This is important because of the different things Kant says about respect as non-interference. It is important to recognize the ways this idea comes to have a general currency within our moral culture. It can be used to enforce the very powers that can make us feel dependent, ignorant and inadequate. It can become part of the process of dispossessing us of the most intimate and personal knowledge of ourselves. It can undermine our trust and self-confidence.

2. Dependence and Independence Kant had a deep understanding of the human importance of people being free to make certain decisions for themselves. He recognizes the importance of this for our development and growth as human beings. This helped him grasp the dangers of one person being dependent upon others for their means of livelihood. He knew this would make it difficult for people to retain a sense of self-respect, because they would no longer be able to feel fully equal to others. To this extent Kant did recognize some of the social foundations for equality between people, since he recognized the *difficulties* of people continuing to regard themselves as equal to others, if they are dependent upon them for their very means of livelihood. At the same time Kant did recognize the ways that dependency can become "almost second nature" to someone. He recognizes the ways that one can even grow fond of it while being "really incapable for the time being of using his own understanding." At times Kant seems to be saying that it is quite possible for us to suffer the consequences of dependency without even realizing that this is happening to us. This raises the critical issue of ideology.[10]

It seems as if it is possible for people to abstract from the relations of power and dependency they are involved in to regard themselves as equal before the moral law, while at the same time suffering the consequences of these very relationships of dependency. This will mean that people are, in some sense, *mystified* about the character of the social relations they are in. People will continue to think of themselves as equal to others, entitled to an equal respect, while all the time being undermined in the ways they think for themselves and identify their own needs, because of the workings of these very relationships

---

[10] It is difficult to do more than hint at these issues here. It shows that it is not simply a question of becoming aware of the relationships of dependency. We can still suffer from their consequences. It involves a much more sensitive discussion of moral psychology and social theory. Within a Marxist tradition it was Georg Lukacs in his *History and Class Consciousness* who glimpsed these issues of 'second nature,' though he does not develop this insight either (London: Merlin Press, 1971). If Wilhelm Reich had a less developed understanding of Marxism theoretically, he had a deeper grasp of the nature of these issues. See the collection *Sex-Pol, Essays 1929-34*, ed. Lee Baxandall (New York: Vintage Books, 1972). This would encourage a much less rationalistic conception of the workings of ideology.

of subordination and dependency.[11] But if people are left feeling that this is simply a consequence of their individual laziness, rather than also of the social relations of power and dominance, they will be left without ways of understanding what makes them think and feel about themselves the way they do. Worse than this, they will become "fond" of a situation that is undermining them all the time, without their realizing what is happening. This can make it so much harder for people to trust in their own understanding. I think that this is why it is useful to think about this as a *process of mystification* which has deep cultural and historical sources.

It is partly because of the ways in which Kant contrasts 'dependence' and 'independence' in his thinking, that he tended to see all forms of human dependency as potentially undermining of people being able to live independent lives.[12] It is crucial within a Protestant tradition because individuals must be seeking their own individual salvation in the eyes of God that any involvement with others must be a 'distraction' from this fundamental relationship. What is more, any sort of emotional relationship with others is easily assumed to make it much more difficult for people to act out of a sense of duty. This helps produce a secular moral culture in which it is easy to assume that we are better on our own. This can make us suspicious of the help of others, particularly within a middle-class culture where this individualistic ethic is so firmly grounded. This can make it difficult for us to accept that we can receive much from others. Whatever meaning our lives are going to have will come from the 'ends' or 'goals' we have set ourselves to achieve. If this tradition can help define our individual goals, it can also make us feel we have to be continually *proving* ourselves. This can make us blind to our individual wants and needs, let alone the support, caring and love we can get from others. Not only is it easy to assume within a capitalist moral culture that others are always trying to get the better of us, but we assume that it is always better if we can do without the emotional support and comfort of others. This is confirmed in the deep division within liberal moral culture between the 'public' realm in which we have to prove ourselves and the 'private' realm of

[11] A difficulty with theorizing relationships of power and dependency is a weakness in the theoretical framework provided by John Rawls, *A Theory of Justice* (Oxford, 1971). It represents a significant blindness in liberal moral and political theory. This is discussed in "Liberalism and the Autonomy of Morality," in my *Kant, Respect and Injustice* (London: Routledge and Kegan Paul, 1986), Chap. 8.

[12] The relationship between freedom and individualism is usefully discussed by Charles Taylor in "Atomism" and "Kant's Theory of Freedom" which have been collected in his *Philosophy and the Human Sciences*, Philosophical Papers 2 (Cambridge University Press, 1985).

emotional support and comfort. This fundamentally fragments our experience. We can even experience ourselves as being very different people in these different realms of our lives.

Because Kant put so much weight upon individuals being free to do their duty, he was suspicious of any kind of involvement with others. There was always the chance that this would leave people feeling obligated to others. For Kant this would mean that people would no longer be free to follow their own ends. This is what led Kant to deny the role which sympathy, kindness and caring can play in our relationships with others, though he seems to think about this again in *The Doctrine of Virtue*. He still tends to see any form of kindness and caring as a way of making us dependent upon others. He is so aware of the dangers of dependency inherent in our relationships with others that he tempts us into thinking and feeling that we would almost be better off without the caring and kindness of others.[13] At some level the sympathy, care and involvement with others cannot give central meaning to our lives, but can only distract us from pursuing the individual ends we have set ourselves. The support and understanding of others cannot have an intrinsic meaning in itself. It can only strengthen our resolve to do what we must do alone. So our need for the love and caring of others can only be incidental to the meaning to be given to our lives through our individual moral achievements.[14] This very much fits in with the prevailing cultural notions of 'individual achievement' and 'individual success.' It makes it easier for people to assume that it is 'sensible,' for instance, to move to a new area because this means promotion in the firm. If this involves sacrificing the close relationships people have built up in an area, then this is a sacrifice people have to be ready to make. It is often implicitly part of the patriarchical ideology within a family ready to organize itself around individual advancement. This involves the readiness of people — often men — to subordinate their relationships, often also with wife and children, so that these career opportunities can be grasped.

Kant sometimes seems to argue that our need for others can only reflect our "weakness" or "inadequacy." It is almost as if it has to be a sign that we

[13] Kant's relationship to altruistic feelings and their place within his moral vision is usefully discussed by Lawrence Blum, *Friendship, Altruism and Morality* (London: Routledge and Kegan Paul, 1980).

[14] The relationship between individuality and community within liberal moral theory is usefully discussed by Michael Sandel, in his *Liberalism and the Limits of Justice* (Cambridge University Press, 1982). Unfortunately he does not connect these issues to questions of dependency and subordination. It is a strength of some feminist theory that it has attempted to draw some of these connections. See, for instance, Jean Grimshaw, *Feminist Philosophers* (Brighton: Harvester Press, 1986).

cannot face the world on our own, so that we need the help of others. This is still most clear within, say, a frontier morality, where the highest value is put upon independence and strength and where it is a sign of weakness and failure to admit you need the help and support of others. In a more muted form this still has an importance within our own individualistic moral consciousness.[15] It's easy for us to feel that needing others threatens to make us dependent upon them. This means that we also have to do without the support of others, even when we need it. In its own way this can encourage us to "close off" from others, as we feel uneasy and even ashamed if they can see and recognize our need. It is so easy for need to be identified with weakness and inadequacy, especially within a male culture. Often we do not want to admit this need to ourselves, since it threatens to lower our self-esteem. This can mean that, especially as men growing up within a competitive culture, we have to harden ourselves against the realization of what we need from others.

Kant implicitly supports those aspects of our moral culture which interpret needing others as a sign of weakness. Kant recognizes that it is difficult for people to maintain their self-respect, if their welfare is dependent upon the generosity of others. It is very important for Kant to maintain an identification between "autonomy," "independence" and "self-sufficiency" so that individuals are free to prove themselves individually. This is at the heart of a competitive morality. If people are dependent upon others, then this has to be a sign of moral weakness. This has to be an avoidable situation for Kant, since it threatens to challenge the very presupposition of the autonomy of morals. This is why it is so crucial for Kant to think about the moral relations between rich and poor. Somehow these social inequalities have to be explained as the consequences of individual moral actions.[16]

Goldsmiths College
University of London

[15] Some of these issues are discussed by Richard Norman in "Does Equality destroy Liberty?" in *Contemporary Political Philosophy*, ed. Keith Graham (Cambridge University Press, 1982).
[16] These issues are further explored in my book, *Kant, Respect and Injustice*. An attempt to take seriously the moral issues raised by relationships of power and subordination even when they challenge the categorical distinction between morality and politics is provided by Simone Weil. She is deeply influenced by Kant, drawing her understanding of oppression from Kant's principle of not treating someone only as a means to one's own ends. This is further discussed by Lawrence Blum and Victor Seidler in *A Truer Liberty: Simone Weil and Marxism* (London: Routledge and Kegan Paul, 1989).

Index

255

Conjectural Beginning of Human History
173 187-193
consensus 220 222 232 233
constructivism 114 196-211
contingency 101
Copernican revolution 77 80 93 94 141
Crawford, D. 109
Critique of Judgment 7 8 20 112 144 172
Critique of Practical Reason 8 9 24 25 33-
37 46 73 74 81 144
Critique of Pure Reason 10 15 19-21 23 64
73 76 79 80 102 106 116 138 139 143
culture (*Kultur*) 88

Davidson, D. 7 8 20
Deleuze, G. 109
dependence 235-254
desires 4 8 14 66 67 69-72 74 80 83 86 91
117 118 162 238
see also inclinations
determinism 3 4 8 26 81
causal 7 17 32 73 79
laws of nature 83 84 91
psychological 3 4 8
devils 72
Dewey, J. 121
Diderot, D. 178
Dilthey, W. 190
discourse 218 220 221
fictional 192
quasi-performative 193
Diskurs Ethik 213
dogmatists 80; *see also* metaphysics
Dreier, R. 154
dream 100
dualism 46 102
ontological 24 31
Dummett, M. 121-123 216
duty 43 50-57 64-69 70 72 90 119 146 151
153 155 223
exemplary 67 68
legal and ethical 154-156
of beneficence 47
perfect and imperfect 43 44
to others and to oneself 60 61 156-157
159
see also obligation

education (*Bildung*) 88 91
emancipation, mental 139
empeiria 101
empirical
character 1-21
knowledge 66 96 97 124 140
objects 97 98 141 142
realism 101 107
synthesis 141 142
empiricism 97 101 141
end(s) 55-60 71; *see also* finality
in itself 34 104 215
kingdom of 133 205
of nature 189
of reason 135-138
Engstrom, S. 23
Enlightenment 88 91 138 248
epistemic
condition 19
vs. practical spontaneity 12 13 94 102
equality 59 60
ethical
perspective 107
self 106 128
see also moral
evil 35-37 46 148
radical 173 179
explanation and understanding (Dilthey)
190
explanation, mechanistic and teleological
7
external world *see* phenomenal

fact 102
of reason 34 39 83 214 217 221 226 232
facticity 101
falsity 100 102
faith, rational 34 146
Fichte 172 175 177 178
finality-adaptation, -solution 168-182
finitude 89
of reason 137
forms of life 235
formula of humanity 41 44
formula of universal law 30 41 50 51
Forschner, M. 68
Foucault, M. 228